# Summary Conviction Law for Paralegals

Gargi Mukherji

emond · Toronto, Canada · 2015

Emond Montgomery Publications Limited
60 Shaftesbury Avenue
Toronto ON  M4T 1A3
http://www.emond.ca/highered

Printed in Canada.
Reprinted November 2019.

We acknowledge the financial support of the Government of Canada. **Canadä**

Emond Montgomery Publications has no responsibility for the persistence or accuracy of URLs for external or third-party Internet websites referred to in this publication, and does not guarantee that any content on such websites is, or will remain, accurate or appropriate.

Publisher, higher education: Mike Thompson
Managing editor, development: Kelly Dickson
Director, editorial and production: Jim Lyons
Developmental editor: Joanne Sutherland
Copy editor: Heather Gough
Proofreader: Laura Bast
Indexer: Paula Pike
Text designer: Shani Sohn
Cover designer: Tara Wells
Cover image: iStockphoto.com / wdstock

**Library and Archives Canada Cataloguing in Publication**

Mukherji, Gargi, author
    Summary conviction law for paralegals / Gargi Mukherji.

Includes index.
ISBN 978-1-55239-594-3 (pbk.)

    1.  Criminal law—Canada—Textbooks.    I.  Title.

KE8809.M84 2015          345.71          C2014-905085-2 ?KF9220.ZA2M84 2015

*To my family, for their encouragement, support, and patience
throughout this journey, and specifically to my sons—
may you always have the freedom to pursue your dreams.*

# Contents

## 4 Compelling Attendance and Bail

## 5 Witnesses

## 6 Disclosure and Pre-Trial Conferences

# 7 Pre-Trial Applications

# 8 The Trial

# 9 Sentencing and Appeals

## Appendixes

# Preface

*Summary Conviction Law for Paralegals* is a criminal law text written solely for paralegals. I first embarked on this project in response to my former students' queries about a criminal law text that brings together the *Criminal Code* and common law in one convenient package. After doing some research, I realized that this did not exist, and hence the idea began to percolate in my mind. My goal was to write a practical textbook that would assist students, professors, and licensed paralegals within the scope of summary conviction law and procedure. In writing this textbook, I have relied upon my own practical experiences as a Crown attorney, as well as my pedagogical experience as a professor in a paralegal program.

This text references the *Criminal Code*, the *Canadian Charter of Rights and Freedoms*, the Law Society of Upper Canada's *Paralegal Rules of Conduct*, and the *Criminal Rules of the Ontario Court of Justice*. Every aspect of a summary conviction matter is discussed—from arrest to conviction and sentencing. Each chapter contains tips and strategies from a defence paralegal perspective. There are numerous references to cases and examples that demonstrate various legal principles. There is a chapter on drafting pre-trial Charter and non-Charter related applications. Each chapter concludes with Short Answer questions and Apply Your Knowledge questions to assist in the application of the content to real-life scenarios.

This text is meant to be a resource not only for students in paralegal programs across Ontario, but also for licensed paralegals beginning to practise in criminal law. *Summary Conviction Law for Paralegals* aims to bridge the gap between criminal law theory and actual day-to-day practice. It is my hope that readers will enjoy using the book as much as I have enjoyed writing it.

Gargi Mukherji
June 2014

# Acknowledgments

This text has been a work in progress for many months. I would like to thank my family for their constant encouragement, support, and patience for putting up with me (and managing without me) during the arduous process of writing and revising. Without you, this project would have been impossible for me to take on.

I would like to thank my former and present students for their ideas, feedback, and words of encouragement. My passion for teaching is rejuvenated by them every day.

I acknowledge the valuable feedback of professors Ana Bernal (Durham College), Christine Hobkinson, JD (legal reviewer), Laurie Nichols (Loyalist College), Shayan Shaffie (Humber College), and Craig Stephenson (Conestoga College). They provided detailed suggestions about the organization of the text, as well as content-specific feedback. Being new to the writing process, their assistance was invaluable to me.

Finally, I acknowledge the support and assistance that I received from the editors at Emond Montgomery and the developmental editor, Joanne Sutherland—they were great at keeping me focused and on task.

# Introduction and Professional Practice

# 1

## LEARNING OUTCOMES

After reading this chapter, you should be able to:

- Distinguish between federal and provincial law-making authority

- Outline the structure and levels of courts in the Canadian criminal justice system

- Understand the layout of the *Criminal Code*

- Explain the duties and scope of practice of a paralegal defence agent

- Discuss the ethical obligations of the paralegal to the client and to the administration of justice

- Distinguish between the roles and responsibilities of the Crown and the police

# Introduction

*Summary Conviction Law for Paralegals* is written for paralegal students and licensed paralegals practising in criminal law. As licensed paralegals in Ontario are governed by the Law Society of Upper Canada, this text is intended to cover the criminal law educational requirements for paralegal programs across Ontario. This text is intended to serve as a comprehensive resource that covers the *Criminal Code*, the *Canadian Charter of Rights and Freedoms*, the *Paralegal Rules of Conduct*, and the *Criminal Rules of the Ontario Court of Justice*, as well as explanations of common law precedents and authority on various issues within criminal law. Both substantive and procedural laws are covered with a practical approach to all aspects of a summary conviction proceeding. The focus of *Summary Conviction Law for Paralegals* is to follow the steps of a criminal prosecution chronologically—from pre-arrest to sentencing from both a defence and Crown perspective.

In Chapter 1, we look at where criminal law comes from and the division of powers between the federal and provincial levels of government. A brief overview of the Canadian court system is provided, followed by a detailed look at the layout of the *Criminal Code*. The role and scope of the defence paralegal in representing a client in a criminal matter is discussed with specific reference to the ethical rules that apply. Finally, the roles of the police and the Crown are examined.

# Origins of Criminal Law

Canada's criminal law is based on common law and statutory law. **Common law** is based on judicial decisions, or **precedents**. Precedents from higher levels of court are more influential than those from lower courts. For example, a Supreme Court of Canada decision carries more weight than a decision from the Ontario Superior Court of Justice. Decisions of the Supreme Court of Canada are binding on all other Canadian courts unless they are distinguishable on the facts of the case. According to the principle of **stare decisis**, all Ontario provincial courts must follow a decision of the Ontario Court of Appeal. However, all Ontario provincial courts are not bound by the decisions of appellate courts of other provinces or by decisions of the Federal Court of Appeal. Canadian common law is constantly evolving based on changing circumstances in society.

Laws, which are created at either the federal or provincial level of government, are called "statutes," "legislation," or "acts." They are referred to as **statutory law**. Parliament may create laws for the entire country, but only for matters over which the federal government has jurisdiction. Similarly, a province or territory may only create laws for matters over which it has jurisdiction. If one level of government encroaches on the jurisdiction of another level of government, then the law is said to be **ultra vires**, or beyond the powers of that level of government. A law that exceeds the scope of its jurisdiction is unconstitutional. If the law is within the powers of the level of government that created it, it is said to be **intra vires**.

---

**common law**
a legal system developed from judicial decisions

**precedent**
principle or rule established in a previous legal case that is binding or persuasive on other courts in deciding similar cases

**stare decisis**
a legal principle that requires judges to follow previous rulings made by other judges in higher levels of court within the same province or territory and rulings of the Supreme Court of Canada on the same issue

**statutory law**
written law passed by Parliament; takes precedence over common law

**ultra vires**
beyond the legal authority of a level of government to create a law

**intra vires**
within the legal authority of a level of government to create a law

> ### EXAMPLE
>
> ### *Ultra Vires*
>
> If the federal government were to pass a law regulating the order in which cases are to be tried within provincial courts on a daily basis, this law would be *ultra vires*. Although the federal government has the power to create criminal laws, the authority over the administration of justice lies with the province.

Section 91 of the *Constitution Act, 1867* (UK), 30 & 31 Vict, c 3, reprinted in RSC 1985, App II, No 5, establishes the jurisdiction of the federal government to pass laws relating to matters of national concern, such as criminal law, trade and commerce, banking, immigration, and national security. Section 92 of the *Constitution Act, 1867* establishes the power of the provinces and territories to regulate matters of local concern, such as health care, energy and natural resources, civil rights, and property laws. Although the federal government has the power to create criminal laws and procedure, the provinces and territories regulate the administration of justice, including their constitution, maintenance, and organization, as well as the procedural rules of the provincial courts. This means that offences under the *Criminal Code* are dealt with by the provincial level of government.

Constitutional law is the highest form of written law, as it governs and shapes statutory laws created and passed by the legislature. The *Constitution Act, 1867* and the *Constitution Act, 1982*, being Schedule B to the *Canada Act 1982* (UK), 1982, c 11, determine whether or not a law is valid. The *Canadian Charter of Rights and Freedoms*, Part I of the *Constitution Act, 1982*, being Schedule B to the *Canada Act 1982* (UK), 1982, c 11 [Charter], guarantees certain political, civil, and legal rights to people in Canada from the policies and actions of all levels of government (federal, provincial, and municipal), subject only to reasonable limits prescribed by law.

# The Canadian Court System

There are four levels of court in Canada that address criminal matters. At the lowest level is provincial court, which deals with the vast majority of criminal cases. In Ontario, the provincial courts are called the Ontario Courts of Justice and are composed of provincially appointed judges and justices of the peace. The Ontario Courts of Justice are located both in major cities and in remote locations across the province of Ontario. As will be discussed in greater detail in Chapter 2, paralegals may only appear on summary conviction matters in provincial court.

The second level of court is superior court, which has **inherent jurisdiction**, or the jurisdiction to hear cases in any area except those limited to a particular level of court. Superior courts are divided into special divisions, such as the criminal division and the family division. More serious criminal cases are dealt with in superior courts, either before a judge and jury or before a judge alone. In Ontario, the superior court is called the Superior Court of Justice and is composed of federally appointed judges.

**inherent jurisdiction**
a concept based on the common law doctrine that a superior court has the authority to hear any matter that appears before it; may be overridden by statute or legislation

The third level of court is the provincial appellate court, which hears appeals from provincial court and superior court. The name of this court in Ontario is the Ontario Court of Appeal, and it consists of a panel of three judges who are federally appointed. Leave to appeal (permission) is required if an appeal to the Superior Court of Justice has already been dismissed.

The last and highest level of court in Canada is the Supreme Court of Canada. It is the final court of appeal from all other courts in Canada. Leave to appeal is not given routinely. It is granted only if the case involves a question of public importance; if it raises an important issue of law or mixed law and fact; or if the matter is, for any other reason, significant enough to be considered by the Supreme Court of Canada. Figure 1.1 shows an outline of Canada's court system.

Federal Court matters are mostly immigration, taxation, administrative law, and public law cases. The Federal Court does not hear criminal cases or appeals.

**FIGURE 1.1    Outline of Canada's Court System**

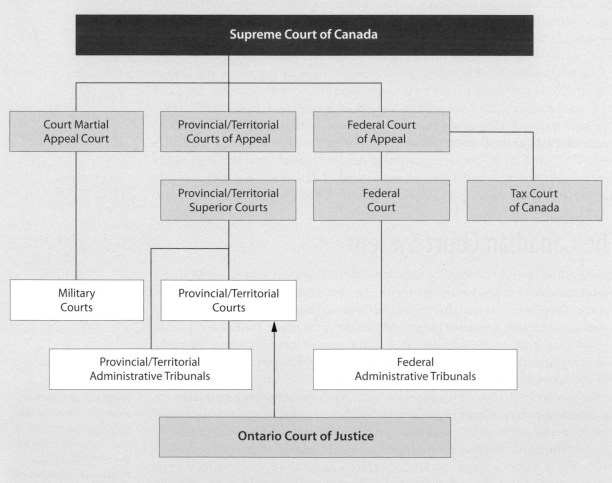

Source: Adapted from Department of Justice, *Canada's Court System* (Ottawa: Government of Canada, 2014), online: <http://www.justice.gc.ca/eng/csj-sjc/ccs-ajc/page3.html>. © Department of Justice Canada, 2005. Adapted with the permission of the Minister of Public Works and Government Services, Canada, 2014.

# Overview of the Criminal Code

The *Criminal Code*, RSC 1985, c C-46 is a federal statute that sets out criminal offences and penalties. Since it is federal legislation, criminal law is the same across all of the provinces and territories of Canada. All persons in Canada are subject to the *Criminal Code* regardless of whether or not they are Canadian citizens. The *Criminal Code* also contains procedures for dealing with criminal offences and sets out the powers of the various levels of criminal courts within Canada.

The *Criminal Code* is divided into various components or parts, which can be found in the Table of Contents. Each part deals with specific types of offences, procedures, and forms. For example, part II.1 of the *Criminal Code* deals with terrorism; therefore, any offences related to terrorism would be found in this part. New offences are placed in the part in which they belong. As of the current date, there are 28 parts in the *Criminal Code*, as well as seven additional point parts. There are also forms included in the *Criminal Code*, which are templates for various documents used in criminal proceedings.

## PRACTICE TIP

Buy a commercial edition of the *Criminal Code*. Commercial editions contain annotations to the text of the Code, including cross-references and leading cases that interpret each section. They may also include other relevant legislation, such as the Charter or the *Canada Evidence Act*, RSC 1985, c C-5 [CEA]. Other standard features include the Table of Cases, Offence Tables, and Forms of Charges.

Tables of Cases list the cases used in the annotations, providing a convenient reference list. Offence Tables set out offences under the *Criminal Code* along with information as to whether the offence is indictable, summary, or hybrid; whether an offence is an absolute jurisdiction offence; the maximum and minimum sentence; available sentencing options; and mandatory and discretionary orders that the court may make. It is important to note that there are different commercial versions of the *Criminal Code*, and the layout may differ according to the version used. Forms of Charges contain the proper wording of various offences, which are followed by police officers when swearing out the information (see Chapter 2).

Use caution when referring to the Offence Tables, as the circumstances of the case will dictate the availability of sentencing options and orders made by the court. Furthermore, statutory conditions must be satisfied and exceptions may apply. It is important to discuss all possible sentencing options with your client before entering a plea.

## Proper Statutory Citation

As a primary source of law, the *Criminal Code* must be cited using the proper statutory citation. The proper citation for the *Criminal Code* is:

*Criminal Code*, RSC 1985, c C-46

| | | |
|---|---|---|
| *Criminal Code* | = | name of the statute |
| RSC | = | the name of the statute series in which the legislation appears (Revised Statutes of Canada) |
| 1985 | = | the year in which the statute was last published in a revised volume |
| c C-46 | = | chapter "C-46" (Note: the letter "C" makes reference to the first letter of the name of the legislation—"*Criminal Code*") |

## Statutes and Acts Related to the Criminal Code

Offences under the *Criminal Code* are prosecuted pursuant to the procedures set out therein. Other federal statutes that follow the procedures set out in the *Criminal Code* include: the *Youth Criminal Justice Act*, SC 2002, c 1; the *Controlled Drugs and Substances Act*, SC 1996, c 19; and the *Firearms Act*, SC 1995, c 39. It is important to note that these statutes are not part of the *Criminal Code* but are separate statutes that may also contain criminal offences or procedures for dealing with criminal offences. Likewise, the *Constitution Act, 1982* and the Charter are often included in commercial publications of the *Criminal Code*, but they do not form part of it.

# Paralegal Authority to Appear as Defence Agent

Paralegals in Ontario are licensed by a governing body. The Law Society of Upper Canada (LSUC) regulates the paralegal profession. In Ontario, licensed paralegals may appear before the Ontario Court of Justice, in Small Claims Court, and before many administrative tribunals.

Both the *Criminal Code* and the LSUC *Paralegal Rules of Conduct* (Rules) make reference to the scope of a paralegal's authority to represent someone charged with a criminal offence.

Section 802.1 of the *Criminal Code* refers to the limitation of the use of agents:

> 802.1.  Despite subsections 800(2) and 802(2), a defendant may not appear or examine or cross-examine witnesses by agent if he or she is liable, on summary conviction, to imprisonment for a term of more than six months, unless the defendant is a corporation or the agent is authorized to do so under a program approved by the lieutenant governor in council of the province.

In Ontario, the *Law Society Act*, RSO 1990, c L.8 further defines the scope of activities for a paralegal licensee. Under the *Law Society Act*, By-law 4, section 6(1)(c), a proceeding includes "a proceeding or intended proceeding ... in a summary conviction court under the *Criminal Code* (Canada)." A "summary conviction" is described in section 787(1) of the *Criminal Code* as an offence punishable by a fine of not more than $5,000 or a term of imprisonment not exceeding six months or both. When read in conjunction with section 802.1 of the *Criminal Code*, this makes it clear that a defence paralegal may not appear as agent when the accused person is liable to a term exceeding six months of incarceration, even though section 802.1 makes reference to exceptions for corporations or approved programs. Since the LSUC is the licensing body for paralegals in Ontario, this by-law trumps the *Criminal Code*, and paralegals may only appear for matters under the *Criminal Code* when the maximum period of incarceration is no more than six months.

A licensed paralegal is authorized to conduct a number of activities with respect to summary conviction matters (see Appendix A).

# Roles and Responsibilities of the Defence Paralegal

## To the Client

The Rules apply to a defence paralegal practising in the area of summary convictions. Rule 3 deals with duties owed to the client. In the context of criminal law, the rules that will be discussed here with particular relevance to a defence paralegal are:

- Rule 3.01 Competence
- Rule 3.02 Advising Clients
- Rule 3.03 Confidentiality
- Rule 3.04 Conflict of Interest
- Rule 3.08 Withdrawal from Representation

### Rule 3.01 Competence

Before agreeing to act for a client in a criminal matter, the defence paralegal must first be satisfied that he or she is competent in that area of law. Competency is not limited to subject matter knowledge but also refers to the ability to identify legal issues and potential defences, advising the client of the possible options and outcomes, implementing a chosen course of action, and advocating on behalf of the client. Rule 4.01 deals with the paralegal's duties as an advocate to the client and to the court. Specifically, rule 4.01(4)(a) states that the paralegal must raise every issue and advance every argument that would assist in the client's defence.

Since there are significant liberty interests at stake in a criminal matter, the paralegal must be vigilant in ensuring that his or her client's legal rights are not placed in jeopardy. Once a course of action is chosen, the paralegal must identify which procedural steps must be followed. For example, if the chosen course of action is to file an application for judicial stay of proceedings due to non-disclosure, the paralegal must identify what items have not been disclosed, that letters have been sent to the Crown requesting disclosure, that the Crown has failed to respond to the request, that the *Criminal Rules of the Ontario Court of Justice*, SI/2012-30 [Criminal Rules] have been followed regarding filing and service of the appropriate application form, and that a hearing date is set for the application.

Even when there is no readily apparent defence available to the client, the client is still entitled to have a trial on the charge, as the burden of proof is on the Crown to prove the case beyond a reasonable doubt. In certain situations, a defence to the charge may only come to light once the trial has started. Often, evidence at a trial may emerge in a different manner than what is expected by Crown counsel or by the defence paralegal. It is therefore important to always be fully prepared for a trial. Once a paralegal has appeared as a representative for the client, he or she is officially on the record and may not withdraw from the case without certain exceptions as set out in the Rules.

### Rule 3.02 Advising Clients

In the context of criminal law, a paralegal must take care not to knowingly assist or encourage any dishonesty, fraud, or illegal or criminal conduct on behalf of the client, as set out in rule 3.02(4) of the Rules. This rule applies to individual clients as well as organizations. A paralegal must also refrain from advising a client on how to violate the law and avoid punishment. It is advisable for the paralegal to discuss the nature of the paralegal–client relationship at the outset, when discussing the scope of the retainer. Clients may be unaware of the legal and ethical boundaries of a paralegal's duty to the client; therefore, it is best to raise this at the beginning of the relationship.

When advising clients, the paralegal also has a duty to provide honest and candid advice, as set out in rule 3.02(2). The client may wish to know how likely it is that he or she will be convicted or acquitted. The paralegal must provide advice that is based on a thorough review of the evidence. It is also important to note that trials are based on the credibility and reliability of witnesses, which is impossible to gauge beforehand. What appears to be a relatively strong case for the Crown may not turn out to be the same at trial. Similarly, what appears to be a strong case for the accused may be fraught with challenges at trial. When giving advice to the client, it is important to avoid providing any guarantees of the outcome of a case.

Rule 3.02(11) indicates that a paralegal should advise and encourage a client to compromise or settle a dispute whenever it is possible to do so on a reasonable basis. Plea negotiations form an important function in the criminal justice system and are discussed in more detail in Chapter 6 and Chapter 8.

### Rule 3.03 Confidentiality

A distinction must be made between the duty of confidentiality and solicitor–client privilege. The duty of confidentiality to the client (and potential clients) extends to all information gathered during the course of a retainer, regardless of whether or not the information itself is confidential. It is a statutory duty that paralegals must abide by, as set out by the Law Society of Upper Canada. Solicitor–client privilege, which extends to licensed paralegals, is a common law doctrine that applies to communications between a licensee and the client for the purpose of legal advice. Communications also include documents or any records that fall on the continuum of legal advice.

A defence paralegal must be aware of the very limited circumstances in which he or she is permitted to disclose information provided by the client. When there is a clear, serious, and imminent threat to public safety, solicitor–client privilege will be set aside. This is known as the public safety exception to solicitor–client privilege. Similarly, rule 3.03(5) permits a paralegal to disclose confidential information where the paralegal has reasonable grounds to believe that there is an imminent risk of death or serious bodily harm, and disclosure is necessary to prevent the death or harm.

Even when appearing before a judge and seeking to withdraw, the paralegal shall only provide the minimal amount of information necessary in order to avoid prejudicing the client and breaching his or her obligations with respect to confidentiality. Indicating that there has been a "breakdown in the paralegal–client relationship" indicates to the court that the paralegal must withdraw for reasons that may not be stated on the record due to obligations of confidentiality.

In the context of representing a client in a criminal matter, what happens when the client discloses evidence indicating involvement in a criminal offence? What are the paralegal's legal and ethical obligations? This issue was considered in one of the most sensational criminal cases in Canadian history (see Case in Point: *R v Murray*).

## CASE IN POINT

# How Far Does Solicitor–Client Privilege Go in Protecting Client Confidentiality?

*R v Murray*, 2000 CanLII 22378 (Ont SC), 48 OR (3d) 544

### Facts

In 1993, Paul Bernardo retained defence counsel Ken Murray to represent him on charges of domestic assault and a number of sexual assaults that took place in Scarborough, Ontario. During this time, police were investigating Bernardo for the murders of Leslie Mahaffy and Kristen French. Police had executed a search warrant at the residence of Bernardo and his wife, Karla Homolka, but had not found anything connecting him to the murders.

Bernardo instructed Murray to attend his residence and retrieve six videotapes from the bathroom ceiling on the second floor of the house. Murray, along with a junior lawyer and his law clerk, found the tapes and made a pact not to reveal the findings to anyone.

Murray made copies of the tapes and kept them locked in his office safe. He did not immediately view the videotapes at the time, on the instructions of Bernardo. The videotapes contained evidence of sexual assaults against Leslie Mahaffy, Kristen French, and two other victims. The tapes clearly depicted Bernardo as the main culprit and Karla Homolka as an active and willing participant in those horrific acts.

In May 1993, Homolka negotiated and struck a plea agreement whereby she would plead guilty to manslaughter with respect to the deaths of Leslie Mahaffy and Kristen French in exchange for a 12-year sentence of imprisonment. As part of this agreement, Homolka agreed to testify against Bernardo at his trial. Murray was aware that Homolka was involved in a plea agreement with the Crown, but he did not notify anyone of the videotapes. Murray held onto the tapes for 17 months in order to attempt to arrange for a plea agreement for Bernardo. Murray's intention was to show that Homolka was the actual killer of the two girls.

In August 1994, Bernardo instructed Murray to suppress the videotapes in order to argue that he did not know Leslie Mahaffy and Kristen French. At this point, Murray arranged for a new defence lawyer to represent Bernardo and applied to withdraw as counsel. Murray also sought instructions from the Law Society as to what he should do with the tapes. He was advised to turn the tapes over to the presiding judge at Bernardo's trial. However, the tapes were turned over to Bernardo's new counsel, John Rosen, with the court's approval. Twelve days after reviewing them, Rosen turned them over to police. Bernardo was subsequently convicted of two counts of first degree murder in the deaths of Leslie Mahaffy and Kristen French.

Ken Murray was charged with attempting to obstruct justice for hiding the tapes, as they contained evidence that incriminated Bernardo for the murders. Moreover, the defence had no legal right to conceal them in the months preceding the trial. Furthermore, Murray came into possession of the tapes prior to Bernardo being charged with the murders. Murray took the position that he was legally entitled to retain the tapes to use at trial in his client's defence.

### Decision

Justice Gravely held that although it was reasonable for Murray to view the tapes first, he had no right to conceal them for as long as he did. However, Justice Gravely ruled that although the *actus reus* of the offence of obstructing justice was proved, there was no evidence of wilful intent on Murray's part to obstruct justice, as he may well have believed that there was no obligation to disclose the tapes. Accordingly, Murray was found not guilty. In the reasons for his decision, Justice Gravely noted that there was a lack of legal authority on the ethical obligations of lawyers regarding incriminating evidence.

Six months later, the Law Society withdrew charges of professional misconduct against Murray, and he escaped from the Bernardo fiasco without any sanctions. Had Murray not hidden the tapes, Homolka would likely have been charged with two counts of first degree murder, not man-slaughter. Unfortunately, little has changed with respect to Ontario's professional conduct guidelines for criminal defence lawyers who come into possession of incriminating physical evidence. Thus, the balance between competing duties to the client and to the administration of justice is left up to individual lawyers to resolve.

### Discussion Question

Do you think the duty to one's client should rank above other ethical obligations? Should it be left to individual practitioners to decide how to resolve any ethical dilemmas that may arise?

## Rule 3.04 Conflict of Interest

**joint retainer**
contractual relationship in which the paralegal represents more than one client in the same matter

A defence paralegal must be careful to avoid a conflict of interest, which may arise in a number of scenarios when defending a client in a summary conviction matter. Typically, conflicts may arise when representing more than one client on a matter as part of a **joint retainer** or acting against a former client in an unrelated matter when the paralegal has previously obtained confidential information from the former client. To avoid this, a joint retainer agreement should specify that if a conflict of interest arises, the paralegal must withdraw from representing both clients.

### EXAMPLE

**Joint Retainers**

Client A and Client B have been charged with theft under $5,000 for stealing candy bars together from a convenience store. Both have asked you to represent them and allege that they did not steal from the store. A few months later, Client A tells you that Client B is the one who stole the candy bars and that she was not aware of this until after they were charged. Can you continue to represent both of them? Can you choose to represent one client?

## Rule 3.08 Withdrawal from Representation

Special rules apply for a paralegal who wishes to withdraw from representing a client in a criminal matter. In certain cases, withdrawal is optional for the paralegal. An example of a situation in which withdrawal is optional—meaning that the paralegal may choose whether or not to withdraw—is when there has been a serious loss of confidence between the paralegal and the client (rule 3.08(2)). Even in situations in which withdrawal is optional, the paralegal may not use the threat of withdrawal to force the client to act in a certain way (rule 3.08(4)). In other situations, withdrawal is mandatory, meaning that the paralegal has no choice but to withdraw. An example of a situation where the paralegal must withdraw is where the client instructs the paralegal to act contrary to the Rules.

### EXAMPLE

**Mandatory Withdrawal**

Your client asks you to represent her for a charge of making harassing telephone calls. The complainant is your client's cousin. Prior to the trial, your client tells you that she wants you to prolong your cross-examination in such a manner as to harrass the complainant, thereby ensuring that she is unable to testify.

Sections 7–9 of rule 3.08 deal with withdrawal in criminal and quasi-criminal cases.

Since the jeopardy faced by a client in a criminal or quasi-criminal matter is much greater than in any other type of case, a paralegal must withdraw far in advance of any approaching trial date to enable the client to obtain other representation and to allow that licensee sufficient time to prepare. This means that even in situations in which the client has not paid the paralegal's fees, the paralegal must apply to withdraw well in advance of the trial date so as not to adversely affect the client's rights. For all other situations, if the paralegal is justified in withdrawing from representation but cannot do so with sufficient notice, then he or she must bring the application to withdraw immediately prior to the commencement of the trial.

A question that often arises is how much information the court is entitled to receive regarding the reasons for withdrawal. On the one hand, the paralegal is bound by a duty of confidentiality to the client, yet on the other hand, the paralegal must be careful not to deceive the court or assist in dishonesty. How does the paralegal reconcile these obligations if a conflict arises with respect to withdrawal? The case of *R v Cunningham* sheds some light on this issue.

## CASE IN POINT

# How Much Information Is the Court Entitled To?

*R v Cunningham*, 2010 SCC 10, [2010] 1 SCR 331

### Facts

Jennie Cunningham was a criminal defence lawyer appointed by Yukon Legal Aid to act as counsel for a defendant charged with sexual offences. Prior to the preliminary inquiry, Yukon Legal Aid notified the accused that his funding would be suspended unless he updated his financial information. When he failed to respond, Cunningham brought an application before the court to withdraw as counsel based on the suspended funding. She indicated that she would be willing to represent him if the funding were reinstated. The lower courts refused her application, but the Court of Appeal allowed her appeal. The matter was then appealed to the Supreme Court of Canada.

### Decision

The Supreme Court of Canada established some guidelines regarding applications to withdraw as counsel prior to trial. In situations where counsel seeks to withdraw far enough in advance of the trial date that an adjournment of the trial will not be necessary, the court will not inquire further into the reasons for withdrawal.

If, however, the timing of withdrawal is at issue, the court is entitled to inquire further. If counsel seeks to withdraw for

ethical reasons, this means that an issue has arisen in the solicitor–client relationship that makes it impossible for counsel to continue to represent the accused in good conscience. An example of this is when the client instructs the paralegal to lie to the court. When the reason for withdrawal is based on ethical grounds, the court must grant withdrawal, as it would be inappropriate to force counsel to continue to act in violation of his or her ethical responsibilities.

If the paralegal seeks to withdraw because of non-payment of fees, then the paralegal must be forthcoming with the court about the reason for withdrawal. It is at the court's discretion as to whether to permit counsel to withdraw for non-payment of fees when the timing of the withdrawal is at issue. In either case, the court must accept counsel's answer at face value and not delve any further so as to avoid encroaching on issues of solicitor–client privilege and confidentiality.

The Court went on to outline a number of factors that judges ought to consider when exercising discretion in deciding whether or not to allow the withdrawal application (para 50):

- whether it is feasible for the accused to represent himself or herself;
- other means of obtaining representation;

- impact on the accused from delay in proceedings, particularly if the accused is in custody;

- conduct of counsel, e.g. if counsel gave reasonable notice to the accused to allow the accused to seek other means of representation, or if counsel sought leave of the court to withdraw at the earliest possible time;

- impact on the Crown and any co-accused;

- impact on complainants, witnesses, and jurors;

- fairness to defence counsel, including consideration of the expected length and complexity of the proceedings;

- the history of the proceedings, e.g. if the accused has changed counsel repeatedly.

The Supreme Court noted that as these factors are independent of the solicitor–client relationship, no privilege should be violated when engaging in this analysis.

### Practice Tip

To avoid the situation of having to withdraw for non-payment of fees close to the trial date, the defence paralegal should diarize regular reviews of the file to ensure that billing is complete and there are enough funds in the trust account to pay for disbursements. Client expectations should be managed at the outset by way of a detailed retainer agreement.

## To the Administration of Justice

Rule 6 deals with a paralegal's duty to the administration of justice and to the courts. Generally, a paralegal has a duty to encourage public respect for the administration of justice.

Often, the issue arises as to whether the defence paralegal ought to make statements to the media about a criminal case. The obligation to the client, to the administration of justice, and to the courts comes first. However, as long as there is no infringement of this obligation and as long as the communications will not materially prejudice a party's right to a fair trial or hearing, a paralegal may make public appearances and provide statements to the media (rules 6.01(4) and (4.1)).

While a criminal defence paralegal must be a vigilant advocate for the client, he or she must also treat the court and other licensees and lawyers with candour, fairness, courtesy, and respect (rule 4.01(1)). While the Rules appear to be clear in terms of which activities are prohibited, in practice, there are situations in which the ethical lines are blurred. For example, rule 4.01(4)(d) states that a paralegal may not attempt to gain advantage from mistakes or oversights not going to the merits of the case. On the other hand, rule 4.01(4)(b) encourages the paralegal to take advantage of every remedy and defence available in law. It may not be clear whether a particular oversight made by a Crown attorney is a potential benefit in the client's case. Is the paralegal in breach of the Rules if he or she does not bring the oversight to the attention of the Crown? Is the paralegal justified in waiting to see if the oversight provides a potential defence in the client's case? These questions must be answered in the context of each individual case.

What is clear is that a paralegal may not become a tool or dupe of the client by assisting the client in deceiving the court or misstating facts or the law. The Rules go as far as to indicate that if the paralegal is aware of any binding authority directly on point, he or she must inform the court if the opponent does not mention it, even if the decision does not assist the paralegal's case (rule 4.01(5)(d)).

A paralegal must encourage public respect for, and take care not to weaken public confidence in, the administration of justice, specifically with respect to commenting on judges or decisions made by judges (rule 6.01). This should be kept in mind particularly in situations in which a ruling is made or a decision is rendered against the client.

> ### EXAMPLE
>
> **Rule 6.01 of the *Paralegal Rules of Conduct***
>
> You are having lunch with two defence paralegals. You are all discussing the topic of appearing in front of Judge Smith, a judge who has a reputation for deciding more cases in the Crown's favour. At one point, you mention the sentencing that took place last week before Judge Smith. Your colleague says, "As soon as you walk in and see Judge Smith, forget about case law   he'll just do what he wants anyway!" What are the implications of this comment?

# Roles and Responsibilities of the Police

The role of the police is to maintain order, enforce the law, and prevent and investigate crime. A police officer or a police agency is responsible for investigating, charging, gathering evidence, and presenting that evidence in court.

Although the Crown and the police work closely together, the roles of each are separate and distinct. Police officers are not agents or employees of the Crown attorney. The police and the Crown have independent roles and responsibilities. While the police investigate and lay charges, Crown counsel will only proceed with those offences when there is a reasonable likelihood of conviction and when it is in the public interest to prosecute the accused. The decision as to whether or not to proceed with an offence is at the sole discretion of the Crown. Once a charge is laid, an investigating police officer cannot tell a Crown attorney what position to take on that charge. A police officer cannot force the Crown to withdraw the charge, refuse to negotiate a plea, or accept a plea. Although the police may recommend to the Crown a specific course of action, the Crown does not have to follow the recommendation. However, the Crown attorney with conduct of a particular case may ask the investigating officer for his or her opinion on a plea offer. In larger and more complex prosecutions, the police often consult the Crown on a regular basis, as legal advice from the Crown may be necessary in the gathering of evidence.

# Roles and Responsibilities of the Crown

Crown attorneys or prosecutors in Canada prosecute offences under the *Criminal Code* and other statutes such as the *Youth Criminal Justice Act* and the *Controlled Drugs and Substances Act*. Crown attorneys in Ontario represent the Ontario Ministry of Justice, Criminal Law Division under the direct supervision of the assistant deputy attorney general. Ultimately, the attorney general is a representative of the Queen. The attorney general has the authority to deal with matters relating to criminal prosecutions. For charges pursuant to federal legislation, such as drug charges under the *Controlled Drugs and Substances Act* or the *Firearms Act*, federal Crown attorneys would have jurisdiction to prosecute. For all other offences, provincial

Crown attorneys would have jurisdiction to prosecute. Within each local Crown attorney office, there is typically one Crown attorney, one or two deputy Crown attorneys, and several assistant Crown attorneys who report to the Crown attorney. In Canada, unlike the judicial system in the United States, Crown attorneys are not elected. However, Crown attorneys must not be politically influenced and are granted broad decision-making latitude. In a criminal trial, the burden of proof rests with the prosecution to prove the case beyond a reasonable doubt.

The Crown attorney chooses the appropriate charge on which to proceed, considers the release of accused persons pending trial, and conducts trials at all levels of court. Additional responsibilities of a Crown attorney include acting as counsel to the coroner during inquests and advising police, lawyers, and the public on general matters related to the administration of justice. A Crown attorney does not seek to win cases but rather fairly presents all of the evidence to arrive at the truth. Crown counsel have a duty to ensure that the criminal justice system operates fairly to the accused, to victims of crime, and to the public. The Supreme Court of Canada outlined the role of a Crown attorney in the case of *R v Boucher*, [1955] SCR 16, saying that Crown counsel "have a duty to see that all available legal proof of the facts is presented: it should be done firmly and pressed to its legitimate strength but it must also be done fairly."

**tunnel vision**
a situation in which a particular suspect is believed by investigators to be guilty of an offence and any evidence inconsistent with this theory is dismissed as irrelevant, incredible, or unreliable; may result in the elimination of other suspects who should be investigated

Crown attorneys should be professional in their demeanour and act fairly and dispassionately without personalizing their role in court. Of particular importance, especially with regard to recent legal history in Canada, is the duty of prosecutors to be open to the possibility of the innocence of accused persons and to avoid **tunnel vision**. Tunnel vision means the single-minded and overly narrow focus on a particular investigative or prosecutorial theory so as to unreasonably colour the evaluation of information received and one's conduct in response to that information (The Honourable Fred Kaufman, CM, QC, *Report of the Kaufman Commission on Proceedings Involving Guy Paul Morin* (Ottawa: Publications Ontario, 1998), online: <http://www.attorneygeneral.jus.gov.on.ca/english/about/pubs/morin/>).

To ensure that a consistent approach is taken in prosecutions across the province, Crown attorneys follow the Crown Policy Manual, which not only conveys the attorney general's instructions, priorities, and rationale behind these policies but also provides the public with information on the guiding principles that Crown attorneys must follow, thereby enhancing public accountability. However, the manual is not intended to replace the discretion exercised by Crown counsel in making decisions on a daily basis.

# CHAPTER SUMMARY

The federal government has power to create laws only on matters over which it has jurisdiction. Similarly, the provincial and territorial governments may only enact laws that fall within provincial or territorial jurisdiction.

There are four levels of court in the Canadian criminal justice system: provincial court, superior court, provincial appellate court, and the Supreme Court of Canada. Currently, paralegals may only appear on summary conviction matters in provincial court.

Most criminal offences and penalties are set out in federal statutes such as the *Criminal Code*. The *Criminal Code* also contains procedures for the disposition of criminal offences and forms related to criminal matters.

A criminal defence paralegal may represent clients on summary conviction matters in the Ontario Court of Justice.

A defence paralegal has several responsibilities to the client, which include competence, advising on procedures, legal issues, potential defences, confidentiality, avoiding conflicts of interest, and advocacy. These rules and responsibilities are set out in the *Paralegal Rules of Conduct*. A defence agent also has duties to the administration of justice and to other licensees and lawyers.

The roles and responsibilities of the Crown and of the police are separate and distinct in relation to a criminal prosecution. While the police are responsible for maintaining order, enforcing the law, gathering evidence, and investigating crimes, the function of Crown attorneys is different. Crown attorneys represent the attorney general and have a duty to fairly present all of the evidence before the court to arrive at the truth.

# KEY TERMS

common law, 2
inherent jurisdiction, 3
*intra vires*, 2
joint retainer, 10
precedent, 2
*stare decisis*, 2
statutory law, 2
tunnel vision, 14
*ultra vires*, 2

# REVIEW QUESTIONS

## Short Answer

1. Distinguish between common law and statutory law.
2. Which level of court hears summary conviction matters?
3. What is the scope of a paralegal's authority to represent someone charged with a criminal offence?
4. What specific considerations apply when a paralegal wishes to withdraw from representation in a criminal or quasi-criminal matter?
5. Summarize the roles and responsibilities of a Crown attorney.

## Apply Your Knowledge

1. Identify which level of government has law-making authority over the following laws:
   a. a law that prevents drivers from using any hand-held devices while driving
   b. a law that prevents passengers on an aircraft from transporting hazardous materials
   c. a law that changes current immigration policies
   d. a law that bans the sale of junk food in schools
   e. a law that changes the current policies on agricultural trade

2. Identify what parts and sections of the *Criminal Code* these offences and topics may be found under:

   a. commencement of proceedings of a summary conviction matter

   b. pretending to practise witchcraft

   c. issue of appearance notice by peace officer

   d. careless use of a firearm

   e. mailing obscene matter

   f. fine option program

   g. counselling or aiding suicide

   h. counterfeiting stamp

3. On the morning of trial, a client asks you if you are familiar with the particular judge who will be hearing his case. He asks you whether this judge is more likely to believe him or the Crown's witnesses. He also wants to know which route he should take (what to say on the stand) in order to be found not guilty. He tells you that he is thinking of lying about his actions in order to avoid being convicted. Can you still represent him? Can you allow him to testify? How would you advise your client?

4. In preparation for a trial, the investigating police officer tells you that she is okay with a guilty plea to a lesser charge. Two weeks later, you walk into the courtroom on the trial date, expecting that this matter will plead out and that there will not be a trial. The Crown informs you that they are not willing to take a plea to a lesser charge and that they are prepared to proceed to trial. Should you make a motion for abuse of process? Should you complain to the Crown attorney? Should you complain to the investigating officer's sergeant? How could this situation have been avoided?

5. Your 19-year-old client is charged with dangerous operation of a motor vehicle, and the Crown has elected to proceed summarily given that your client has no previous criminal record. Your client has advised you that he wishes to plead guilty to the charge. The Crown's position, as disclosed on the particulars, is a 60-day jail sentence. Based on your research, this is a harsh position on sentencing under the circumstances. You have made attempts to meet with an assistant Crown to discuss the matter, but since it has not yet been set for trial, no one has been assigned to the case. Should you set the matter down for trial? Should you convince your client to plead not guilty based on what the Crown is seeking in terms of a sentence? What should you do?

# Preliminary Matters

# 2

## LEARNING OUTCOMES

After reading this chapter, you should be able to:

- Describe the burden and standard of proof in a criminal proceeding

- List and explain the two basic elements of any criminal offence

- Understand what inchoate offences are

- Explain how identification evidence may be presented

- Distinguish between summary, hybrid or dual procedure, and indictable offences

- Locate the penalty provision for an offence under the *Criminal Code*

- Highlight the significance of the information

- Outline the process to lay a charge and issue process

- Describe what counts are and how they are set out

# Introduction

Paralegals have a limited scope of practice within criminal law. In this chapter, we will review how offences are classified under the *Criminal Code* with a view to ascertaining whether a particular offence falls within the scope of practice of paralegals. We will examine the elements of an offence that the Crown must prove as part of its case against an accused person and discuss how to find penalties for offences under the *Criminal Code*. Finally, we will look at the procedure for laying a charge and issuing process.

# Burden of Proof and Standard of Proof

In any criminal matter, there are always two parties involved: the Crown and the accused. Since the Crown represents the Queen or King, the official head of Canada, cases are always brought under his or her name. The Latin word for queen is *Regina*; for king, the word is *Rex*. Therefore, in a criminal case, the Crown is listed as *R*, which is short for *Regina* or *Rex*. The accused is identified by his or her last name. For example, if the accused's last name is Smith, the case citation would be *R v Smith*. Whichever party initiated the proceeding would be named first in the case citation. Therefore, if the Crown is prosecuting the accused, the Crown would be named first. If the accused is convicted and wants to appeal the conviction, the accused would be named first in the appeal (*Smith v Her Majesty the Queen*).

Occasionally, certain groups or organizations who may have an interest in the outcome of the proceedings may be granted **intervenor status**. These groups must apply to the court for leave to intervene. If leave is granted, the person or group is given legal standing to participate in the proceeding as an intervening party. This particularly occurs in cases where a non-party group or organization's rights may be affected by the outcome of a decision. Typically, this happens in appellate proceedings, but it may also happen at a trial. If there is a constitutional issue, the federal government may intervene as of right, meaning that there is no need to be granted leave by the court.

In a criminal matter, the Crown always bears the **burden of proof**. This means that the **onus** is on the Crown to prove its case against the accused person. When the onus shifts to the accused within a trial, it is referred to as a **reverse onus** situation. One example of when the onus shifts is in a Charter application in which an accused person is arguing that her right to counsel was violated. In this example, the Crown bears the burden of proving the elements of the case against the accused. However, the accused must prove that a Charter violation has occurred.

Another example of a reverse onus situation may arise in a bail application when the accused was already on a form of release when committing an offence and now has the onus of showing cause why he or she ought to be released again from custody pending the trial (see Chapter 4 for a discussion about the reverse onus situation in the context of bail). Both of these examples of reverse onus are procedural—where the accused bears the onus of proof as a matter of procedure. A

**intervenor status**
a legal status granted to a non-party to an offence to participate in the proceedings

**burden of proof**
obligation of a party to prove what it is asserting

**onus**
responsibility or obligation to prove

**reverse onus**
situation in which the burden of proving or disproving something shifts from the Crown to the accused

reverse onus situation may also result in the accused bearing the burden of disproving an element of the offence or a presumption (see Case in Point: *R v Oakes*).

## CASE IN POINT

# Reverse Onus: Onus on the Accused

*R v Oakes*, [1986] 1 SCR 103

### Facts

David Edwin Oakes was charged with unlawful possession of a narcotic for the purpose of trafficking pursuant to section 4(2) of the *Narcotic Control Act*, RSC 1970, c N-1. Oakes was found in possession of eight 1-gram vials of cannabis resin in the form of hashish oil. When the police searched him at the station, he had $619.45 on him. Oakes told the police that he had bought ten vials of hashish oil for $150 for his own use and that the remainder of the money was from a workers' compensation cheque.

At his trial, Oakes did not call any evidence as to his possession of the narcotic. Section 8 of the *Narcotic Control Act* provided that when an accused person was found in possession of a narcotic, the trier of fact must conclude that the accused possessed the narcotic for the purpose of trafficking unless the trier of fact was satisfied by evidence to the contrary that it was simple possession—that is, for the accused's own personal use. Oakes argued that section 8 of the *Narcotic Control Act* imposed a burden on the accused to prove that he or she was not in possession for the purpose of trafficking. This burden violated the presumption of innocence guaranteed under section 11(d) of the Charter.

### Decision

The Supreme Court of Canada held that section 8 of the *Narcotic Control Act* did violate section 11(d) of the Charter, in that it required Oakes to prove on a balance of probabilities that he was not in possession of the narcotic for the purpose of trafficking. The Supreme Court of Canada went on to say that the violation could not be saved under section 1 of the Charter. Therefore, section 8 of the *Narcotic Control Act* was struck down.

### Discussion Question

Do all reverse onus situations violate section 11(d) of the Charter? Does it matter whether a reverse onus situation is related to a procedure or to an element of the offence? Should reverse onus provisions be removed in criminal law, or are there situations in which they are justified?

The **standard of proof** is the extent to which the facts must be proven. The standard of proof that the Crown must meet is beyond a reasonable doubt. This does not mean having to prove with absolute certainty that the accused is guilty, but rather that there is no *reasonable* doubt in the mind of the trier of fact as to the guilt of the accused. Contrast this with a civil matter, in which the standard of proof is on a balance of probabilities, which is a much lesser burden. The reason for such a high evidentiary burden on the Crown is that under the Charter, the accused is presumed to be innocent until proven guilty. The accused also has Charter-protected liberty interests at stake in a criminal prosecution.

**standard of proof**
level or extent to which facts must be proven

# Elements of an Offence

There are two elements in any criminal offence: *actus reus* and *mens rea*.

## Actus Reus

**actus reus**
a Latin term for the "guilty act"; wrongful physical acts that make up the offence

**Actus reus** is a Latin term that means "the guilty act." The Crown must prove that the accused committed the guilty act beyond a reasonable doubt. An example of the *actus reus* components for the offence of assault, pursuant to section 265(1) of the *Criminal Code*, is outlined below. There are three different ways in which the *actus reus* for assault may be carried out:

(a) application of intentional force to another person, directly or indirectly, without the consent of that person;

(b) attempting to threaten or threaten, by an act or a gesture, to apply force to another person when the other person believes on reasonable grounds that the accused has the ability to carry out the threat; or

(c) while openly wearing or carrying a weapon or an imitation weapon, accosting or impeding another person, or begging.

**commission**
execution of an act that causes harm

**omission**
failure to do an act that one has a legal duty to do that results in harm

Not all criminal offences involve the **commission** of an act. Some offences involve an accused person failing to do something that he or she has a legal duty to do, which is referred to as an **omission**. An example of an offence made out by omitting to do something is the offence of failing to provide the necessaries of life to a child under the age of 16 years old, pursuant to section 215(1)(a) of the *Criminal Code*. The *actus reus* of this offence is made out by failing to provide food or shelter to a young child.

In another category of *actus reus*, simply being present at a location or having possession of an item is enough to prove the *actus reus* element. An example of this is the offence of possession of goods obtained by the commission of a crime, pursuant to section 354(1) of the *Criminal Code*.

---

### EXAMPLE

**Possession of Stolen Goods**

The police receive a complaint of loud noise coming from a residence. When they attend to investigate, they are allowed in by the homeowner, Harry. Once inside the residence, police see a stolen item of jewellery that they recognize as being taken during a recent robbery at a pawn shop. It does not matter whether Harry committed the robbery; for the purpose of this offence, the *actus reus* involves proving that he is in possession of the item that was obtained by the commission of a crime (the robbery).

---

The accused's mental state is not considered when looking at whether the *actus reus* is made out. For example, Person A holds a gun to Person B and tells Person B to steal lottery tickets from a convenience store; Person B then steals lottery tickets from the store out of fear for his personal safety. The *actus reus* of theft is made out even though Person B felt compelled to steal the lottery tickets.

This example demonstrates that in addition to the guilty act, there is a mental element to the offence that must be considered. For example, the *actus reus* must be voluntary and not a result of a reflex or convulsion. Similarly, if someone commits a criminal offence while under a hypnotic state, the *actus reus* cannot be said to be voluntary, assuming that there is evidence of a true hypnotic state; these defences will be discussed further in Chapter 8.

---

**EXAMPLE**

**Reflex or Convulsion**

Mary suffers from undiagnosed seizures. While driving, she suffers from a seizure and loses control of her vehicle. The vehicle swerves onto the sidewalk, striking and killing a pedestrian. In this case, although Mary committed the *actus reus*, her actions were involuntary. Therefore, Mary cannot be convicted of an offence.

---

In most cases, an action or omission is not enough to support guilt—it must be accompanied by a guilty mind.

## Mens Rea

**Mens rea** is a Latin term meaning "the guilty mind." In addition to proving elements of the *actus reus*, for criminal offences that require intent, the Crown must prove that the accused possessed the requisite mental intent to commit the offence. There are two types of *mens rea*: subjective and objective.

Subjective *mens rea* involves inquiring into what was in this particular accused's mind at the time of the offence. In other words, the Crown must prove beyond a reasonable doubt that the accused intended his or her actions. This is not always easy to do, especially in cases when the accused has not provided any statements to the police and does not testify at trial. The trier of fact must consider the evidence in determining what the accused actually intended, knew, or believed.

Although the offences of murder and manslaughter are indictable and do not fall within the paralegal scope of practice, subjective *mens rea* is best explained when looking at the offence of culpable homicide. Culpable homicide, found in section 222 of the *Criminal Code*, involves causing the death of a person either by an unlawful act, criminal negligence, fear, violence or deception, or wilfully frightening a vulnerable person. However, the penalties for culpable homicide vary depending on the intent of the accused. An accused person who commits a homicide may be charged with first degree murder, second degree murder, manslaughter, or criminal negligence causing death—in all of these cases, a death has resulted. The difference in these categories is in the actual sentence handed down to the accused, which is based on the accused's moral blameworthiness or subjective *mens rea*.

**mens rea**
a Latin term for "the guilty mind"; the criminal intention or knowledge of committing an offence

For first degree murder, the Crown must prove that the act was planned and deliberate. For example, if the accused person has planned the death of his spouse, purchases a gun two days before the murder, arranges for an alibi, and then kills her, he would be charged with first degree murder. If the victim dies in the course of a sexual assault, forcible confinement, kidnapping, or the hijacking of a plane, the accused would be charged with constructive first degree murder. He or she did not plan on killing the victim, but the victim died during the commission of another offence, and the accused was therefore responsible for the death. An accused person would also be charged with first degree murder in the death of a police officer acting in the course of his or her duty. Conviction of first degree murder results in an automatic sentence of life imprisonment with no chance of parole for at least 25 years.

Second degree murder is defined under the *Criminal Code* as all other murder other than first degree murder. An example of second degree murder is an accused person who gets into an argument with someone else, goes to her car to get a knife, and stabs the person with whom she argued. In this case, the murder was not planned in the sense of being calculated, with the consequences considered and weighed beforehand. It is also not deliberate, since the pros and cons of the killing were not thought out before the action. The minimum penalty for adults upon conviction for second degree murder is life imprisonment with no chance of parole for at least 10 years. If the Crown can prove that a culpable homicide occurred but cannot prove that it was planned and deliberate, then the accused will be convicted of second degree murder.

Manslaughter occurs when the accused commits an unlawful act that results in the death of another person. There are two different forms of manslaughter: voluntary manslaughter and criminal negligence causing death. Voluntary manslaughter is also referred to as unlawful act manslaughter—when the accused commits an unlawful act that results in the death of another person. The accused does not have the *mens rea* to cause the death of the other person; therefore, he cannot be charged with murder. This is where objective *mens rea* comes into play, which is the objective foresight of the risk of bodily harm that is not trivial or transient (*R v Creighton*, [1993] 3 SCR 3). This is sometimes referred to as a modified objective test: the Crown must prove that the accused had the *mens rea* to commit an unlawful act (subjective test) and that a reasonable person in the same circumstances as the accused would have foreseen the risk of non-trivial and non-transient bodily harm (objective test). It is not necessary for the Crown to prove that a reasonable person would have foreseen that death would have occurred.

An example of voluntary manslaughter is an accused person who gets into an argument with the victim in a parking garage and then punches the victim in the face. As a result of the blow, the victim hits his head on a concrete wall and dies two days later. While the accused did not intend to kill the victim and likely did not foresee that the punch would lead to the death of the victim, he did intend to punch the victim. Therefore, *mens rea* for the unlawful act exists. The Crown would also have to prove that a reasonable person in the same circumstances as the accused would foresee that as a result of the punch, the victim could fall and strike his head on the concrete wall, resulting in serious bodily harm.

The second form of manslaughter is criminal negligence causing death. In this category of manslaughter, there is no intent to commit any serious criminal offence; therefore, the accused's responsibility for causing death is constructed from either the commission or omission of an act. The *mens rea* element for criminal negligence is **recklessness**, or consciously disregarding the fact that the action may result in a substantial and unjustifiable risk of harm to another person. A famous example of criminal negligence causing death is the case of Francisco José Garzón Amo, the driver of a Spanish train that derailed, causing the death of 79 people.

Therefore, culpable homicide is an offence for which, depending on the level of *mens rea* of the offender, the penalty varies greatly. This is based on the premise that offenders should be penalized according to their level of moral blameworthiness.

**recklessness**
consciously disregarding the fact that an action may result in a substantial and unjustifiable risk of harm to another person

---

**EXAMPLE**

**Francisco José Garzón Amo**

On July 12, 2013, in one of Europe's worst rail disasters, 79 people died in a train crash in Spain. Francisco José Garzón Amo, the driver, was charged with numerous counts of criminal negligence causing death. Evidence from the black box recorder showed that the train was travelling at 95 mph (153 km/hr), with speeds of up to 119 mph (192 km/hr) in a 50 mph (80 km/hr) speed limit. The train derailed on a curve in the tracks and smashed into a concrete wall. There was evidence that Garzón Amo slammed on the brakes seconds before the crash instead of braking four kilometres before the curve as typical. There was also evidence that Garzón Amo had been on the phone with railway officials and had been reading a document at the time of the crash.

---

## How to Determine the Level of Mens Rea in Offences Under the Criminal Code

The intention requirement for offences is typically described by using words such as: "intentionally," "with intent to," "for the purpose of," "knowingly," "wilfully," "as a means to," or "recklessly." As discussed above, the Crown may be required to prove beyond a reasonable doubt that the accused's purpose was to commit a criminal offence (subjective test) or that a reasonable person in the accused's circumstances would have foreseen the risk of harm in committing the act(s) leading up to the offence (modified objective test). Depending on the wording used in the description of the offence, either a subjective, objective, or modified objective test would apply in determining the level of *mens rea* of the accused. As can be seen in the table below, the level of *mens rea* may vary depending on the offence.

Many provincial offences, which are **quasi-criminal** in nature, require a much lower level of *mens rea*; these are called strict liability offences. Those that contain no *mens rea* element at all are called absolute liability offences. Since these types of offences do not involve significant liberty interests and are regulatory in nature, the *mens rea* component is minimal or non-existent. However, all criminal offences require the Crown to prove some level of *mens rea*.

**quasi-criminal**
non-criminal but may carry a penalty similar to that of a criminal offence

**Mens Rea Continuum: From Proof of Higher Levels of Intent to Lower Levels**

| Level of Mens Rea | Definition | Wording in the Offence Section* | Example |
|---|---|---|---|
| *Intention*† | Accused fully intends to commit the *actus reus*. In other words, the accused foresees it and desires it. | "intentionally," "with intent," "wilfully," "purposely" | Vinh plans to go to a bar where Amit will be present so that Vinh can punch Amit. |
| *Knowledge* | Accused must have knowledge of certain facts in order to have the requisite *mens rea*. | "knowingly," "with knowledge" | Sally was caught by the police with a bag of marijuana. The Crown must prove that Sally knew that the baggie contained marijuana. |
| *Wilful blindness* | Accused has suspicions about the illegal act but deliberately chooses not to investigate or inquire any further. | "wilfully," "knowingly," "with knowledge," "deliberately" | Mario is walking through a park at midnight and is approached by someone who wants to sell a box of ten brand new iPhones, still in their packaging, for $200. |
| *Recklessness* | Accused is aware of the danger or risk in an action and persists in doing it anyway. | "reckless," "recklessly," "disregarding" | Preet throws an empty beer bottle toward his neighbour's house that shatters the window. |
| *Criminal negligence* | Accused does not realize the consequences of his or her actions, but a reasonable person would have. | "with negligence," "negligently," "neglectfully" | Magda is driving 20 km over the speed limit in a rain storm, fiddling with her CD player, and talking on a cell phone. She hits a pedestrian, instantly killing him. |

\* Even without the use of these words, the offence may include acts that involve the requisite level of *mens rea*. It is not necessary that offences include specific words describing the level of *mens rea*.

† Intention should not be confused with premeditation—it is not a requirement that the accused plan the *actus reus* ahead of time.

# Inchoate Offences

**inchoate offences**
offences that are not fully completed; the *mens rea* is present but not all of the elements of the *actus reus* are present

**attempt**
intention to commit the offence, along with actions that extend beyond mere preparation

**conspiracy**
agreement between two or more parties to commit an offence

**counselling**
deliberately encouraging or actively inducing another person to commit an offence

**Inchoate offences** involve some action toward the completion of an offence—simply thinking about committing an offence is not sufficient to constitute a crime. Although the Crown must prove the *mens rea* of the accused, the *actus reus* of the offence is not complete. There are three types of inchoate offences: an **attempt**, a **conspiracy**, or **counselling** someone to commit an offence.

An attempt involves the accused trying but either failing or not following through with all of the steps of the *actus reus*. Some offences under the *Criminal Code* make specific reference to an attempt related to that particular offence. Section 24(1) of the *Criminal Code* defines the offence of attempt and stipulates that the Crown must prove the intention of the accused to commit the offence. The Crown must further prove that the defendant's actions or omissions go **beyond mere preparation** to commit the offence. Whether the defendant took steps beyond mere preparation to commit the offence is a question of law for the trial judge, pursuant to section 24(2) of the *Criminal Code*.

**beyond mere preparation**
a legal test applied by a judge to determine whether the accused has taken steps toward committing the offence beyond simply planning it

The Supreme Court of Canada has stated that in determining whether the actions of the accused go beyond mere preparation, the court must consider the significance of the accused's actions and how close the accused came to actually completing the offence (*Deutsch v The Queen*, [1986] 2 SCR 2). It is also important to note that even if circumstances make it impossible for the accused to commit the offence, he or she may still be convicted of an attempt. Section 463 of the *Criminal Code* sets out penalties for attempts, and in the case of an attempted summary conviction offence, the accused will be found guilty of a summary conviction offence. An example of a case involving an attempt is set out in the Case in Point: *R v Lucas*.

The offence of conspiracy to commit an offence is set out in section 465(1) of the *Criminal Code*. The offence of conspiracy is complete upon the agreement of two or more parties to commit an illegal act. The Crown must prove that all of the parties actually intended to carry out the act. Unlike the offence of attempt, the Crown does not have to prove that any steps were taken toward completing the act—the *actus reus* is complete once an agreement is made. In most cases, the penalty for a conviction for conspiracy is the same as the penalty for carrying out the actual offence.

The offence of counselling involves the accused person deliberately encouraging or actively inducing another person to commit or become a party to a criminal offence. Counselling is set out in section 22(1) of the *Criminal Code*, and it is not a requirement that the offence be carried out in the manner in which it is counselled. As long as the actual offence committed is one that the accused person knew or ought to have known was likely to be committed as a result of his or her counselling, the offence is made out. Section 464(b) creates an offence of counselling even when the offence is not ultimately committed. Counselling a summary conviction offence that is not committed is an offence punishable by summary conviction.

---

### EXAMPLE

#### The Irksome Ex

Simi is upset with her ex-boyfriend. One day, while she is having a few drinks after work, she starts thinking of ways to get back at him. She discusses her ideas with an undercover police officer sitting at the bar. Simi tries to recruit the police officer into going to her ex-boyfriend's house and damaging his new sports car. Even though Simi is unaware that she is speaking to an undercover police officer who has no intention of carrying out her plan, Simi could be charged with counselling to commit mischief.

## CASE IN POINT

# Attempt Break and Enter

*R v Lucas*, 2013 ONCJ 280

### Facts

The accused, Isaac Lucas, was observed on video surveillance to be walking back and forth on the main floor of a building containing an automated teller machine. Lucas was then seen to exit the building and return shortly after with a set of wire cutters. He was observed to climb up on a radiator, snip the cord off of the glass break sensor, and pocket the sensor before leaving the building. Lucas then got into a Cadillac Escalade and left the area. Approximately 2–3 weeks later, Lucas was arrested for an unrelated break and enter offence, at which time he was identified as the suspect on the surveillance video. He was charged with an attempt break and enter with intent to commit an indictable offence.

The Crown argued that the actions captured on the video constituted an attempt to commit the offence of break and enter into the building, and that the actions of disabling and stealing the glass break sensor went beyond mere preparation to commit the offence. Furthermore, the Crown argued that there was no other rational explanation for the accused to disable the security system other than an intention to break into the building at a later date.

### Decision

Justice Baldwin of the Ontario Court of Justice held that the fact that there was no actual break and enter into this particular building close in time to when the glass break sensor was disabled was of no significance. In finding the accused guilty of the offence of an attempt to commit a break and enter, the Court found that not only did the accused steal the sensor, but he was also observed to clean up the mess and stuff the wires back into the ceiling, conceivably to hide what he did. The images of him walking back and forth into the lobby area, constantly looking around him, were evidence of him casing-out the building. It was clear that Lucas had the *mens rea* to commit the offence of break and enter. The Court further concluded that Lucas' actions went beyond mere preparation. Justice Baldwin commented that to be guilty of an attempt, the accused person must have progressed a sufficient distance (that is, beyond mere preparation) down the intended path.

### Discussion Questions

Where is the line to be drawn between mere preparation and an attempt? How close to the actual offence must the accused be in order to be convicted of an attempt? Does it matter if the accused changed his or her mind about carrying through with the offence?

# Identification

**identification**
evidence showing that a person charged with an offence is the one who committed the offence

**circumstantial evidence**
evidence that relies on an inference or reasoning to connect it to a conclusion of fact

**Identification**, although not a separate element, is something that the Crown must prove in any criminal offence. In other words, the Crown must prove beyond a reasonable doubt that the accused person charged with the offence is the one who committed the offence. Identification evidence may be present in several different ways: by forensic evidence, such as fingerprints or bodily substances belonging to the accused; by eyewitness identification; by video surveillance; or by written or verbal confessions from the accused and/or co-accused(s). In certain cases, there may be no real evidence linking the accused to the offence, but several pieces of **circumstantial evidence**, when considered together, point to the culpability of the accused person.

> ### PRACTICE TIP
>
> Defence agents do not have to have their clients sit with them at counsel table. Once the accused is arraigned and the trial begins, the accused may sit in the gallery. This is especially important to remember in a case in which the defence believes that eyewitness identification will be problematic. Sometimes the witness may not be sure of the accused's identity but just points to the person sitting at counsel table, as he or she expects the accused to be sitting there. Note that if the defence paralegal uses this tactic and the witness is able to successfully point out the accused, this may result in strong identification evidence for the Crown, especially if the gallery is filled with people! Therefore, the defence will have to use caution before engaging in this practice.

In Canada, **forensic identification specialists** are responsible for collecting physical evidence from a crime scene. These specialists are police officers with specialized training in the location, collection, and preservation of evidence, which is then submitted to a laboratory for analysis.

**forensic identification specialist**
specially trained police officer responsible for the collection of physical evidence from a crime scene

# Classification of Offences in the Criminal Code

There are three main types of offences in the *Criminal Code*: indictable offences, hybrid offences, and summary conviction offences.

## Indictable Offences

The most serious category of offences is that of **indictable offences**. Examples of indictable offences include but are not limited to: murder, manslaughter, robbery, sexual assault causing bodily harm, aggravated assault, drug trafficking, and acts of terrorism. Greater penalties are involved for indictable offences. For certain indictable offences, such as murder, the potential maximum penalty is life imprisonment. There is no **limitation period** in proceeding with an indictable offence, meaning that the police may charge a person at any time with an indictable offence, provided that there is sufficient evidence against the person.

In most cases, a person charged with an indictable offence has the right to choose his or her mode of trial: before a provincial court judge, a superior court judge alone, or before a judge and jury in Superior Court. A person charged with an indictable offence may also have the right to a **preliminary inquiry**. Sections 535–551 of the *Criminal Code* deal with the procedure of preliminary inquiries.

Not everyone charged with an indictable offence is entitled to a trial before a judge and jury, or to a preliminary inquiry. Section 553 of the *Criminal Code* deals with **absolute jurisdiction offences**; in those cases, a provincial court judge has absolute jurisdiction to try an accused person charged with certain offences, such as theft, fraud, false pretences, and mischief. For absolute jurisdiction offences, there is no right to a preliminary inquiry.

**indictable offences**
the most serious category of offences under the *Criminal Code*, which may only be tried on indictment

**limitation period**
specific time period by which a charge must be laid

**preliminary inquiry**
evidentiary hearing during which the Crown must prove that there is sufficient evidence to proceed with an indictment against the accused

**absolute jurisdiction offences**
offences for which a provincial court judge has absolute jurisdiction to try an accused person charged with certain offences

## Hybrid Offences

The second category of offences is **hybrid offences**, which cover the majority of offences under the *Criminal Code*. Hybrid offences are sometimes referred to as **dual procedure offences**. This is because the Crown may make an election as to whether to proceed by summary conviction or by indictment. If no election is made, the offence is considered to proceed by way of indictment. However, if no election is made on a hybrid offence and it proceeds to trial before a summary conviction court, there is a presumption that the Crown has elected to proceed summarily (*R v Dudley*, 2009 SCC 58, [2009] 3 SCR 570).

*Limitation period is 12 months!*

### Crown Election

The Crown's election as to whether to proceed by way of summary conviction or by indictment may be based on several factors, such as: the number of prior convictions on the accused person's record, the seriousness of the offence, the Crown's position on sentencing, the desire for a quick trial process, the length of time that the matter has been pending in the court system, whether the information was sworn outside of the limitation period for a summary conviction offence, and other relevant considerations. The decision as to how the Crown wishes to proceed is a discretionary one and not subject to review by any court unless the Crown exercises a deliberate abuse of process. The Crown may make its election at any time prior to a plea being entered.

## Summary Conviction Offences

The third category of offences is **summary conviction offences**, which are generally less serious types of offences. Although part XXVII of the *Criminal Code* deals with summary convictions, summary conviction offences are found throughout all sections of the *Criminal Code*. There are few criminal offences that are strictly summary. Some examples include causing a disturbance, trespassing at night, public nudity, possession of marijuana under 30 grams, and harassing telephone calls. For a purely summary conviction offence or an offence for which the Crown elects to proceed by way of summary conviction, the accused person must be charged with the offence within six months of when the "subject-matter of the proceedings arose," pursuant to section 786(2) of the *Criminal Code*. If the information is laid outside of the six month limitation period for a pure summary conviction offence, the information is defective, as there is no jurisdiction to proceed on it. An exception to this arises if both the Crown and the defence consent to the information being laid outside of the six month limitation period.

Summary conviction trials take place in provincial court, and there is no option for a jury trial. Police powers of arrest with or without a warrant, as well as fingerprinting procedures, are distinguished for summary conviction offences, as will be discussed in Chapter 3. Most summary conviction offences, or hybrid offences for which the Crown elects to proceed by way of summary conviction, carry a maximum penalty of six months' incarceration and/or a fine not exceeding $5,000. There are exceptions to this general penalty, as discussed below.

There is a "fourth" category of offence that is not officially recognized under the *Criminal Code* but carries a higher maximum penalty than the general penalty for summary conviction offences. These are **super-summary offences**, or summary conviction offences that are punishable by a maximum of 18 months' incarceration and/or a $10,000 fine. Super-summary offences are distinguished from summary conviction offences only in terms of the penalty that they carry. The penalty for these offences is higher, yet they still fall under the umbrella of summary conviction and allow flexibility to the Crown in avoiding a preliminary inquiry. Examples of super-summary offences include sexual assault, assault with a weapon, impaired driving, and any offence involving a child under the age of 18.

> **PRACTICE TIP**
>
> As paralegals do not have authority to appear on indictable offences, or on super-summary offences for which the penalty exceeds six months of incarceration, it is best to ask the Crown early on in the matter as to how the Crown is proceeding. If the attending Crown does not make an election, ask the Crown to undertake to provide their position by the next court appearance. While the Crown is not obligated to make an election at the first court appearance, the defence paralegal wants to avoid a situation in which he or she has been acting on behalf of the client throughout the proceedings and then discovers that the Crown is proceeding by indictment.

**super-summary offences**
a category of hybrid or summary conviction offences that carry a greater penalty than the general penalty for summary conviction offences

# Determining the Penalty Provision for an Offence

The penalty for a summary conviction or hybrid offence may be found in one of three locations in the *Criminal Code*.

Certain offences have the penalty set out in the offence section itself. An example of this is found for the offence of manufacturing, promoting, or selling instruments or literature for illicit drug use, pursuant to section 462.2 of the *Criminal Code*.

> 462.2. Every one who knowingly imports into Canada, exports from Canada, manufactures, promotes or sells instruments or literature for illicit drug use is guilty of an offence and liable on summary conviction
>> (a) for a first offence, to a fine not exceeding one hundred thousand dollars or to imprisonment for a term not exceeding six months or to both; or
>> (b) for a second or subsequent offence, to a fine not exceeding three hundred thousand dollars or to imprisonment for a term not exceeding one year or to both.

As can be seen from the excerpt, the offence itself is described under section 462.2, and the penalties are set out in the same section under paragraphs (a) and (b). From the wording of the section, it is clear that this is a pure summary conviction offence. The penalty for a first offence is a maximum fine of $100,000 and/or six months' incarceration. For a second or subsequent offence, the penalty is a maximum fine of $300,000 and/or one year incarceration. Therefore, a paralegal would not be able to represent someone facing a charge pursuant to this section, given that the penalty is outside of the permissible scope of practice.

Another example of an offence for which the penalty is set out in the offence section itself is the offence of unlawfully causing bodily harm, pursuant to sections 269(a) and (b) of the *Criminal Code*:

269.  Every one who unlawfully causes bodily harm to any person is guilty of
    (a)  an indictable offence and liable to imprisonment for a term not exceeding ten years; or
    (b)  an offence punishable on summary conviction and liable to imprisonment for a term not exceeding eighteen months.

As can be determined from the wording of this section, this is a hybrid offence, punishable by indictment or by summary conviction. The penalty in either case is set out in the offence section itself. Even if the Crown were to proceed by way of summary conviction, a defence paralegal would not be authorized to represent an accused person, since the maximum penalty is 18 months' incarceration (a super-summary offence). It is important to note that the paralegal jurisdiction to appear stems from the penalty provision set out for the particular offence and is not based on what the Crown is actually seeking as a penalty. The reason for this is that the judge is not bound by the Crown's sentencing recommendation and may potentially impose the maximum penalty authorized under the *Criminal Code*.

Some offences do not have the penalty provision set out in the description of the offence itself; rather, it is found in close proximity to the offence. The only way to determine this is to read the sections following the offence section in order to look for the penalty. An example of this for a pure summary conviction offence is unlawful assembly, pursuant to section 63(1) of the *Criminal Code*:

63(1)  An unlawful assembly is an assembly of three or more persons who, with intent to carry out any common purpose, assemble in such a manner or so conduct themselves when they are assembled as to cause persons in the neighbourhood of the assembly to fear, on reasonable grounds, that they
    (a)  will disturb the peace tumultuously; or
    (b)  will by that assembly needlessly and without reasonable cause provoke other persons to disturb the peace tumultuously.

*Lawful assembly becoming unlawful*
(2)  Persons who are lawfully assembled may become an unlawful assembly if they conduct themselves with a common purpose in a manner that would have made the assembly unlawful if they had assembled in that manner for that purpose.

*Exception*
(3)  Persons are not unlawfully assembled by reason only that they are assembled to protect the dwelling-house of any one of them against persons who are threatening to break and enter it for the purpose of committing an indictable offence therein.

From the reading of the offence itself, there is no mention of the type of offence that it is (summary, hybrid, or indictable) or the penalty for it. Reading further down from this section, the penalty is mentioned under section 66 of the *Criminal Code*:

*Punishment for unlawful assembly*
66.  Every one who is a member of an unlawful assembly is guilty of an offence punishable on summary conviction.

Another example of an offence for which the penalty section can only be found by reading the sections following the offence is assault, pursuant to section 265(1) of the *Criminal Code*:

265(1)  A person commits an assault when
(a)  without the consent of another person, he applies force intentionally to that other person, directly or indirectly;
(b)  he attempts or threatens, by an act or a gesture, to apply force to another person, if he has, or causes that other person to believe on reasonable grounds that he has, present ability to effect his purpose; or
(c)  while openly wearing or carrying a weapon or an imitation thereof, he accosts or impedes another person or begs.

While this is a detailed description of the various ways in which the offence of assault may be made out, there is no reference to the penalty provisions or to the type of offence. Reading on, section 266 makes mention of the penalty:

266.  Every one who commits an assault is guilty of
(a)  an indictable offence and is liable to imprisonment for a term not exceeding five years; or
(b)  an offence punishable on summary conviction.

Therefore, assault is a hybrid offence, and a defence paralegal may represent someone charged with assault if the Crown proceeds by way of summary conviction.

Finally, some offences only make reference to the fact that the offence is punishable on summary conviction and do not mention a specific penalty. This is the case for assault when the Crown proceeds summarily; section 266(b) does not specifically mention what the penalty is. Another example is found for the offence of trespassing at night, pursuant to section 177 of the *Criminal Code*:

177.  Every one who, without lawful excuse, the proof of which lies on him, loiters or prowls at night on the property of another person near a dwelling-house situated on that property is guilty of an offence punishable on summary conviction.

Again, the specific penalty is not set out for the offence of trespassing at night. When the *Criminal Code* does not make specific mention of the penalty other than to state that it is punishable upon summary conviction, where does one look for the actual penalty? The answer is found in section 787(1) of the *Criminal Code*, the general penalty section for summary conviction proceedings:

787(1)  Unless otherwise provided by law, everyone who is convicted of an offence punishable on summary conviction is liable to a fine of not more than five thousand dollars or to a term of imprisonment not exceeding six months or to both.

Therefore, section 787(1) of the *Criminal Code* tells us that when there is no penalty specified for a summary conviction proceeding, the general penalty is a maximum fine of $5,000 and/or imprisonment not exceeding six months.

# The Information

**information**
charging document for
criminal offences that is
sworn and commences
the prosecution

As mentioned earlier in this chapter, for a pure summary conviction offence, or for a hybrid offence for which the Crown wishes to proceed summarily, the limitation period to lay charges is six months. Charges or offences are set out in an **information**, which is the charging document for criminal offences. Pursuant to section 788(1) of the *Criminal Code*, proceedings are commenced by laying an information in Form 2. In order for an information to be laid, the police must have **reasonable grounds** to believe that an offence—or offences—has been committed and that the person being charged has committed the offence. Reasonable grounds is a much

**reasonable grounds**
a set of facts or circum-
stances that would cause a
person of ordinary and prudent judgment to believe
beyond a mere suspicion

lower standard than proof beyond a reasonable doubt. However, it is much more than a hunch. The grounds put forth by the police officer must demonstrate that there is a probability that an offence has occurred and that the accused has committed the offence. This is an objective test, meaning whether a reasonable person, standing in the shoes of the police officer, would also believe that reasonable grounds exist for an offence, or offences, to have been committed by the accused person.

For summary conviction matters, the police officer must lay an information in writing and under oath before a justice of the peace or before a provincial court judge (section 789(1)(a) of the *Criminal Code*). A sample information is found at Form 2 of the *Criminal Code* (see Appendix B). The information is accompanied by a sworn summary of the evidence.

The procedure for laying an information for indictable and hybrid offences varies depending on whether or not the accused is under arrest at the time of the laying of the information. For indictable and hybrid offences, if the accused has not yet been arrested, the justice must hear and consider the allegations at a **pre-enquete hearing**. This means that the hearing is not open to the public. The justice may also hear the evidence of witnesses when it is necessary or desirable to do so.

**pre-enquete hearing**
private hearing in the
absence of the parties

# Issuing Process

**issuing process**
a procedure in which a
justice issues a summons
or warrant or confirms
the form of release that
the accused is on

If the justice decides that there are enough grounds to proceed with laying the sworn information and have the accused person attend court, then the justice may decide to issue a summons or a warrant, or confirm the form of release that the accused is already on. This is known as **issuing process**. Pursuant to section 788(2) of the *Criminal Code*, one justice may receive the information and issue a summons or warrant with respect to the information. On the other hand, if the justice is not satisfied that the requisite grounds exist for laying the sworn information, then process will not be issued. When the accused person has already been released by the police officer on an appearance notice, a promise to appear, or a recognizance, the justice may cancel the form of release.

If the accused has been arrested and released by the police officer to attend court, the information must be laid as soon as practicable and before the accused's first appearance in court (section 505 of the *Criminal Code*). It should be noted that the Crown does not lose jurisdiction over the offence in situations in which the information is not laid before the first appearance; however, if the charge has not been laid, then the form of release will be of no further force or effect. In this situation, a new summons or warrant will have to be issued for the accused in order to compel his or her attendance in court. Forms of release will be discussed in greater detail in Chapter 4.

For any public prosecution, the person laying the information, or **informant**, is usually a police officer. However, any person who has reasonable grounds to believe that an offence has been committed by a known person may swear an information on oath by appearing before a justice. This is known as a private prosecution. In this case, although the justice must receive the information, he or she must also refer the matter to a provincial court judge, who then holds a special hearing to determine whether the person named in the information should be compelled to attend court. The attorney general must be provided with a copy of the information and notice of the hearing.

**informant**
person who has reasonable grounds to believe that an offence has been committed and who appears before a justice to swear an information on oath

# Counts

An information may set out more than one offence, but the facts supporting each offence must be clearly set out in a separate **count**. Each count sets out the specifics of an offence in sufficient detail so that the accused knows exactly what the details of the offence are. This allows the accused to understand the case that he or she has to meet. Typically, the date of the offence, the location of the offence, and the name of the complainant are listed for each count. If the exact date or location is not known, an approximate date or location may suffice.

If the accused is charged with committing the same offence against several people, then each count will deal with each named complainant. If an accused is charged with a number of different offences against one complainant, then each count will deal with each offence. If two offences are set out in a single count, it violates the **rule against duplicity**, and the defence paralegal may seek a motion to amend the count on the basis that it is too ambiguous. Similarly, if there is any defect in the information or the counts, the defence paralegal may bring a motion to quash the information or the counts, pursuant to section 601(1) of the *Criminal Code*. Where two or more co-accused are charged together, the defence paralegal for one accused may bring a **motion to sever** the co-accused being tried together. The judge will hear arguments from the Crown and defence before ruling on the motion to sever. Section 591(3) refers to whether it is "in the interests of justice" to sever the accused and the counts. An accused person may also seek to join charges on separate informations when the offences are related to the same transaction. This is referred to as **joinder** of counts. Joinder may also be used to join co-accused who wish to be tried together.

**count**
specific details pertaining to an offence that are set out in the information

**rule against duplicity**
rule against duplicate or ambiguous offences set out in one count

**motion to sever**
application to separate co-accused or charges from being heard together on an information

**joinder**
joining charges or co-accused together

## PRACTICE TIP

Although section 601(1) of the *Criminal Code* refers to amending defects in an indictment, section 795 of the *Criminal Code* indicates that part XX applies to summary conviction matters. Section 601(1) is in part XX of the *Criminal Code*; therefore, the sections pertaining to amending counts and indictments apply equally to an information and the counts contained in it.

## Multiple Counts

**multiple count information**
information that contains more than one count

An information that has several counts is referred to as a **multiple count information**. Each count relates to a separate offence but arises from the same transaction for which the accused was arrested. For example, Mary had too many alcoholic drinks at a bar, got into a fight and punched someone, smashed a window at the establishment, and proceeded to drive home while her ability to operate a motor vehicle was impaired by alcohol. Mary would be charged with assault, mischief under $5,000, and driving while impaired. The information would contain these three counts, as they arose out of the same transaction.

Using the same example, perhaps Mary had too much to drink at the bar and then drove home without punching anyone or breaking the window. On the way home, Mary was pulled over by the police and charged with driving while impaired. Mary was released the next day, but two days later, she was still upset with one of the servers for serving her too much alcohol. Mary returned to the bar and punched the server, and on her way out of the bar, she smashed a window. The police were called, and Mary was charged with assault and mischief under $5,000. Since the charges of assault and mischief under $5,000 did not arise from the same circumstances as the impaired driving offence, they would form part of a separate transaction. Therefore, these charges would appear in a separate information. In this case, there would be little use in joining these charges together, as they involve separate circumstances and Mary would likely want the benefit of having two separate trials.

## CHAPTER SUMMARY

The burden of proof in a criminal matter is always on the Crown, and the standard of proof is beyond a reasonable doubt. This is due to the gravity of a criminal prosecution and the liberty interests at stake for an accused person. For evidentiary or procedural issues, the onus may shift to the accused.

The two basic elements for any *Criminal Code* offence are *actus reus* and *mens rea*. In most cases, the Crown must prove these elements beyond a reasonable doubt. The *actus reus* may involve the commission or omission of an act. The level of *mens rea* varies for different offences.

An accused person may also be convicted on an inchoate offence, such as an attempt, a conspiracy, or counselling to commit an offence that is not complete. In order to prove an attempted offence, the Crown must show that the accused took steps beyond merely preparing to commit the crime.

For all criminal offences, the Crown must prove the identification of the accused. This means that the accused person is the one who committed the offence. Identification evidence may be present in several different forms.

All criminal offences can be classified as indictable, hybrid or dual procedure, or summary conviction offences. Indictable offences are the most serious type. Hybrid or dual procedures offences refer to those for which the Crown has the option of proceeding either by indictment or by summary conviction. Summary conviction offences are the least serious category of offences.

There are three methods of locating a penalty for a summary conviction *Criminal Code* offence: within the offence section itself; within close proximity to the offence section; or, where no penalty is specified, the general penalty section for summary conviction offences (section 787(1)). The offence section and surrounding sections must be read carefully in order to determine where the penalty may be found.

When the police have reasonable grounds to believe that a criminal offence has occurred, they must swear an information on oath before a justice. The information is the charging document for criminal offences and is accompanied by a sworn summary of the evidence.

If the justice is satisfied that reasonable grounds exist for a charge to be laid, he or she must issue process by issuing a summons or warrant for the accused, or by confirming the form of release that the accused is on.

The facts that support each offence must be set out in a separate count in the information. Each count must contain sufficient detail so that the accused person is aware of the nature of the criminal charge. When there are several offences involved as part of one transaction, these are set out in a multiple count information.

## KEY TERMS

# REVIEW QUESTIONS

## Short Answer

1. For which of the following offences may a paralegal represent a client?

    a. taking a motor vehicle without owner's consent

    b. harassing telephone calls

    c. uttering threats to cause bodily harm

    d. criminal harassment

    e. defacing current coins

    f. robbery

    g. assault causing bodily harm

    h. keeping a gaming or betting house

2. Identify the offence section, penalty section, and actual penalty upon the Crown proceeding by way of summary conviction for each of the following offences:

    a. personating someone at an exam

    b. disarming a peace officer

    c. causing unnecessary suffering to a bird by poison

    d. mailing obscene matter

    e. unauthorized recording of a movie

    f. contempt of court

    g. forcible confinement

3. Name the two essential components of every criminal offence that the Crown must prove. Describe what each term means.

4. What are three types of inchoate offences and how is the *actus reus* component different from a regular offence?

5. What are the steps in laying a charge and issuing process?

## Apply Your Knowledge

1. On August 20, 2013, at 10 p.m., Police Constable Singh is called to Shooter's Bar in Anytown, Ontario. When he attends to the address at 123 Anyplace Street, he meets with the owner, Joe. Joe tells Constable Singh that he was robbed exactly two weeks ago at Shooter's Bar by a regular patron named Dave. According to Joe, Dave was playing darts at the bar with some other friends. Dave was so drunk that he kept losing, and this made him angry. At 2 a.m., Joe told Dave that it was time to close up. Dave threatened to stab Joe with the sharp end of the dart unless Joe gave him a bottle of rum. Fearing for his safety, Joe gave him a new bottle of rum from behind the bar. Dave left quickly and had not returned to the bar until tonight. Constable Singh asks Joe why he had not called the police at the time of the robbery. Joe tells Constable Singh that he did not wish to make any trouble for Dave. However, Dave returned tonight, approached Joe, and told him that if he spoke to the police about the previous incident, he would come back and knock Joe's teeth out. Dave also slashed Joe's tires before leaving tonight. Joe tells Constable Singh where Dave can be found. Dave is subsequently arrested.

    a. Constable Singh is appearing before a justice of the peace to lay the information. Which offences should Dave be charged with?

    b. What other details from this fact scenario would need to be listed in the information?

2. Stan decides to earn some cash on the side by creating fake tickets to a sold-out music concert. He uses a high quality laser printer to print the tickets, which look authentic. Two days before the concert, Stan posts an online ad indicating that he has tickets available for purchase. His plan is to meet the buyers in front of the concert arena five minutes before the show so that they will not have any time to verify whether the tickets are real. Several people contact Stan and indicate that they are interested in buying the tickets from him.

    On the day of the concert, there is a severe ice storm, resulting in the concert being cancelled. Three days later, Stan is arrested as a result of his roommate tipping off the police. Do you think Stan is guilty of an offence? What can he be charged with? Provide reasons for your answer.

3. Jessica works in a bulk foods store. Jessica dislikes her manager, as he is very rude and condescending toward her. At the end of a particularly difficult shift, Jessica purposely knocks over a glass jar of peanuts, shattering it near the candy bins, which are being stocked by another employee at the time. Jessica makes no attempt to clean it up, since she is finished for the day.

    The next morning, a six-year-old boy is rushed to the hospital for a severe allergic reaction to ingesting peanut fragments, which were found in a plastic bag of candy that his mother purchased for him from the bulk food store. The candy was from an open bin in the same area where Jessica knocked over the jar of peanuts. All of this is later discovered on a store surveillance tape. Can Jessica be charged with an offence? Why or why not?

# Investigatory Police Powers and the Charter

# 3

## LEARNING OUTCOMES

After reading this chapter, you should be able to:

- List the legal rights under the *Canadian Charter of Rights and Freedoms* that pertain to an accused person in a summary conviction matter

- Outline the process for obtaining a search warrant and describe the legalities of a search with or without a warrant

- Distinguish between a warrantless arrest and an arrest with a warrant

- Outline the components of the right to counsel

- Explain the protections available under the right to silence and the right against self-crimination

- Identify the circumstances in which a statement or confession made by an accused person will be admissible in court

- Describe the test for exclusion of unlawfully obtained evidence

# Introduction

In the Canadian criminal justice system, there is a fine balance between the powers of the police to investigate crime and the preservation of the rights of the accused. In this chapter, we will look at police investigatory powers and procedures of arrest and search, both with and without a warrant. We will also examine specific legal rights under the *Canadian Charter of Rights and Freedoms* that most frequently apply to an accused person in a criminal proceeding. These include the right to be secure against unreasonable search or seizure, the right against arbitrary detention, the right to counsel, and the right to silence. We will discuss the intersection of the common law as it applies to warrantless searches, as well as to the statements and confessions of an accused person. Finally, we will identify the remedy for situations where evidence has been obtained as a result of a violation of the accused's rights.

# The Canadian Charter of Rights and Freedoms

The Charter, which came into effect on April 17, 1982, is the most important piece of legislation in Canada that protects the rights of the individual against govern-

**The Canadian Charter of Rights and Freedoms: Common Legal Rights Involved in Criminal Law**

| Charter Section | Legal Right |
|---|---|
| Section 7 | Right to life, liberty, and security of the person and the right not to be deprived thereof except in accordance with the principles of fundamental justice |
| Section 8 | Right to be secure against unreasonable search or seizure |
| Section 9 | Right against arbitrary detention or imprisonment |
| Section 10(a) | Right to be informed promptly of the reasons for arrest or detention |
| Section 10(b) | Right to retain and instruct counsel without delay and to be informed of that right |
| Section 10(c) | Right to have the validity of the detention determined by way of habeas corpus |
| Section 11(a) | Right to be informed without unreasonable delay of the specific offence |
| Section 11(b) | Right to be tried within a reasonable time |
| Section 11(c) | Right not to be compelled to be a witness in proceedings against that person in respect of the offence |
| Section 11(d) | Right to be presumed innocent until proven guilty according to law in a fair and public hearing by an independent and impartial tribunal |
| Section 11(e) | Right not to be denied reasonable bail without just cause |
| Section 24(1) | Enforcement of guaranteed rights and freedoms |
| Section 24(2) | Exclusion of evidence bringing administration of justice into disrepute |

ment intrusion. It applies to any act of the federal or provincial government. Since provincial governments have the power to create municipalities, the Charter applies to municipal governments as well. The Charter guarantees certain political, civil, and legal rights to people in Canada regarding the policies and actions of all three levels of government. It is important to note that the Charter applies to all people residing within the country, regardless of whether or not they are Canadian citizens. However, the Charter does not apply to disputes between private parties. Within the context of criminal law, the Charter applies to the actions or inactions of the federal and provincial Crown, police agencies, and correctional staff.

The Charter provides certain fundamental freedoms in section 2: freedom of conscience and religion; freedom of thought, belief, opinion, and expression; freedom of peaceful assembly; and freedom of association. While a multitude of cases have arisen in Canada involving one or more fundamental freedoms guaranteed under section 2, it is the legal rights provided under the Charter that usually arise in criminal law jurisprudence. Notably, section 1 of the Charter allows for reasonable limits to be placed on these guaranteed rights as long as those limits can be demonstrably justified.

An excerpt of the legal rights guaranteed under the Charter, which will be the focus of this chapter, is included in Appendix C.

# Life, Liberty, and Security

Section 7 of the Charter provides the right to life, liberty, and security of the person. In the context of criminal law, examples of rights that would fall under section 7 include the right to silence, the right against self-crimination, and the right to have full disclosure of the Crown's case. Section 7 rights are not absolute—the right to life, liberty, and security exists unless it is taken away in accordance with the **principles of fundamental justice**. An example of a principle of fundamental justice includes the requirement that all criminal offences that are punishable by a period of incarceration have a *mens rea* element. Another example of a principle of fundamental justice is the right of an accused person to make full answer and defence.

**principles of fundamental justice** core values within the justice system that society believes ought to prevail over an individual's right to life, liberty, and security

# Search and Seizure

Section 8 of the Charter provides protection from unreasonable search or seizure. The purpose of section 8 is to protect people from unjustified government intrusion. There must be a balance between a suspect's or accused's right to privacy and the state's interest in crime prevention.

The accused's right is limited to a "reasonable expectation of privacy." In other words, section 8 of the Charter is only triggered once the accused establishes that he or she has a reasonable expectation of privacy. How does the court determine whether the accused has a reasonable expectation of privacy in the place being searched by police? Does the accused's reasonable expectation of privacy vary according to the type of privacy rights being affected?

## Types of Privacy Interests

The Supreme Court of Canada distinguished between three types of privacy interests in *R v Tessling*, 2004 SCC 67, [2004] 3 SCR 432 [*Tessling*]: personal privacy, territorial privacy, and informational privacy. Since **personal privacy** concerns the bodily integrity of an individual, it affords the greatest protection. Personal privacy includes searching a person's body for bodily substances such as hair or blood, collecting DNA by using buccal swabs, obtaining bodily impressions such as fingerprints or teeth impressions, and taking photographs of the person. **Territorial privacy** involves a sliding scale of privacy, with one's home having the greatest privacy interest and one's car, school locker, or even prison cell having fewer privacy interests. Finally, **informational privacy** involves a determination of how much information to reveal, to whom, and under what circumstances. Informational privacy includes digitally stored information.

Therefore, privacy can be categorized into different types. Once it is determined what type of privacy right is affected, the next step is to ascertain whether an accused person has a reasonable expectation of privacy.

**personal privacy**
privacy rights relating to the bodily integrity of an individual

**territorial privacy**
privacy rights relating to places where an individual has a reasonable expectation of privacy

**informational privacy**
privacy rights relating to when, how, and to what extent personal information is communicated to others

## Reasonable Expectation of Privacy

In the case of *R v Edwards*, [1996] 1 SCR 128, 132 DLR (4th) 31 [*Edwards*], the Supreme Court of Canada held that in order to determine whether a person has a reasonable expectation of privacy, it is necessary to look at the totality of the circumstances by assessing a number of factors. Such factors include:

- The person's presence at the time of the search
- The possession or control of the property or place being searched
- The ownership of the property or place
- The historical use of the property or item
- The ability to regulate access, including the right to admit or exclude others from the place

The criteria in *Edwards* were expanded upon by the Supreme Court of Canada in *Tessling* and *R v Patrick*, 2009 SCC 17, [2009] 1 SCR 579 [*Patrick*]. Other factors to consider in deciding whether or not there is a reasonable expectation of privacy include:

- The place where the alleged "search" occurs
- Whether the informational content of the subject matter is in public view
- Whether the informational content of the subject matter has been abandoned
- Whether such information is already in the hands of third parties; if so, is it subject to an obligation of confidentiality?
- Whether the police technique is intrusive in relation to the privacy interest
- Whether the use of this evidence-gathering technique is itself objectively unreasonable
- Whether the informational content exposes any intimate details of the appellant's lifestyle or information of a biographical nature

In the case of *R v Cole*, 2012 SCC 53, [2012] 3 SCR 34, the Supreme Court of Canada adopted the factors set out in *Edwards*, *Tessling*, and *Patrick* and set out a four-part test to determine whether a person had a reasonable expectation of privacy based on the totality of the circumstances. The four-part test is as follows:

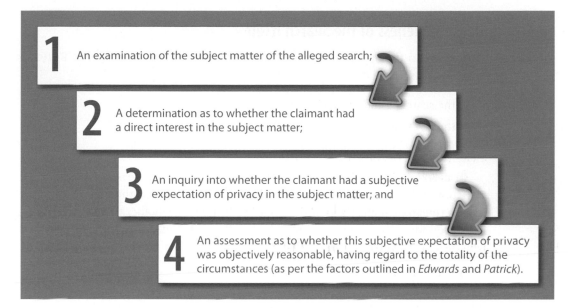

**1** An examination of the subject matter of the alleged search;

**2** A determination as to whether the claimant had a direct interest in the subject matter;

**3** An inquiry into whether the claimant had a subjective expectation of privacy in the subject matter; and

**4** An assessment as to whether this subjective expectation of privacy was objectively reasonable, having regard to the totality of the circumstances (as per the factors outlined in *Edwards* and *Patrick*).

Once it is established that the accused had a reasonable expectation of privacy, the next step is for the court to determine whether the search was conducted reasonably.

---

**E X A M P L E**

**Was There a Reasonable Expectation of Privacy?**

Tom and Navjeet are friends. Navjeet has invited Tom over to his house for a party. Tom starts to smoke a marijuana joint in the kitchen. Suddenly, the police arrive at Navjeet's house in response to a loud noise complaint. Navjeet gives the police permission to enter his house. The police see Tom smoking the marijuana joint, and they arrest him for possession of marijuana. Because it is Navjeet's residence, Tom does not have a reasonable expectation of privacy.

## Absence of a Search Warrant

Whenever feasible, prior authorization from a justice—by way of a search warrant— must be obtained in order for a search to be reasonable (*Hunter et al v Southam Inc*, [1984] 2 SCR 145). "Feasible" does not mean when it is possible or convenient; rather, it means that a police officer who has reasonable opportunity to obtain a search warrant must do so. Such authorization is to be given by a neutral, impartial person acting in a judicial capacity. The justice must be satisfied that there are reasonable grounds for believing that an offence has been committed and that a search of the place for which the warrant is sought will reveal evidence related to that offence. If an accused person establishes that a search was conducted without a warrant, it is presumed that the search was unreasonable. For any search carried out without a warrant, the Crown must establish that the search was reasonable.

## Reasonableness of the Search Itself

According to the Supreme Court of Canada in *R v Collins*, [1987] 1 SCR 265, a search is reasonable if:

- the search is authorized by law;
- the law that authorizes the search is reasonable; and
- the manner in which the search is carried out is reasonable.

In determining whether the law authorizing the search is reasonable, the court will look at the reasonableness of the warrant: whether it was authorized prior to the search (meaning that a warrant was obtained by police), whether there were reasonable grounds to issue the warrant, whether it was based on sworn evidence, and whether the decision to grant it was made judiciously (*R v Caslake*, [1998] 1 SCR 51 [*Caslake*]).

## Prior Authorization for the Search

A search warrant is an order from a justice of the peace or a judge, pursuant to statute, that permits law enforcement personnel to enter into a place, search the place, and seize items mentioned in the warrant. If the police obtain a warrant, then consent of the owner of the place is not required in order to gain entry. Examples of *Criminal Code* provisions that allow police to obtain a search warrant include:

- Section 487—basic search warrant
- Section 164—warrant of seizure for obscene materials
- Section 186—authorization to obtain wiretap evidence
- Section 256—warrant to obtain blood samples for impaired driving
- Section 492.2—authorization to obtain telephone records

Section 487 of the *Criminal Code* provides for the most common type of search warrant in criminal law. Section 487 grants a justice the authority to issue a search warrant with the power to search a building, a place, or a receptacle. Before a search warrant may be obtained, the police officer must establish that there are reasonable grounds to believe that an offence has been committed or is about to be committed and that evidence relating to the offence will be found at the place of the search.

**information to obtain**
document setting out reasonable grounds for the basis of a search warrant

The police officer must submit an **information to obtain** (ITO) along with a draft version of the search warrant to the justice of the peace. The information to obtain a warrant must set out the reasonable grounds for the basis for the warrant and must be under oath or include an affidavit from the informant. The grounds may be based on personal knowledge or information from secondary sources; however, there must be a sufficient factual basis to support the application. The ITO should be clear and concise but does not have to include all details of the police investigation. On the other hand, if it does not contain sufficient detail, it may be subject to a Charter challenge to have the results of the search excluded as evidence.

The ITO must also contain:

- the name of the applicant or informant;
- a description of the offence that was committed or is suspected of having been committed, including the date and time of the offence; the name of the complainant, the manner of the offence, and the section number of the offence;
- a list of the items to be seized described in sufficient detail so as to be able to identify them; and
- a description of the building, place, or receptacle to be searched, with the address listed.

An ITO pursuant to section 487 of the *Criminal Code* is Form 1 of the *Criminal Code* (see template in Appendix D). The search warrant is Form 5 of the *Criminal Code* (see template in Appendix E).

**PRACTICE TIP**

If a search warrant is challenged prior to trial, an application to quash the warrant may only be brought on the basis of jurisdictional error. The only test for a valid search warrant is whether there was sufficient evidence before the justice that a warrant should have been issued. Any challenge to the validity of the search, the items seized pursuant to the warrant, or the sufficiency of the grounds used to obtain the warrant should be raised by way of a Charter application at trial.

## Plain View Doctrine

What happens if the police obtain a search warrant for a residence, attend the residence, and find items that are not in the search warrant but are clearly evidence of another criminal act? The **plain view doctrine** permits police officers who are lawfully executing a search to seize items that constitute evidence of a crime. Therefore, if the police have a search warrant to seize marijuana plants, and they come across illegal weapons, under the plain view doctrine, they may seize the illegal weapons without the necessity of having to obtain another warrant for these additional items. Section 489(2) of the *Criminal Code* essentially codifies the plain view doctrine and permits police officers to seize anything that has been obtained by the commission of an offence, has been used in the commission of an offence, or will afford evidence with respect to an offence. Section 489(2) also grants police officers the ability to seize items in plain view even when they do not have a warrant but are acting in the lawful execution of their duties.

**plain view doctrine**
common law authority that permits the police to seize illegal items that are in plain sight while in the execution of a lawful search

**EXAMPLE**

**In Plain View**

Police Constable Chen pulls over a driver for speeding. While issuing the offence notice, Constable Chen sees a butterfly knife on the front passenger seat—an object that is a prohibited weapon pursuant to section 84(1) of the *Criminal Code*. Since Constable Chen is acting in the lawful execution of her duties as a police officer and the knife is apparently illegal, the plain view doctrine would allow Constable Chen to seize the knife.

Another exception to the requirement for a search warrant is when an accused has abandoned his privacy interest in an item. For example, the police may seize and search bags of garbage that have been placed "at or within reach of the lot line" (*Patrick*, *supra*). The location of the items and the intention of the accused are key factors used to determine whether or not the privacy interest has been abandoned.

## Types of Searches for Which a Warrant Is Not Required

The six types of searches that do not require the police to obtain a warrant are described below.

| Type of Search | Description |
|---|---|
| Consent searches | when police request permission to search from the owner/ occupier of the premises, and permission is granted |
| Search incident to arrest | police may search the person under arrest and the immediate area surrounding the person for weapons and/or destruction of evidence |
| Inventory search | police may conduct a search of a person being placed in custody in order to secure his/her personal possessions |
| Search to protect the safety of the public | police may search an area if there is a reasonable fear that the safety of the public is in imminent danger |
| Search necessary to prevent destruction of evidence | police may search an area when there is imminent danger that evidence will be lost, be removed, be destroyed, or disappear if the search is delayed (this is known as **exigent circumstances**)* |
| "Hot pursuit" searches | when the police enter a dwelling-house to apprehend a person when they believe that entry is necessary in order to prevent imminent bodily harm or death to any person, or to prevent the imminent loss or destruction of evidence |

**exigent circumstances**
danger that evidence will be lost, removed, or destroyed

* When exigent circumstances do not exist, police are required to obtain a warrant to arrest a person in a dwelling-house (*R v Feeney*, [1997] 2 SCR 13, 146 DLR (4th) 609).

All of the search powers described above, for which the police are not required to obtain a warrant, are derived from common law.

### Consent Search

The criteria for a valid consent to a search or seizure were set out by the Ontario Court of Appeal in the case of *R v Wills*, [1992] OJ No 294, 70 CCC (3d) 529:

**express consent**
consent that is clear and unmistakable; may be given verbally or by gestures

**implied consent**
consent that is inferred from a person's actions or silence based on the circumstances of the situation

1. there must be **express consent** or **implied consent**;
2. the party consenting had the authority to consent;
3. the consent was voluntary and not due to any oppression, coercion, or other conduct that would negate the freedom to choose not to consent;
4. the party was aware of the nature of the police conduct that he or she was being asked to consent to;

5.  the party knew that he or she had the ability to refuse the search; and

6.  the party was aware of the potential consequences and jeopardy of the search or seizure.

While the police do not have a duty to notify the accused of his or her right to refuse to give consent, a failure to do so may result in a finding by the court that the consent was not informed.

### Search Incident to Arrest

The legal principles governing search incident to arrest were set out by the Supreme Court of Canada in *Caslake*. The Court stated that the police must have a valid purpose that is "truly incidental" to the arrest in order to justify a warrantless search. The three main purposes of a search incident to arrest are:

1.  to ensure the safety of the police and the public;

2.  to secure evidence; and

3.  to discover evidence.

If the justification for the search is to discover evidence, there must be a reasonable prospect that the evidence will relate to the offence for which the accused has been arrested. The purposes outlined by the Supreme Court of Canada in *Caslake* were affirmed in the more recent case of *R v Nolet*, 2010 SCC 24, 1 SCR 851, which is discussed in the Case in Point later in this chapter.

The common thread behind warrantless searches, which are justified under the common law, is the reasonableness of the police conduct in the totality of the circumstances in each case. The standard of reasonableness is always evolving, given the breadth of cases in the area of search or seizure and section 8 of the Charter.

## CASE IN POINT

# Search for Officer and Public Safety

*R v MacDonald*, 2014 SCC 3

### Facts

The police were called about a noise complaint at the home of the accused, MacDonald. When MacDonald opened his front door, the officer noticed that he had an object in his hand hidden behind his leg. The officer twice asked MacDonald what was in his hand. When the accused did not answer, the officer pushed the door slightly further open in order to see. MacDonald and the officer engaged in a struggle, and MacDonald was disarmed of a loaded handgun.

MacDonald was charged with several firearms-related offences and was convicted at trial. The Court of Appeal upheld most of the convictions but reduced MacDonald's sentence. Both the accused and the Crown appealed to the Supreme Court of Canada.

### Decision

The officer's action of pushing the door further open did invade the accused's reasonable expectation of privacy and constituted a breach of section 8 of the Charter. However, the warrantless search fell under the common law police duty to protect the lives and safety of the public and constituted a "safety search," which may justify a Charter breach if it is found to be reasonably necessary. In determining whether the search was reasonably necessary, the Supreme Court considered several factors and balanced the duty of the police to protect the public against the accused's liberty interests. These factors included "the importance of the duty to the public good; the necessity of the infringement for the performance of the duty; and the extent of the infringement."

In this case, the officer had reasonable grounds to believe that there was an imminent threat to public and police safety. The door was pushed open a few inches further only after the accused was asked what he had behind his leg and had failed to answer. Furthermore, the search itself was minimally intrusive. In the result, the Supreme Court held that the section 8 Charter breach was justified and dismissed the accused's appeal.

### Discussion Question

While the decision of the Supreme Court of Canada was unanimous in this case, the Court was divided as to whether the police require reasonable grounds to *believe* an individual is armed and dangerous in order to conduct a safety search or reasonable grounds to *suspect* an individual is armed and dangerous in order to conduct a safety search. Explain the difference between these two standards. Which do you think ought to apply and why?

# Arrest and Detention

The police have powers to arrest someone with or without a warrant. These powers are codified in the *Criminal Code*.

## Arrest Without a Warrant

Section 495(1) of the *Criminal Code* outlines the circumstances in which the police may arrest a person without a warrant:

- a person has committed an indictable offence, or the officer has reasonable grounds to believe a person has committed or is about to commit an indictable offence;
- a person is found to be committing any criminal offence; or
- the officer has reasonable grounds to believe that a warrant of arrest for a person is in effect in the jurisdiction in which the person is found.

It is important to note that certain categories of indictable offences are exempt from this provision. Also, if the officer is satisfied on reasonable grounds that the public interest would be satisfied without having to arrest a person for a hybrid or summary conviction offence, then he or she is obligated not to do so. As discussed in Chapter 2, "reasonable grounds" refers to the probability that an offence has occurred and that the accused has committed the offence. Under section 495(2)(d) of the *Criminal Code*, the factors that the officer must consider in determining whether or not to arrest without a warrant include the need to establish the identity of the person, to secure or preserve evidence relating to the offence, or to prevent the continuation or repetition of the offence or the commission of another offence; the officer must also have no reasonable grounds to believe that the person will fail to attend court if not placed under arrest.

The hot pursuit exception, discussed earlier for searches, is applicable to arrest without a warrant. When the police are in hot pursuit of a suspect, and the suspect enters a dwelling-house, the police may also enter the dwelling-house to make the warrantless arrest. Unless there are exigent circumstances present, the police must knock  on the door or ring the doorbell, identify themselves as police officers, and state the reason for their entry.

The police may not enter a dwelling-house simply to investigate or to arrest a person who is residing there; in those situations, a warrant would be required. Rather, the hot pursuit exception allows police to enter a dwelling-house and arrest a person without a warrant if there is a continuous transaction between the commission of the offence, the pursuit by the police, and the capture of the person. The police powers to enter a dwelling-house without a warrant and exigent circumstances for doing so are set out in section 529.3(1) and (2) of the *Criminal Code*. Exigent circumstances include imminent bodily harm or death to any person, or the imminent loss or destruction of evidence.

## Arrest with a Warrant

An arrest warrant is issued by a justice when there are reasonable grounds to believe that a person has committed an offence. In order to obtain an arrest warrant, a police officer must appear before the justice and swear an information with allegations of the offence. The warrant must contain the name of the accused or his or her description, a brief description of the alleged offence, and an order that the accused be arrested. A warrant remains in force and effect until the accused is arrested. Section 29 of the *Criminal Code* imposes a duty on police officers to have the warrant when executing it and to produce it, if feasible. Notice of the warrant should also be given to the person being arrested, when feasible, as well as the reason for the arrest.

Sections 529 and 529.1 of the *Criminal Code* allow for a justice to grant an arrest warrant with the authorization for police to enter a dwelling-house if there are reasonable grounds to believe that the person is or will be present at the location. This is referred to as a "Feeney warrant" after the famous case of *R v Feeney*. Provisions also exist in section 529.4 for a justice to authorize a police officer to enter a dwelling-house without having to announce entry.

## CASE IN POINT

# Warrantless Entry to Arrest the Accused When No Exigent Circumstances Exist

*R v Feeney*, [1997] 2 SCR 13, 146 DLR (4th) 609

### Facts

Frank Boyle was an 85-year-old man who was last seen alive on June 7, 1991 in the small town of Likely, BC. On June 8, a neighbour noticed that Frank's garage door was open, and when he went inside to investigate, he found Frank's body in the living room. Frank had been hit on the head several times. Money, cigarettes, and beer were missing from his house. Frank's truck was found in a ditch a short distance from his house with a bloody crowbar inside.

Police interviewed witnesses, who saw the accused, Michael Feeney, on that day in the vicinity of the victim's truck. Other witnesses who had been partying with Feeney on June 7 mentioned that Feeney had been taking beer and cigarettes from them because he said that he did not have any money. The police found out that Feeney was living in a trailer on the property of one of the witnesses, and they quickly went over to the trailer without obtaining a search warrant.

The police knocked on Feeney's trailer door, and when there was no answer, they walked in. They found Feeney sleeping, so they shook him awake and asked him to step outside where it would be easier to see him in the light. When Feeney stepped outside, the police noticed bloodstains on his clothing. He was then arrested for Frank Boyle's murder.

A number of forensic items were seized from Feeney's trailer, including:

- a pair of Feeney's shoes with blood on them that was later found to match the victim's blood; the soles of the shoes matched shoe prints found at the crime scene;
- a package of cigarettes matching the brand of those found at the victim's residence; and
- a blood-spattered T-shirt that Feeney was wearing that was later found to match the victim's blood.

Later, the police also found a fingerprint on the door of the victim's fridge and another fingerprint on a beer can in the victim's trunk—both found to match Feeney's fingerprints.

At Feeney's first trial in 1992, the Crown relied on the forensic evidence found in the trailer. Feeney was convicted of second degree murder, and he appealed the conviction to the Court of Appeal, arguing that the evidence from the trailer ought to be excluded, as it had been illegally obtained by police. The Court of Appeal denied the appeal and upheld the conviction. Feeney appealed to the Supreme Court of Canada.

## Decision

The Supreme Court of Canada overturned the conviction, agreeing with defence counsel. The Court stated that the police needed to have reasonable and probable grounds to believe that Feeney committed the murder before they could effect a lawful arrest. The police officer who entered the trailer had testified that he had suspected that Feeney had been involved but did not have reasonable and probable grounds to arrest him before entering the trailer. The Supreme Court of Canada also indicated that exigent circumstances did not exist for the police to simply walk into Feeney's trailer to search it without obtaining a warrant first. There were no reasons to believe that someone was in imminent danger or that evidence would be lost or destroyed. The Court ruled that none of the evidence found in the trailer could be used against Feeney in court and ordered a new trial.

At Feeney's second murder trial in 1999, the police matched the saliva from a cigarette butt found on the victim's property to Feeney using DNA testing, and they relied upon the fingerprint evidence. Feeney was again convicted of second degree murder. His appeal to the Court of Appeal was dismissed.

## Practice Tip

A "Feeney warrant" is required to enter a residence to effect an arrest when there is no consent or permission to enter, when exigent circumstances do not exist, and when the police are not in hot pursuit of a suspect.

## Bench Warrants

Arrest warrants may also be issued in situations other than the commission of an offence. An arrest warrant may be issued when:

- a suspect is evading arrest;
- an accused person fails to attend court while on a form of release (summons, appearance notice, promise to appear, or recognizance);
- a person avoids service of court documents;
- a person fails to respond to a subpoena or is evading service of a subpoena; or
- an accused person fails to show up for fingerprinting.

**bench warrant**
warrant issued by the court

This is referred to as a **bench warrant**, since it is issued by the court when someone violates an order or condition of the court.

Most warrants are only valid in the province within which they are issued. However, if a police officer comes into contact with a person for whom a warrant is outstanding in another province, he or she may arrest the person and contact the police in the province in which the warrant was issued. The police in the issuing province have the option of requesting that the person be transported back to the issuing province or that the person be released from custody. However, before an out-of-province warrant may be executed, it must first be endorsed by another justice in that province (section 528(1) of the *Criminal Code*).

## Canada-Wide Warrants

For serious indictable offences, the police may apply for a Canada-wide warrant, which authorizes police officers to arrest, detain, and transport a person found anywhere in Canada. Even in the case of a Canada-wide warrant that is issued in another province, a justice in the province in which the arrest is made must endorse the warrant. Pursuant to section 703 of the *Criminal Code*, Canada-wide warrants may only be issued by a superior court justice.

## Arbitrary Detention

In the previous section, we have reviewed under what circumstances a police officer may arrest a person either with or without a warrant. However, there are situations in which a person is being investigated by the police, and there are no reasonable grounds for which to arrest him or her. Typically, the person is referred to as a suspect or a person of interest in the investigation. Do the police have unlimited powers of investigation when they are dealing with a person of interest?

Section 9 of the Charter deals with **arbitrary detention**. Detention means any restraint of liberty; therefore, a person may be detained even when he or she has not been arrested. Detention occurs when the conduct of the police physically or psychologically deprives a person of his or her choice to simply walk away (*R v Grant*, 2009 SCC 32, [2009] 2 SCR 353 [*Grant*]).

Not all forms of detention are a breach of section 9. For it to constitute a breach, the detention must be *arbitrary*, meaning capricious, random, unjustified, or unpredictable. Therefore, if the police are conducting an investigation, and they come across a person of interest whom they wish to interview, they may detain the person even though there is no general power of detention for investigative purposes. The police may detain a person of interest if they have reasonable grounds to suspect that the person is connected to a particular crime and that the detention is reasonably necessary based on an objective look at the circumstances (*R v Mann*, 2004 SCC 52, [2004] 3 SCR 59). Simply acting on a "hunch" that a person is guilty is not enough. If called upon to justify the detention, the police officer must be able to state the objective grounds for it. Persons who are detained for investigative purposes must be advised of the reasons for their detention in clear and simple language.

Certain arbitrary detentions, such as randomly pulling over a motorist to check for sobriety, are a breach of section 9 of the Charter but are justified under section 1. Section 1 of the Charter allows for reasonable limits to be placed on guaranteed Charter rights as long as the limits can be demonstrably justified.

**arbitrary detention**
a random or unjustified restraint of liberty

## CASE IN POINT

# Random Vehicle Stops

*R v Nolet*, 2010 SCC 24, 1 SCR 851

## Facts

The accused, Regent Nolet, and his passengers were operating a commercial tractor-trailer on the highway when they were pulled over by an RCMP officer for a spot check pursuant to the Saskatchewan *Highways and Transportation Act, 1997*, SS 1997, c H-3.01. The officer noticed an expired fuel sticker on the outside of the vehicle, which was a provincial offence. The officer asked for the driver's licence, vehicle registration, and logbook. Nolet told the officer that they had unloaded cargo in Edmonton and Moose Jaw, but these stops were not noted in the logbook. The officer also found other problems with the vehicle's registration.

The officer asked if he could inspect the trailer, as well as any documents inside, to confirm or dispute the contents of the logbook, and Nolet agreed to this. The officer found a small duffle bag behind the driver's seat in the sleeping compartment of the cab. When the officer touched the bag, its contents crackled like paper, so the officer opened the bag on the presumption that it contained other logbooks or travel documents. However, the bag actually contained $115,000 in small denominations. The officer immediately suspected that the money was the proceeds of drug transactions, and he arrested the accused for possession of the proceeds of crime. All of this took place within nine minutes of the stop.

The officer called for assistance from other RCMP officers, and further inspection revealed that the interior of the trailer measured three feet less than the exterior length, indicating the presence of a hidden compartment. The trailer was driven to the RCMP detachment, where officers opened up the hidden compartment and found 392 pounds of packaged cannabis marijuana, valued between $1.1 and $1.5 million. The officers did not obtain a search warrant for any of the inspections, searches, and seizures.

The trial judge acquitted the accused, stating that the warrantless searches were unreasonable. The Court of Appeal found that no Charter breaches had occurred and ordered a new trial. The accused appealed to the Supreme Court of Canada.

## Decision

The Supreme Court of Canada stated that random roadside stops must be limited to their intended purposes and cannot be turned into unfounded general inquisitions or unreasonable searches. However, the Court recognized that roadside stops can sometimes be unpredictable, because they are not static events. Accordingly, as information emerged, the RCMP were entitled to investigate further.

The Court held that there was a valid reason for stopping the vehicle in the first place. Therefore, the initial stop did not violate the accused's section 9 Charter rights. Furthermore, the continued detention of the accused was also not arbitrary, since the officer had the statutory authority to search for further evidence related to the *Highways and Transportation Act* offences. The Court noted that the reasonable expectation of privacy in the cab area of the tractor-trailer was limited, given that it was a resting place but also a work place and therefore subject to random checks related to highway transport matters. The officer did not immediately open the duffle bag until after he had felt through the bag to determine that it was likely relevant to the regulatory search. Therefore, it was not unreasonable for the officer to open the bag. At this point, Nolet was arrested, and the search of the trailer occurred incidental to the arrest.

It is of note that the following day, an RCMP officer again searched the tractor-trailer, this time for the purposes of doing inventory. The officer came across trucking documentation. The Court held that this additional search did not meet the requirements of a valid warrantless search, because the purpose of this search was incidental to administrative procedures and not the arrest. Therefore, this additional search was in breach of section 8 of the Charter. However, the evidence gathered from this additional search was nevertheless admissible under section 24(2). The Court followed the test set out in *Grant*, discussed below under "Unlawfully Obtained Evidence," and held that this search constituted a technical breach that minimally impacted the accused, and society's interest in having the charges adjudicated on their merits prevailed.

In the result, the Supreme Court of Canada held that the accused's Charter rights were not violated and dismissed the appeal.

## Discussion Question

Does it matter that the search of the cab occurred approximately two hours after the arrest? Does a search incident to arrest have to occur close in time to the arrest in order to be a lawful search?

(Hint: Look at what the Supreme Court of Canada said in *Caslake* and the length of time that passed between the arrest and the search.)

# Reasons for Arrest and Right to Counsel

Upon arrest or detention, sections 10(a) and (b) of the Charter are triggered. These two sections are related. An accused person must be informed of the reasons for the arrest or detention under section 10(a) so that he or she may make an informed choice as to whether to exercise the right to counsel based on the extent of the jeopardy that he or she is facing. The purpose of section 10(b) of the Charter is twofold: to give the accused initial instruction about the right to consult with counsel (the informational component) and to provide the accused with a reasonable opportunity to do so (the implementation component). The following table outlines the nature of the informational and implementation components of the right to counsel.

**Right to Counsel Components**

| Informational Component | Implementation Component |
|---|---|
| • Once a suspect is detained, information on the right to counsel must be given immediately, subject only to concerns for officer or public safety | • Police must provide the detainee with a reasonable opportunity to contact counsel and to have questioning curtailed until the reasonable opportunity has ceased (*R v Bartle*, [1994] 3 SCR 173, 118 DLR (4th) 83) |
| • The informational duty of police is triggered at the outset of an investigative detention (*R v Suberu*, 2009 SCC 33, [2009] 2 SCR 460) | • Whether the detainee decides to exercise or waive the right to counsel, he or she must be capable of communicating with counsel to instruct counsel, understand the function of counsel, and understand that he or she may dispense with counsel (*R v Whittle*, [1994] 2 SCR 914, 116 DLR (4th) 416) |
| • Detainees must be provided information about access to counsel free of charge and about access to duty counsel who provide immediate legal advice regardless of financial status | |
| • Information must be presented in a timely and comprehensible manner | • The detainee must invoke the right to counsel before there is a correlative duty on police to provide a reasonable opportunity to contact counsel and refrain from eliciting evidence |
| • If the police are aware of any language difficulties, intoxication, or mental disability on the part of the suspect, they must take appropriate steps to enable comprehension | • Any waiver of the right to counsel must be given freely and voluntarily. In addition, the accused must know what he or she is giving up in order for the waiver to be valid |
| • If there is a change in circumstances, such as a change in the accused's jeopardy or reason to believe that the accused may not have understood the initial right to counsel given by the police, then the section 10(b) right is triggered again | |

## The Right to Counsel Trilogy

On October 8, 2010, the Supreme Court of Canada released decisions in three landmark cases, all involving the right to counsel under section 10(b) of the Charter: *R v Sinclair*, 2010 SCC 35, [2010] 2 SCR 310; *R v McCrimmon*, 2010 SCC 36, [2010] 2 SCR 402; and *R v Willier*, 2010 SCC 37, [2010] 2 SCR 429.

While the facts of each case are different, the Court came up with clear guidelines for what the right to counsel does and does not entail. Invoking the right to silence is not final or absolute—the police may ignore a suspect's choice to remain silent and attempt to change the suspect's mind about that choice. An accused person does not have the right to have counsel present during the police interview.

After consulting with counsel, accused persons do not have the right to re-consult with counsel unless there is a change of circumstances: a change in the jeopardy faced by the accused, a change to the investigative procedures used by the police, or reason to believe that the accused did not understand the initial advice given by counsel. Examples of a change of procedure or a non-routine procedure used by the police, as identified by the Supreme Court of Canada, include a request that the accused participate in a lineup or submit to a polygraph test. The practice of investigating officers presenting real or fake evidence to exaggerate the strength of the case against the accused is insufficient to constitute a change in investigative procedure.

> **EXAMPLE**
>
> **Change in Accused's Jeopardy Warranting a Right to Re-Consult with Counsel**
>
> Ester is charged with aggravated assault against Linda. While Ester is being interviewed by police, the police receive information that Linda has died as a result of her injuries from the assault. Ester is now going to be charged with manslaughter, and the legal jeopardy that she now faces is obviously much greater. Therefore, she must be provided with her right to counsel again before the police decide to interview her further.

# Right to Silence and Right Against Self-Crimination

**self-crimination**
a statement made or action taken by a person that supports a finding of guilt

Sections 7, 11(c), and 13 of the Charter provide the right to silence and protection against self-crimination. The right to silence and right against **self-crimination** cover both testimonial evidence (statements and confessions made by an accused person) and non-testimonial evidence (bodily samples and other forms of physical evidence).

## Right to Silence

The right to silence includes the right to make a free and meaningful choice as to whether to speak or remain silent. When an accused person has chosen to exercise the right to remain silent, the right is not absolute. It does not prevent the police from questioning an accused in the absence of counsel who has been retained by the accused. The police may use persuasion to question an accused as long as it does not deny the accused the freedom to choose whether to remain silent or not.

The Supreme Court of Canada, in the case of *R v Singh*, 2007 SCC 48, [2007] 3 SCR 405 [*Singh*], reiterated that the right to silence includes the right of the detainee to make a meaningful choice as to whether or not to speak to the police. However, the Court also stated that it is inappropriate to impose a rigid requirement on the police that they refrain from questioning a suspect who has indicated that he or she does not wish to speak to the police. When the police persist in continued questioning despite repeated assertions from the accused that he wishes to remain silent, this may lead to the conclusion that the subsequent statement was not given out of the accused's own free will, depending on the circumstances of the case. It should be noted that in *Singh*, the accused asserted his right to silence 18 times throughout police interviews. On each occasion, the interviewing officer either affirmed that Singh had the right to not say anything or explained that he (the officer) had a duty to present the evidence to the accused. The officer continued on with the interview. The Supreme Court of Canada upheld Singh's conviction, stating that the right to remain silent does not mean that a person has the right not to be spoken to by the police. Questioning a suspect is vital to the investigative role of the police.

The police may use undercover agents to observe the accused. However, there is a distinction drawn between the use of undercover agents to observe the accused and the use of agents to actively elicit information from the accused. Common law holds that it does not matter if a police agent (whether undercover or not) lies to the accused, permits himself or herself to be misidentified, or engages in subterfuge, as long as the accused's responses are not actively elicited or result from interrogation during which the accused has chosen to exercise his or her right to remain silent (*R v Liew*, [1999] 3 SCR 227, 177 DLR (4th) 302).

When the accused exercises his or her right to remain silent in the face of accusations made by the police, no inferences may be drawn at trial from the accused's decision to remain silent.

## Right Against Self-Crimination

Section 11(c) of the Charter protects a person from being compelled or forced to be a witness in proceedings against that person with respect to an offence. Therefore, if a person is called as a witness in a matter and provides sworn testimony, that sworn testimony may not be used in a subsequent trial against that person unless that person chooses to testify.

### EXAMPLE

**Self-Crimination: Testimonial Evidence**

Elena testifies for the defence in a case in which her friend, Andre, is being charged with assault. Under direct examination, Elena admits that she was also involved in the assault. As a result of her testimony, the police charge Elena with assault. At her assault trial, unless Elena chooses to take the stand and testify, the Crown may not use the transcript of Elena's evidence from Andre's trial against her. Elena has the right not to be forced to provide evidence against herself. However, if Elena chooses to testify, the Crown may be able to cross-examine her on credibility issues based on the evidence that she provided under oath at Andre's trial.

If two co-accused are charged with the same offence in separate informations, each of them may be compelled to testify as a Crown witness in the other's trial.

The Crown is permitted to cross-examine the accused at a second trial on inconsistent testimony given at the first trial. Unlike a witness, who can be compelled to testify, an accused person cannot. Therefore, any testimony from an accused is not compelled evidence.

As discussed earlier, evidence may be testimonial or non-testimonial. The right against self-crimination protects non-testimonial evidence as well, such as evidence that would not have been obtained but for the statement of the accused. This is referred to as **derivative evidence**.

**derivative evidence**
evidence obtained as a direct result of violating the accused's legal rights

**EXAMPLE**

**Derivative Evidence**

The police interview Salman for five hours without giving him his right to counsel. In his statement, Salman discloses where he has hidden illegal weapons. As a result of the Charter breach, not only is Salman's statement inadmissible, but so are the weapons. If it were not for Salman's statement, the police would not have found out about the location of the weapons.

**rule of inevitable discovery**
exception to the inadmissibility of derivative evidence when the evidence would have been discovered regardless of the Charter breach

The exception to derivative evidence is the **rule of inevitable discovery**: if the police would have found out about the location of the evidence anyway, such as through the statement of another witness, then the evidence may be used regardless of the Charter breach, because it would have been discovered in any event.

# Statements and Confessions

## The Common Law Confessions Rule

The common law confessions rule developed as a result of the realization that a **confession** could be obtained through improper means, thereby calling into question its reliability. Under what circumstances can a statement made by an accused person be used against him or her at trial? Two factors are key: the voluntariness of the confession and the status of the person to whom the confession is made. A confession is a statement suggesting guilt made to a **person in authority**. A person in authority "refers to those formally engaged in the arrest, detention, examination or prosecution of the accused and so applies to police officers and prison officials or guards" (*R v Hodgson*, [1998] 2 SCR 449, 163 DLR (4th) 577). Persons in authority are not limited to these categories—based on the situation, other people may be persons in authority. The accused's perception that the statement was given to a person in authority is taken into account as long as it is a reasonable belief.

**confession**
written or verbal statement made by the accused suggesting or implicating guilt

**person in authority**
person who is formally engaged in the arrest, detention, examination, or prosecution of the accused

## CASE IN POINT

# Who Is a Person in Authority?

*R v Hodgson*, [1998] 2 SCR 449, 163 DLR (4th) 577

## Facts

The complainant alleged that the accused, Hodgson, sexually assaulted her numerous times while babysitting her when she was between the ages of 7 and 11 years old. She disclosed these incidents to her mother when she was 13 years of age. The complainant, her parents, and her stepfather confronted Hodgson at his workplace. They all testified that Hodgson confessed to the sexual assaults and apologized to the complainant. The complainant's mother left to call the police, and when she returned, she struck the accused. The complainant's father also held a knife to the accused's back and testified that he did this in order to prevent the accused from fleeing before the police arrived.

The accused denied making a confession; he testified that although he was shocked and upset by the confrontation, he was not frightened or threatened by it. He did not object to the evidence of the confession at trial and was convicted. On appeal, the issue was whether the complainant, her parents, and her stepfather were "persons in authority." The Court of Appeal declined to deal with this issue, citing that since they did not fall under the conventional definition of a person in authority (someone engaged in the arrest, detention, examination, or prosecution of an accused person), the onus was on the defence to raise the issue at trial and to request that a *voir dire* take place to determine whether these individuals were in fact persons in authority. Since the accused did not raise the issue at trial, the Court of Appeal dismissed the appeal. Hodgson appealed to the Supreme Court of Canada.

## Decision

The Supreme Court of Canada dismissed the accused's appeal. Beyond the traditional group of persons held to be persons in authority (police officers, prison officials, prison guards),

those persons who the accused reasonably believes are acting on behalf of the state and could influence or control the proceedings against him may also be persons in authority. The viewpoint of the accused must be considered—did the accused have knowledge of the person's status? There must also be a reasonable basis for the accused's belief that the person hearing the statement was a person in authority. Therefore, the accused has the evidentiary burden of proving that there is a valid issue to consider. If the accused meets this threshold burden, the Crown must prove beyond a reasonable doubt that the recipient of the statement was not a person in authority, or even if he or she was a person in authority, that the confession was made voluntarily. The Supreme Court also noted that when the potential person in authority is further removed from this conventional characterization, it may be less likely that a trial judge will initiate a *voir dire*, because the need to do so may be less apparent. Consequently, when it is less clear that a person is a person in authority, the accused has an increased obligation to raise the issue.

In this case, there was nothing to suggest that the complainant or her family members had already spoken to the police when they confronted Hodgson. Nor was there anything to suggest that the accused subjectively believed the family to have control over the criminal proceedings. Therefore, the Supreme Court held that the trial judge's obligation to hold a *voir dire* was not triggered, and the evidence of the accused's confession was properly admitted into evidence.

## Practice Tip

The further away the recipient of the statement is from the conventional category of persons in authority, the greater the onus is on the accused to alert the trial judge about the need to hold a *voir dire* on the admissibility of the confession.

---

If a statement is not made to a person in authority, it is not a confession but rather an admission. A statement made by an accused against his or her interests to another person is admissible in court as an exception to the hearsay rule. However, if a statement is made by the accused to a person in authority, it is inadmissible unless the Crown can prove that it was a voluntary statement. A **voir dire** is required to determine the voluntariness of the statement.

**voir dire**
trial or a hearing held within a trial, typically to determine the admissibility of contested evidence or the eligibility of prospective jurors

The common law confessions rule, as outlined in the case *R v Oickle*, 2000 SCC 38, [2000] 2 SCR 3, requires that a statement made to a person in authority be voluntary—meaning free from inducements, oppressive circumstances, and unfair trickery—and made with an operating mind.

**Inducements** are threats or promises in the form of words or gestures made by a person in authority. An example of a promise would be preferential treatment for the accused in exchange for a confession. In considering whether something is an inducement, the court will consider whether something is promised for the confession.

**Oppressive circumstances** may include being interrogated over a long period of time, the physical conditions in the interview room, a denial of the basic human dignity of the accused, and/or confronting the accused with fabricated evidence. Any atmosphere that takes away the accused's ability to make a meaningful choice about whether or not to speak to the authorities may be considered to be oppressive.

Lack of an operating mind may result if the accused lacks the cognitive ability to understand what he or she is saying and what is being said to him or her. Severe intoxication and mental shock are examples of lack of an operating mind.

Finally, unfair police trickery, which would have the effect of shocking the community, would likely render a confession inadmissible. An example of unfair police trickery is a situation in which a police officer pretends to be a priest and offers to take a confession from the accused.

The following worksheet provides an effective analysis for determining whether a confession is voluntary:

**inducements**
threats or promises made by a person in authority that are meant to influence or persuade someone to do something

**oppressive circumstances**
circumstances that deprive an accused person of basic necessities or the right to counsel and serve to overbear the accused's will

### Worksheet: Voluntariness of the Statement

| What was the statement? | | |
|---|---|---|
| 1. Was the statement made to a person in authority? | NO | YES—who was the person? |
| 2. Was the statement made voluntarily? Answer the questions below—if your answer is YES, provide an explanation. | NO | YES |
|    a. Were there any threats or promises made by the person in authority that had an effect on the accused? | | |
|    b. Was the accused under oppressive circumstances when the statement was made? | | |
|    c. Did the person making the statement lack an operating mind when he or she made the statement? | | |
| 3. Was any unfair trickery used by the police to get the person to make the statement? | | |

If the answers to all of the questions under Questions 2 and 3 are "no," then the statement is considered to be voluntarily given and therefore ought to be admissible.

# Unlawfully Obtained Evidence

The accused bears the burden of proving that his or her Charter rights have been breached. Once the accused proves this on a balance of probabilities, what happens to the evidence that was obtained as a result of the Charter breach? Section 24(1) provides that if the court finds that a person's Charter right has been breached, a person may apply to "a court of competent jurisdiction to obtain such remedy as the court considers appropriate and just in the circumstances." For a summary conviction matter, the court of competent jurisdiction is the Ontario Court of Justice.

The remedy for breach of a Charter right is found under section 24(2) of the Charter, which holds that if a court concludes that evidence was obtained "in a manner that infringed or denied any rights or freedoms guaranteed by this Charter, the evidence shall be excluded if it is established that, having regard to all the circumstances, the admission of it in the proceedings would bring the administration of justice into disrepute."

In the case of *Grant*, the Supreme Court of Canada revisited the test for exclusion of evidence under section 24(2). The majority of the Court in the *Grant* decision revised the test for exclusion of evidence, focusing on three parts:

- seriousness of the Charter-infringing conduct;
- impact on the Charter-protected interests of the accused; and
- society's interests in adjudication on the merits.

An analysis of the test under section 24(2) of the Charter, based on the *Grant* decision, is set out in the worksheet below. The evidentiary remedy under section 24(2) is the exclusion of evidence.

## Worksheet: Exclusion of Evidence

| | | |
|---|---|---|
| Was the evidence obtained by the authorities in a way that infringed (limited) or denied a right or freedom guaranteed in the Charter? | NO | YES— Section. Explanation. |
| Would admitting the evidence harm the reputation of the justice system (i.e., society would think less of it or lose respect for it)? To determine this, answer the three questions below: | NO | YES— explain: |
| 1.  Is it a serious breach or just technical/minor? Fairness is a fundamental principle of the justice system. Consider: | | |
|    a.  Was the violation committed in good faith or was it wilful and deliberate? | | |
|    b.  Was it serious or technical? | | |
|    c.  Was the violation due to urgency? | | |
|    d.  Could the authorities have used other investigative tools? | | |
| 2.  What is the impact on the individual's protected interests? The more serious the impact on the accused's protected interests, the greater the risk that admission of it would undermine public confidence in the system. | | |
| 3.  What is the societal interest in adjudication on the merits of the case? Consider the reliability of the evidence and whether the truth-seeking function of the criminal justice system is better served by admitting the evidence or excluding it. | | |

Other remedies that a court may grant for the breach of a Charter right include a judicial stay of proceedings or an adjournment. The remedy to be sought depends on the nature of the breach. In Chapter 7, we will look at how to draft an application for a specific remedy based on a breach of Charter rights.

# CHAPTER SUMMARY

Sections 7–11 of the Charter most commonly affect accused persons in the criminal justice system. These legal rights affect an accused person during the course of a police investigation all the way through to trial and sentencing.

Section 8 of the Charter provides protection from unreasonable search and seizure, but it is only triggered when the accused establishes a reasonable expectation of privacy. There are three types of privacy interests: personal privacy, territorial privacy, and informational privacy. Furthermore, the search itself must be reasonable, and when feasible, a warrant must be obtained for the search. This involves submitting an information to obtain a warrant based on reasonable grounds.

However, not all searches require the police to obtain a warrant. A search warrant is not required when the plain view doctrine applies, when there is consent to the search, for a search incidental to arrest, for an inventory search, when a search is necessary to protect public safety, and when exigent circumstances exist.

Police may arrest a person with or without a warrant, depending on the circumstances present. A warrant is not required when the accused person has committed or is found to be committing an offence, or when the police have reasonable grounds to believe that the accused person has committed or is about to commit an offence. Police are also not required to obtain a warrant when they are in hot pursuit of a suspect.

Section 9 of the Charter provides protection from arbitrary detention. Upon detention, sections 10(a) and (b) of the Charter apply: police must inform an accused of the reasons for arrest or detention and of the right to counsel. The right to counsel involves an informational component (being given initial instruction about the right to consult with counsel) and an implementation component (being given a reasonable opportunity to contact counsel).

Sections 7, 11(c), and 13 of the Charter provide the right to silence and protection against self-crimination. The right to silence involves being able to make a meaningful choice as to whether to speak or to remain silent. The right against self-crimination includes both testimonial and non-testimonial forms of evidence.

Before a confession is admissible against the accused, it must be proven to have been made voluntarily to a person in authority and to have been free from threats, promises, or oppressive circumstances. The confession must also be made with an operating mind and in the absence of unfair police trickery.

Finally, if evidence is obtained unlawfully, the accused may apply to a court of competent jurisdiction for an appropriate remedy under sections 24(1) and (2) of the Charter. Evidence may be excluded depending on the seriousness of the breach, the impact on the accused, and society's interests in the adjudication of the case on its merits.

# KEY TERMS

arbitrary detention, 49
bench warrant, 48
confession, 54
derivative evidence, 54
exigent circumstances, 44
express consent, 44
implied consent, 44
inducements, 56
informational privacy, 40

information to obtain, 42
oppressive circumstances, 56
person in authority, 54
personal privacy, 40
plain view doctrine, 43
principles of fundamental justice, 39
rule of inevitable discovery, 54
self-crimination, 52
territorial privacy, 40
*voir dire*, 55

# REVIEW QUESTIONS

## Short Answer

1. What right is provided under section 8 of the Charter, and when does it apply to an accused person in a criminal matter?

2. What right is provided under section 9 of the Charter, and how is it defined?

3. Describe the twofold duty on police officers in order to comply with section 10(b) of the Charter.

4. Which sections of the Charter provide the right to silence and protection against self-crimination? Give two examples of types of evidence that fall under self-criminatory evidence.

5. Which sections of the Charter apply to unlawfully obtained evidence, and what is the test to have evidence excluded?

## Apply Your Knowledge

1. Jim Wood is pulled over for speeding. While issuing the offence notice, Constable Snow sees an open duffle bag on the passenger seat of Jim's car. Constable Snow asks Jim to bring the bag closer to the driver's side window. Jim complies, and Constable Snow uses a flashlight to push aside the opening. Several plastic freezer bags with suspicious green leafy substances resembling marijuana leaves are clearly visible inside the bag. Jim Wood is arrested for possession of marijuana for the purpose of trafficking. At Jim's trial, his defence counsel brings an application to exclude the drugs pursuant to section 24(2) of the Charter on the grounds that Jim was subjected to an unlawful search in violation of section 8 of the Charter. Was the search unreasonable? Should the evidence be excluded? Why or why not?

2. Eduardo Rico takes his laptop to Feature Shop to have it repaired. He tells the technician that he will pick it up at 4 p.m. At 3:45 p.m., the technician discovers child pornography on the laptop and calls the police. The police seize the laptop without a warrant. At trial, Eduardo's defence counsel brings a Charter application to exclude the evidence on the laptop based on a warrantless search. Should the evidence be excluded? Why or why not?

3. Sonia Smith is arrested on a charge of conspiracy to commit robbery. Detective Doe reads Sonia her rights pursuant to sections 10(a) and (b) of the Charter. Sonia speaks with her defence counsel and advises police that she does not wish to make a statement. Sonia is then placed in a jail cell with another inmate. The other inmate is actually an undercover police officer named Detective Flynn. Detective Flynn introduces herself to Sonia as "Lucy Lopez" and pretends to confide in Sonia. Sonia then provides several incriminating statements to "Lucy Lopez." Would Detective Flynn be considered a "person in authority"? Should Sonia's statements be admissible at trial? Why or why not?

# Compelling Attendance and Bail

# 4

## LEARNING OUTCOMES

After reading this chapter, you should be able to:

- Outline the options available to a police officer to compel an accused person to attend court

- Describe the procedure involved in judicial interim release

- Describe the duties of a surety

# Introduction

In this chapter, we will identify options available to a police officer in determining whether to release or detain an accused person who is charged with a criminal offence. Various forms of release will be discussed, with reference to conditions placed on an accused person to secure his or her attendance in court. The process of a bail hearing will be examined with respect to the grounds for detaining an accused person, as well as situations in which the obligation shifts from the Crown to the accused to show cause why he or she ought to be released pending trial.

# Procedures to Compel Attendance in Court

When the police determine that a person is to be charged with a criminal offence, there are four different procedures to compel that person's appearance in court, depending on the circumstances:

- when the person is not arrested, issuing an appearance notice for court;
- when the person is arrested, release by the officer in charge;
- when the information is laid first, the issuance of a summons or arrest warrant for the person; or
- when the person is arrested and not released by the officer in charge, to be brought before a justice.

## When There Is No Arrest

Pursuant to section 495(2) of the *Criminal Code*, a police officer may not arrest a person for a summary conviction or hybrid offence when the public interest would be satisfied without the need to arrest the person. Factors for the police officer to take into account in determining whether the public interest would be met are:

- whether the identity of the person can be established; or
- the need to preserve or secure evidence; or
- to prevent a continuation or repetition of the offence or the commission of another offence; and
- there are no reasonable grounds to believe that the person will fail to attend court if he or she is not arrested.

**appearance notice**
formal document, signed by the accused, that sets out details of the accused's first court appearance and is given to the accused before he or she is charged with an offence

If these conditions are met, the police officer must not arrest the accused and may issue an **appearance notice** to the person to compel his or her attendance in court pursuant to section 496 of the *Criminal Code*. A sample of Form 9 of the *Criminal Code*—an appearance notice—can be found in Appendix F. An appearance notice sets out the name of the accused, the offence, the date and time of the court appearance, the courtroom number, and the court location. For a hybrid or indictable offence, the appearance notice sets out the date, time, and location that the accused must attend for fingerprinting. The notice indicates that failing to attend court is an offence pursuant to section 145(5) of the *Criminal Code*, with the penalties listed in the same section. The notice contains the date and location of issue, and it must be signed by the police officer and the accused.

## When Person Is Arrested Without a Warrant and Released by Officer Without Conditions

As discussed in Chapter 3, section 495(1) of the *Criminal Code* outlines the circumstances in which the police may arrest a person without a warrant:

- a person has committed an indictable offence, or the officer has reasonable grounds to believe that a person has committed or is about to commit an indictable offence;
- a person is found to be committing any criminal offence; or
- the officer has reasonable grounds to believe that a warrant of arrest for a person is in effect in the jurisdiction in which the person is found.

It should be noted that hybrid offences are considered to be indictable until the Crown makes an election.

If a person is arrested, the police may decide to release the person to appear in court on the charge(s). Pursuant to section 497(1)(a) or (b), a police officer must release a person charged with a hybrid or summary conviction offence on a summons or an appearance notice when the public interest would be satisfied without the need to continue to hold the accused in custody. Factors for the police officer to take into account in determining whether the public interest would be met are the same as those discussed above, or if there is a need to ensure the safety and security of any victim or witness to the offence.

When the person is released on an appearance notice or a summons, no conditions are placed on the accused person other than to attend court and to attend for fingerprinting. Form 6 of the *Criminal Code* is a template for a **summons** and can be found in Appendix G. Similar to the information contained in an appearance notice, a summons must set out the charge, the date and time of the court appearance, the courtroom number, and the court location. If it is a hybrid or indictable offence, the summons must include the date, time, and location where the accused needs to attend for fingerprinting. The consequences for failing to comply with a summons, along with penalties, are also set out. A summons must be endorsed by a justice of the peace or a judge.

Pursuant to section 509(2) of the *Criminal Code*, a summons must be served by a peace officer either directly on the accused or by leaving it at the accused's last known address or usual place of residence with a person who appears to be at least 16 years of age.

**summons**
formal document served on the accused after a charge is laid that sets out the details of the accused's first court appearance and compels the accused to attend court

## When Person Is Arrested Without a Warrant and Released by Officer with Conditions

When a person is arrested without a warrant for a hybrid or a summary conviction offence and there are no reasonable grounds to believe that the public interest would not be met by releasing him or her, the police have the discretion to release the person on a form of release with conditions attached. Pursuant to section 498(1)(b), (c), or (d), the police officer may release the person on their giving a **promise to appear** or on the person entering into a **recognizance** before a police officer.

**promise to appear**
formal document, signed by the accused, in which he or she promises to appear in court on a certain date

Form 10 of the *Criminal Code* is a template for a promise to appear and can be found in Appendix H. A promise to appear is filled out as a condition of the accused's release. In order to be released from custody, the accused must promise to attend court on the date, time, and location set out, as well as attend for fingerprinting on the date, time, and location set out, if it is a hybrid or indictable offence. The penalty for not complying with a promise to appear is stated in the form, which is dated and signed by the accused.

**recognizance**
form of release whereby an accused person agrees to be bound by a monetary amount and certain conditions in order to secure his or her release from custody

Form 11 of the *Criminal Code* is a template for a recognizance entered into before a police officer and can be found in Appendix I. The recognizance may be for an amount not exceeding $500. This does not mean that the accused has to pay the money up front; if the accused breaches any conditions set out in the recognizance, then default may be noted on it, and the accused may be liable for the specified amount of money to the court. When an accused person is not a resident of the province in which he or she is being held in custody, or when he or she lives more than 200 kilometres away from the place where he or she is being held, the police officer may require the person to pay a cash deposit of a maximum amount of $500 as part of the recognizance. The cash deposit will be forfeited if the accused does not appear in court.

Whether it includes a cash deposit or not, the recognizance must set out the charge; the date, time, and location of appearance; and for hybrid or indictable offences, the date, time, and location of fingerprinting. The recognizance also specifies the offence and penalty for failing to attend court, and it must be signed and dated by the accused.

## When Person Is Arrested with a Warrant and Released by Officer

When a police officer swears an information before a justice and obtains an arrest warrant, or when the accused is otherwise arrested on the strength of a warrant, pursuant to section 499(1), the police officer may release the accused only if the warrant is endorsed for release by the justice authorizing the arrest. The police officer may release the accused on a promise to appear or on a recognizance with or without a cash deposit, as discussed above. However, in addition to these forms of release, a police officer may also require the person to enter into an **undertaking** with conditions pursuant to section 499(2) of the *Criminal Code*. In order to be released, the accused person must undertake or promise to do certain things.

**undertaking**
formal document, signed by the accused, in which the accused promises to do or refrain from doing certain things in order to be released

The conditions that may be attached to an undertaking include one or more of the following:

- remaining within the jurisdiction specified;
- notifying a police officer of changes in the accused's address, employment, or occupation;

- not communicating with a victim, witness, or other identified person, or not attending to a place specified;
- depositing a passport with a police officer;
- abstaining from possessing a firearm and a licence or registration to possess a firearm;
- reporting to a police officer on dates and times specified;
- abstaining from consuming alcohol and non-prescription drugs; and
- complying with other conditions specified in the undertaking.

Section 499(3) of the *Criminal Code* allows an accused person to apply to a justice to replace the undertaking prior to or at the first court appearance; however, the accused would then have to apply for release from custody before a justice. Section 499(4) permits the Crown to apply for the undertaking to be replaced at the court appearance or with three days' notice to be given to the accused. These sections also allow the accused or the Crown to apply to vary or change conditions at a later date.

Form 11.1 of the *Criminal Code* is a template for an undertaking to a police officer and can be found in Appendix J. An undertaking must include the offence that the accused is charged with, the conditions that are attached to the undertaking, an acknowledgment that the person may apply to have the undertaking vacated, and the penalty and offence provision for failure to comply with the conditions. The undertaking must be dated and signed by the accused. It should be noted that when an accused fails or refuses to sign an appearance notice, a promise to appear, or a recognizance, the lack of signature does not invalidate the form (section 501(4) of the *Criminal Code*).

## Confirmation of Process and Failure to Appear

At the accused's first court appearance, whether released by appearance notice, summons, promise to appear, recognizance, or undertaking, the judge must confirm the process—which is the form of release—or cancel it. A defect in the form of release does not invalidate the Crown's ability to proceed on the charge. However, in order to enforce any of the conditions on the form of release, a new form must be served and processed on the accused.

An accused person who fails to appear for fingerprinting at the date, time, and location specified or at the first court appearance may have a warrant issued for his or her arrest. However, before a warrant can be issued, the form of release must be confirmed by a judge.

## When Person Is Brought Before a Justice

When a police officer is not satisfied that the public interest may be met by releasing an accused person on a form of release, he or she must take the person before a justice within 24 hours of the arrest pursuant to section 503(1) of the *Criminal Code*; when a justice is not available within 24 hours, this must occur as soon as possible.

> **PRACTICE TIP**
>
> If a client is charged with failing to attend for fingerprinting, it is a defence to the charge if the form of release has not been confirmed. When the form of release has not yet been confirmed on the date of attendance for fingerprinting, the accused cannot be convicted for failure to appear. Therefore, it is important to check with the clerk of the court whether the judge has confirmed process.

During this time period, if the police officer believes that the person should be released, he or she must do so on a form of release as discussed above, either with or without conditions.

Failure to bring an accused person before a justice within 24 hours of arrest constitutes arbitrary detention under sections 9 and 10(c) of the Charter. Section 10(c) of the Charter provides that an accused person has the right "to have the validity of the detention determined by way of **habeas corpus** and to be released if the detention is not lawful." Section 11(e) of the Charter provides for the accused's right not to be denied reasonable bail without just cause. "Reasonable bail" refers not only to release but also to the restrictions placed on the accused's liberty while on bail (*R v Pearson*, [1992] 3 SCR 665). In the next section, we will look at the grounds for the detention of an accused person.

**habeas corpus**
a Latin term for the accused's right to be brought before a judge

# Judicial Interim Release

**judicial interim release**
formal term for bail; the release of an accused person before trial or sentencing

**show cause hearing**
another term for a bail hearing, during which the Crown prosecutor must show cause why the accused should continue to be detained

Section 515 of the *Criminal Code* deals with **judicial interim release**. Judicial interim release is commonly referred to as a **show cause hearing** or a bail hearing, a process whereby the Crown prosecutor must show cause why continued detention of the accused in custody is justified. The accused does not have to enter a plea at this stage, nor does the Crown have to make a formal election as to how to proceed on the charge. The only consideration is whether or not the accused should be released on bail. An accused person may be physically transported to the courtroom by police or sheriff's officers for the hearing, or the justice may allow the accused to appear by any suitable telecommunications device, such as closed-circuit television.

Section 515(1) of the *Criminal Code* requires the accused to be released on an undertaking without conditions unless the Crown is able to show cause why the accused should be detained in custody or why a different order should be made. The rationale behind this section is twofold: the accused person is presumed innocent until proven guilty according to law, and every accused person has the right not to be denied reasonable bail without just cause. These are rights guaranteed under sections 11(d) and (e) of the Charter, and they apply to bail hearings.

If the Crown prosecutor is not able to show cause why the accused ought to be detained in custody, the justice must order that the accused be released on an undertaking or on a recognizance with conditions and with or without sureties and a cash deposit, depending on the circumstances. The Crown may also consent to the accused's release on a recognizance with conditions, including a cash deposit.

As mentioned above, the onus is on the Crown not only to show cause why the accused should not be released but also to justify why a more onerous form of release ought to be considered instead of an undertaking without conditions as prescribed under section 515(1). The forms of release set out under section 515(2) are similar to rungs on a ladder: the Crown must consider whether a less onerous form of release would be justified under the circumstances, as illustrated in the figure below. Pursuant to section 515(3), the justice shall not make an order under sections 515(2)(b) to (e) unless the Crown "shows cause why an order under the immediately preceding paragraph should not be made."

The justice must consider whether or not to release the accused. The following diagram outlines the forms of release that a justice may consider, from least onerous to an order of detention.

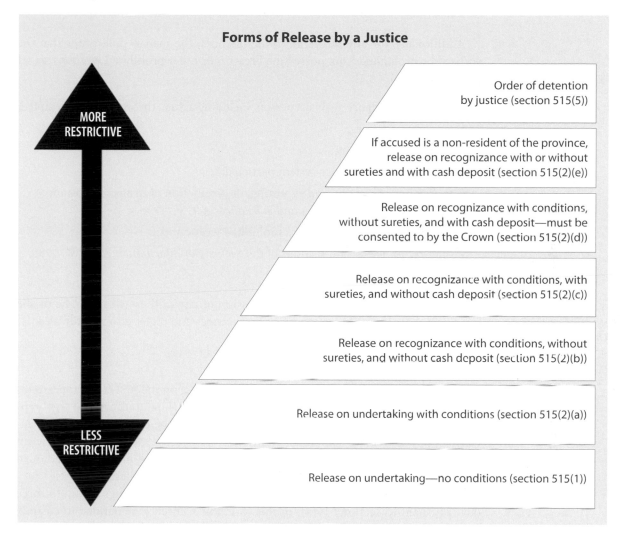

**Forms of Release by a Justice**

MORE RESTRICTIVE

LESS RESTRICTIVE

Order of detention by justice (section 515(5))

If accused is a non-resident of the province, release on recognizance with or without sureties and with cash deposit (section 515(2)(e))

Release on recognizance with conditions, without sureties, and with cash deposit—must be consented to by the Crown (section 515(2)(d))

Release on recognizance with conditions, with sureties, and without cash deposit (section 515(2)(c))

Release on recognizance with conditions, without sureties, and without cash deposit (section 515(2)(b))

Release on undertaking with conditions (section 515(2)(a))

Release on undertaking—no conditions (section 515(1))

The justice may release the accused on any one or more of the following conditions, as set out in section 515(4) of the *Criminal Code*:

- report on the dates and times specified in the order to a police officer or other designated person;
- remain in the jurisdiction specified;
- notify the police of any changes in address, employment, or occupation;
- abstain from communicating with a victim, witness, or other person specified in the order, or to refrain from going to a place specified in the order;
- deposit a passport with the court or police;

- comply with any other condition deemed necessary to ensure the safety of any victim or witness; and
- comply with any other reasonable condition deemed by the justice to be desirable.

Additionally, for any of the following offences, the justice shall order that the accused be prohibited from possessing firearms or other prohibited weapons, as set out in section 515(4.1):

- offences of violence against a person, including actual, threatened, or attempted;
- terrorism offences;
- criminal harassment;
- intimidation of a justice system participant;
- trafficking, importing and exporting, or production of drugs or substances under the *Controlled Drugs and Substances Act*, SC 1996, c 19;
- offences involving the use of a prohibited weapon; and
- offences under certain sections of the *Security of Information Act*, RSC 1985, c O-5.

If the accused person has lawful possession of any of these weapons, he or she must surrender them along with his or her licences and registration certificates.

## Show Cause Hearing

An accused person is entitled to a show cause hearing on the first court appearance before a justice, if he or she so desires. By way of disclosure, the accused's legal representative will be provided with a police narrative of the details and with the accused's criminal record. Sometimes additional disclosure is available, such as victim and witness statements or police officers' notes. The accused may wish to adjourn the matter for further disclosure before applying for judicial interim release.

The Crown prosecutor may request to adjourn the proceedings for up to three days pursuant to section 516(1). In this case, the accused is remanded to custody without his or her consent, but only for a maximum of three days, unless the accused consents to a longer period. The request for the adjournment may be based on the Crown requesting the police to conduct a further investigation, the laying of additional charges, obtaining additional particulars of the offence, or bringing forward pending charges for which the accused has already been released on bail. During the period of the adjournment, the justice may order the accused not to contact or communicate with any victims, witnesses, or other specified persons.

If the Crown is able to show cause why the detention of the accused is justified, the justice must order the accused to remain in custody until the matter is dealt with, either by way of a guilty plea, a trial, or at a bail review proceeding in Superior Court. If the justice makes an order of detention, it must be followed with a statement of the reasons for making such an order. This is particularly important if the accused wishes to appeal the order of detention.

## Reverse Onus Situations

Under certain circumstances, according to section 515(6) of the *Criminal Code*, the onus shifts to the accused to show cause why he or she ought to be released on bail. For example, when the accused has already been released on bail for the commission of an indictable offence and then appears before the justice on another indictable offence, the onus shifts to the accused to show cause why detention is not justified. When the accused has been released on an indictable offence and has been charged for failing to comply with a condition contained in the form of release, the onus shifts to the accused to show why he or she should not be detained.

It should be noted that indictable offences include hybrid offences until the Crown makes an election to proceed either by way of summary conviction or by indictment. Since the Crown rarely makes an election at this early stage, if the accused is charged with a hybrid offence while on release for another hybrid offence, it will typically result in a reverse onus situation. There are other situations in which a reverse onus will result, but they are not within the purview of the paralegal scope of practice in criminal law. The reverse onus provision of judicial interim release has been subject to Charter challenges but has been upheld as constitutional (see Case in Point: *R v Morales*).

If a justice agrees to release an accused in a reverse onus situation, the justice must include the reasons for making an order of release. In a reverse onus situation, if the justice agrees to release the accused, the former bail will typically be revoked and the accused will be released on one recognizance for all of the pending charges. This is done for simplicity, so that the accused is bound by one court order instead of multiple orders with varying or conflicting conditions. The justice may impose additional conditions on the new recognizance unless the accused is able to show cause why the additional conditions should not be imposed.

## CASE IN POINT

# Charter Challenge to the Reverse Onus Provision

*R v Morales*, [1992] 3 SCR 711

### Facts

The accused, Maximo Morales, was arrested and charged with drug trafficking and importing narcotics. The allegations were that the accused was part of a major network to import cocaine into Canada. At the time that the accused was arrested, he was awaiting trial on the indictable offence of assault with a weapon. Morales was denied bail on the drug charges but was subsequently released by the Superior Court at a bail review hearing. Constitutional challenges were brought regarding the secondary ground (section 515(10)(b), discussed below) and the reverse onus provision (section 515(6)).

### Decision

The Supreme Court of Canada held that section 515(6) did not violate the section 11(e) Charter right to be granted bail unless just cause is demonstrated. For just cause to exist, the Supreme Court held that two factors must be present: the denial of bail must only occur in narrow circumstances, and the denial of bail must be necessary to promote the proper functioning of the bail system. Even though the reverse onus provision requires the accused to show why detention is not justified, the Supreme Court held that section 515(6) meets these two requirements and therefore does provide just cause to deny bail. For example, the reverse onus provision is limited in its scope; it only applies to indictable offences, and it is utilized only when a person has been charged with an indictable offence while on bail for another indictable offence and does not show cause why detention is not justified. Furthermore, the Supreme Court held that the denial of bail is necessary to promote the proper functioning of the bail system, as the objective behind section 515(6) is to stop criminal behaviour. Accordingly, the Supreme Court held that the reverse onus provision, section 515(6), is constitutional.

## Discussion Question

All hybrid offences are considered to be indictable offences until the Crown makes an election to proceed summarily. Therefore, if an accused person is arrested for a hybrid offence while already out on bail for another hybrid offence, this will be considered to be a reverse onus situation unless the Crown has already made an election to proceed by way of summary conviction on the first charge. Do you think that this is fair? Should the Crown be forced to make an election prior to the bail hearing?

## Grounds for Opposition to Release

For non-reverse onus situations, the onus is on the Crown to show cause why detention is justified. The burden of proof is on a balance of probabilities. At a show cause hearing, hearsay evidence is allowed—the Crown prosecutor reads in the facts according to the disclosure provided by the police. The Crown has limited grounds that it may argue to justify the continued detention pursuant to section 515(10) of the *Criminal Code*. There are three grounds that the Crown may rely upon at a show cause hearing, referred to as the primary, secondary, and tertiary grounds.

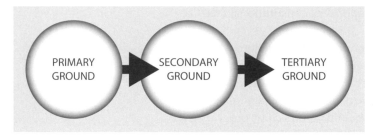

### Primary Ground

Primary ground concerns (section 515(10)(a)) are raised when detention is claimed to be necessary to ensure the accused's attendance in court. Factors that the court may consider in determining whether there are primary ground concerns are whether the accused has a history of failing to attend court, whether the accused has any permanent ties to the community, or whether the accused has made comments about leaving the jurisdiction if released.

Primary ground concerns may be addressed by the defence by showing that the accused has ties in the community (family or employment), that the accused is willing to surrender his or her passport until the charge is dealt with, or that there are conditions that the accused is willing to abide by to ensure attendance in court, such as reporting to the police or attending all court appearances.

### EXAMPLE

**A Primary Ground Concern**

Bryan has been arrested for assault. He has been kicked out of his apartment and has no fixed address. He also has a previous record for failing to attend court on other non-related charges. The Crown is opposed to Bryan's release on the primary ground unless he can provide the court with the address where he will be residing and unless he is willing to personally attend all of his court appearances.

## Secondary Ground

Secondary ground concerns (section 515(10)(b)) are raised when detention is claimed to be necessary for the protection or safety of the public, including victims, witnesses, or any person under the age of 18 years, with regard to any substantial likelihood that the accused will commit a criminal offence or interfere with the administration of justice. Factors that the court may consider in determining whether there are any secondary ground concerns include the accused's previous criminal record, patterns of behaviour that are similar to the current charges, a history of breaching conditions of bail, comments or threats made to the victims or witnesses involved, or a history of substance abuse issues.

> **EXAMPLE**
>
> **A Secondary Ground Concern**
>
> Jenna has been charged with criminal harassment against her ex-boyfriend. Jenna has two previous convictions for assaulting him, and she is bound by two probation orders with conditions that she not have any contact or communication with him. In the past year, Jenna has been convicted three times for breaching this condition. The Crown is opposed to Jenna's release on the secondary ground: there are concerns for the safety of the victim.

Secondary ground concerns may be addressed by the defence by demonstrating to the court that any past conduct can be distinguished from the charges that the accused is now facing. The defence may also be able to provide a secure plan for release that addresses any risk factors, such as substance abuse or anger management, including counselling or treatment programs while the charges are before the court. It should be noted that before the defence paralegal proposes any conditions to be attached to a recognizance, he or she must discuss these conditions with the accused and be satisfied that the accused will be able to abide by these conditions.

## Tertiary Ground

Tertiary ground concerns (section 515(10)(c)) are raised when detention is claimed to be necessary to maintain confidence in the administration of justice. Factors that must be taken into account by the court include:

- the strength of the Crown's case;
- the seriousness of the offence;
- circumstances surrounding the commission of the offence, including whether a firearm was used; and
- whether upon conviction, the accused is facing a lengthy term of imprisonment, or when the offence involves a firearm, a minimum period of three years of imprisonment.

The tertiary ground is used sparingly—only in those cases when release of the accused would result in real harm to the administration of justice (*R v RD*, 2010 ONCA 899). The tertiary ground is only invoked when the primary and secondary grounds have already been considered and do not pose a concern with respect to the accused's release. The constitutionality of section 515(10)(c) was challenged in the case of *R v Hall*, 2002 SCC 64, [2002] 3 SCR 309 (see Case in Point: *R v Hall*).

## CASE IN POINT

# Charter Challenge of the Tertiary Ground

*R v Hall*, 2002 SCC 64, [2002] 3 SCR 309

### Facts

The accused, David Scott Hall, was charged with first degree murder in the death of his cousin's wife. The victim had been stabbed 37 times in her neck, face, shoulders, arms and back. Her neck had been cut to the vertebrae. The Crown's case against Hall was strong: there were traces of his blood in the victim's home; footprint impressions in the victim's blood that matched the type of shoes worn by the accused were found in the kitchen; and a surveillance photo showed the accused wearing those shoes on the night of the murder. A police officer testified that there was a general sense of fear that the killer was at large.

The accused applied for judicial interim release, and the judge denied bail on the tertiary ground. Neither the primary nor the secondary ground was of concern, given that the accused had community and family ties, sufficient sureties were proposed, and there were no reasons to believe that the accused would commit another offence if released on bail with the proper conditions. However, the judge felt that the accused's detention was justified on the tertiary ground: to maintain confidence in the administration of justice, in light of the aftermath of the murder and the strength of the evidence against the accused.

The judge's decision to deny bail was upheld by the Superior Court and the Ontario Court of Appeal. The accused appealed to the Supreme Court of Canada, arguing that section 515(10)(c) should be declared unconstitutional, as it violated the Charter-guaranteed right of the presumption of innocence and the right not to be denied reasonable bail except for just cause.

### Decision

The Supreme Court of Canada held that the specific provision under section 515(10)(c) permitting detention "on any other just cause being shown" was unconstitutional, as it allowed for open-ended judicial discretion to refuse bail. The provision was too vague and imprecise. However, the balance of section 515(10)(c) was held to be valid. This section provided a basis for denial of bail not covered by the primary and secondary grounds. It may not have been used frequently, but it did provide a means to deny bail when public confidence was essential to the proper functioning of the judicial system. There was a proper balance between the rights of the accused and the need to maintain justice in the community.

In dismissing the appeal, the Supreme Court held that the offending phrase "on any other just cause being shown, and without limiting the generality of the foregoing" ought to be severed from section 515(10)(c), and that the remainder of the provision was constitutionally valid.

### Discussion Question

In a situation in which the primary and secondary grounds do not pose a concern in terms of the release of the accused, are the specific factors listed under the tertiary ground simply a means of satiating the public, or are these valid considerations in determining whether or not an accused should be released on bail? Do factors such as the strength of the Crown's case and the seriousness of the offence have an impact on whether the accused is a suitable candidate for bail?

If the Crown is able to show cause, on a balance of probabilities, why the detention of the accused is justified, then the justice must detain the accused in custody until the charges are dealt with by way of a guilty plea or trial. The justice may also include an order that the accused not have any contact or communication with any victim, witness, or other specified person while in custody.

Pursuant to section 523(1)(b), the accused's form of release and conditions remain in effect until the trial is completed, and if the accused is found guilty at trial, until he or she is sentenced. The only exception to this is if a justice vacates the previous form of release and releases the accused on a new recognizance.

If a justice is satisfied that there are reasonable grounds to believe that an accused person has breached or is about to breach any form of release, or has committed an indictable offence while on a form of release, the justice may issue an arrest warrant for the accused pursuant to section 524(1) of the *Criminal Code*. The warrant may be an **endorsed warrant**, meaning that the arresting officer may release the accused on a form of release, or the warrant may be an **unendorsed warrant**, meaning that the arresting officer must detain the accused in custody and bring him or her before a justice to apply for bail. A police officer who has reasonable grounds to believe that an accused person has breached or is about to breach any form of release, or has committed an indictable offence while on a form of release, may arrest the accused without a warrant pursuant to section 524(2) of the *Criminal Code*.

> **PRACTICE TIP**
>
> There are two differing views on the best strategy when applying for judicial interim release. Some believe that making an early application for release is best since the Crown's case is skeletal—there may be witness statements that are missing and police notes that are not yet complete at the time of the application. Based on this, the defence may argue that the Crown's case against the accused is not a strong one. Another strategy is to wait until further particulars are available in order to put forward a strong defence to the charge(s). By having full disclosure, the defence is able to anticipate and address the Crown's concerns by having a good plan in place for the accused's release.

**endorsed warrant**
type of warrant in which the justice authorizes the accused to be released after arrest

**unendorsed warrant**
type of warrant that requires the accused to be brought before a justice to apply for bail after his or her arrest

## Sureties

The Crown may consent to releasing an accused on a recognizance if he or she can come up with one or more sureties. Even when the Crown does not consent to release, the justice may be satisfied that the Crown's grounds for opposition may be addressed by the court by requiring that the accused be released on his or her own recognizance, along with one or more sureties.

A person must qualify to act as a **surety**; he or she must provide financial information to the court and information about his or her character and personal background. Persons with criminal records are not qualified to act as sureties. A surety may be cross-examined by the Crown about his or her qualifications. A surety must also be in a position to supervise the accused.

A surety pledges to pay a certain amount of money to the court if the accused breaches his or her conditions of release, and the surety must ensure that the accused will abide by each condition on the recognizance, including appearances in court. The surety's duties continue until the accused is either acquitted or found guilty and sentenced. If the accused does breach a condition of the recognizance, the Crown may ask the court to note default on the surety and take **estreatment proceedings** against the surety to collect the amount pledged.

**surety**
person who agrees to take responsibility for and supervise the accused while he or she is out on bail

**estreatment proceeding**
an application brought by the Crown to collect the money promised by a surety when the accused breaches a condition or conditions of bail

Pursuant to section 767 of the *Criminal Code*, if the surety is concerned that he or she is unable to supervise the accused or no longer wishes to act as a surety, then he or she must bring the accused to court and ask to be relieved of the responsibility. Alternatively, the surety may apply in writing to the court to request that he or she be relieved of the obligations, pursuant to section 766(1). When a surety withdraws, the accused's recognizance is considered to be vacated, and the accused must apply for judicial interim release. If the surety is unable to bring the accused to court, then an arrest warrant will be issued for the accused. An exception to this is if the justice agrees to substitute one surety for another, in which case the new surety would sign the recognizance.

# CHAPTER SUMMARY

A police officer may release the accused on an appearance notice, a summons, a promise to appear, an undertaking, or a recognizance. Various factors are considered when choosing which method of release to utilize. Such factors include:

- whether the accused has been arrested;
- whether there are any concerns with respect to establishing the identity of the accused;
- the need to preserve or secure evidence;
- the need to prevent the commission of another offence;
- securing the accused's attendance in court; and
- ensuring the safety of victims and witnesses.

If a police officer does not release the accused, he or she must bring the accused before a justice within 24 hours of arrest.

When the accused is brought before a justice, if the police do not release the accused, the accused is entitled to judicial interim release. If the Crown is opposed to the release of the accused, the Crown may raise three grounds in opposing the

accused's release: ensuring the accused's attendance in court, protecting the public, and maintaining confidence in the administration of justice. The onus is typically on the Crown to show cause as to why the accused should be detained in custody. However, a reverse onus situation may result when the accused has already been released on an indictable offence and is before the court on another indictable offence. In a reverse onus situation, the onus shifts to the accused to show cause as to why detention is not justified.

As part of the conditions of release, the justice may require the accused to come up with one or more sureties, who will ensure that the accused abides by any conditions placed on him or her. Before a person may act as a surety, he or she must pledge to pay a certain amount of money to the court if the accused breaches the bail conditions. The surety must also provide personal information to the court and be in a position to supervise the accused. If a surety is no longer able or willing to act as a surety, he or she must request to be relieved of the obligation.

# KEY TERMS

appearance notice, 62
endorsed warrant, 73
estreatment proceeding, 73
*habeas corpus*, 66
judicial interim release, 66
promise to appear, 64
recognizance, 64
show cause hearing, 66
summons, 63
surety, 73
undertaking, 64
unendorsed warrant, 73

# REVIEW QUESTIONS

## Short Answer

1. A person can be arrested without a warrant for a summary conviction offence. With reference to the relevant section of the *Criminal Code*, list the conditions that an officer needs to consider when arresting someone without a warrant.

2. After a person is arrested by police for an alleged summary conviction offence, what three options do the police have in dealing with the person who is in custody?

3. Explain the three grounds that the Crown may rely upon in opposing the release of an accused person.

4. Under what circumstances will a reverse onus situation arise in bail court?

5. List four things that a surety must demonstrate in order to qualify as a surety.

## Apply Your Knowledge

For each of the following scenarios, identify what concerns the Crown may raise in opposing the accused person's release. As the defence paralegal, describe how you would address those concerns before the judge. What conditions would you suggest would be suitable to address the Crown's concerns?

1. Suman has been charged with assault; the complainant is her husband. Suman has been charged with similar offences in the past three years but only has two convictions on her record: one for domestic assault (against her husband) and one for uttering threats (against her neighbours who tried to intervene). For the other offences, her husband has always come to court and asked the Crown to drop the charges. Suman and her husband do not have any children. Suman's aunt lives in the same city and has offered to allow Suman to live with her on a temporary basis.

2. Romeo is charged with impaired driving and driving while suspended. His licence is currently suspended due to another impaired driving conviction from seven months earlier. Romeo has been working in a factory for ten years. He has a few convictions on his record for assaulting other persons in a bar, for causing a disturbance (he was inebriated and harassing people on a street), and for possession of marijuana. While he was being arrested by the police, Romeo told them that he was going to "drive to Florida to get away from the cops." Romeo's supervisor is in court to show his support.

3. Melissa has been charged with failing to comply with conditions of an undertaking. She was previously charged with four counts of mischief under $5,000 for spraying graffiti on a number of office buildings after 6 p.m. She failed to appear at a court date during which trial dates were going to be set for the charges. Melissa is a full-time student at a local college and lives at home with her parents. She has a criminal record from four years ago for theft under $5,000 and for failing to attend the police station to have her fingerprints taken.

# Witnesses

5

## LEARNING OUTCOMES

After reading this chapter, you should be able to:

- Define competency and compellability as they apply to witnesses

- Identify how witnesses are compelled to attend court

- Discuss special provisions that may be sought to encourage witnesses to provide a full and candid account before the court

- Explain which ethical considerations apply to a paralegal interviewing a witness

- Summarize the rules regarding speaking to witnesses who are giving testimony in a case

# Introduction

This chapter will look at witnesses who *can* testify in court and who may be *forced* to testify in court. We will review procedures used to procure witnesses' attendance, as well as the consequences that arise from the failure to appear at a court proceeding. Special provisions for witness testimony in criminal trials will be outlined. Finally, we will discuss the Rules as they apply to interviewing and communicating with witnesses.

# Competence and Compellability of Witnesses

## Competence

A witness may testify in court as long as he or she is competent to do so. All witnesses are presumed to be competent to give evidence and may do so as long as it is material to the case. The only exception to this is with respect to spouses, as discussed below. The burden of proof is on the party challenging the **competence** of a witness to show on a **balance of probabilities** that the witness is not competent. This is typically done by way of a *voir dire* before the witness is sworn in or affirms to tell the truth.

**competence**
ability of a witness to testify and give evidence in court

**balance of probabilities**
standard of proof based on more likely than not

Witnesses who are under the age of 14 are presumed to be competent to testify. However, if the witness's capacity is challenged and the judge is satisfied that an issue exists, then the judge must inquire into whether the witness is able to understand and respond to questions, pursuant to section 16.1(5) of the *Canada Evidence Act*, RSC 1985, c C-5 (CEA). A witness under the age of 14 must promise to tell the truth and does not need to swear an oath or make a solemn affirmation before giving testimony.

Witnesses over the age of 14 who are competent must swear an oath or make a solemn affirmation before being permitted to testify. If the competency of a witness over the age of 14 is challenged, the judge must inquire into whether the witness understands the nature of an oath or solemn affirmation and whether the witness is able to communicate the evidence. If the witness is unable to understand the nature of an oath or solemn affirmation but is able to communicate the evidence, the witness may still testify upon promising to tell the truth, pursuant to section 16(3) of the CEA.

Whether a witness swears an oath or makes a solemn affirmation, both have the same force and effect in law. This means that if a witness lies while giving evidence, he or she may be charged with perjury, regardless of whether the testimony was under oath or solemn affirmation.

### Spousal Competence

In common law, there is a presumption that spouses of accused persons are only competent to testify for the defence. Spouses of accused persons are incompetent to testify for the Crown, except in cases that involve the spouse's person, health, or liberty (*R v Hawkins*, [1996] 3 SCR 1043, 141 DLR (4th) 193 [*Hawkins*]). The traditional justification for this rule was that spouses were deemed to share the same interest; therefore, this would result in a breakdown in marital harmony if one spouse was permitted to testify against the other. The traditional rule did not include common law partners in the definition of spouses. This was recently changed by the Ontario Superior Court of Justice in the case of *R v Hall*, 2013 ONSC 834 [*Hall*], in which Justice Lofchik held that the application of the spousal incompetency rule discriminated against unmarried couples living in common law relationships, which violated section 15(1) of the Charter. Therefore, Justice Lofchik held that common law spouses can also rely on spousal incompetence and may not be called to testify for the Crown. *Hall* is a marked departure from the traditional case law, so paralegals and paralegal students alike should follow subsequent cases and commentary considering *Hall*, as well as any appeals of this decision.

The CEA, while somewhat consistent with the common law rule regarding spousal incompetence, creates exceptions for certain enumerated offences, as discussed in the section on compellability. A distinction should also be made between spousal incompetence and **spousal privilege**: spousal incompetence applies to testimonial evidence, while spousal privilege applies to any communications between spouses. Spousal privilege may be waived by the spouse who is receiving the communication, but spousal incompetence may not be waived.

Interesting issues arise when the accused and his or her spouse get married shortly before the hearing or when there is a breakdown in the relationship—does spousal incompetence still prevent the spouse from testifying for the Crown in these cases? These issues were considered by the Supreme Court of Canada in two cases that were decided over ten years apart from each other: *Hawkins* and *R v Couture*, 2007 SCC 28, 280 DLR (4th) 577 [*Couture*]. In *Hawkins*, the Crown's key witness was the girlfriend of the accused, Hawkins. At the preliminary inquiry, the girlfriend, Graham, provided incriminating statements against Hawkins under oath. After the hearing, Graham hired her own counsel and successfully sought to recant key portions of her earlier statements in court.

After the preliminary inquiry, Graham and Hawkins were legally married. At trial, the Crown attempted to have Graham testify. Alternatively, the Crown sought to read in Graham's statements from the preliminary inquiry as evidence. Both the trial judge and the Court of Appeal held that Graham was not a competent witness for the prosecution. The Supreme Court of Canada agreed with the lower courts, ruling that Graham was not a competent witness, but they permitted her evidence from the preliminary inquiry to be read in as evidence, pursuant to the principled exception to the hearsay rule.

Although the Crown argued that the marriage was solemnized after the indictment was issued, the Supreme Court was unwilling to make any changes to the common law rule regarding spousal competence. The Supreme Court went as far as to say that even when a marriage is motivated by a desire to take advantage of this rule, it may still be a true marriage and is deserving of the law's protection.

The Supreme Court of Canada had the opportunity to revisit this rule in the case of *Couture* (see Case in Point: *R v Couture*).

**spousal privilege**
a legal concept that recognizes that communications between spouses are confidential and do not have to be revealed in court

---

**CASE IN POINT**

## Spousal Incompetence: Nature of the Relationship

*R v Couture*, 2007 SCC 28, 280 DLR (4th) 577

### Facts

Before their marriage, the accused's spouse, Darlene Couture, had been his volunteer counsellor in the prison in which the accused, David Couture, had been serving a sentence for other charges. During the course of counselling, the accused confessed to murdering two women several years earlier. These murders were unsolved at the time of the accused's confession. After the accused was released from jail, he began to live with Darlene, and the two of them started a relationship.

Sometime later, Darlene gave two statements to the police about what the accused had disclosed to her, and the police began their investigation into the accused's involvement in the murders. Before the accused's murder trial on the two charges, the accused and Darlene reconciled and were legally married. At the trial, the Crown was not able to call Darlene based on the spousal incompetence rule, but the trial judge allowed her statements to the police as admissible evidence based on the principled exception to the hearsay rule and following the decision in *Hawkins*. The British Columbia Court of Appeal ruled the statements to be inadmissible and ordered a new trial. The Crown appealed to the Supreme Court of Canada.

### Decision

The Supreme Court of Canada dismissed the Crown's appeal, concluding that permitting the Crown to rely on Darlene Couture's statements would violate the rule against spousal competence. The Court distinguished the *Hawkins* case, as the statements made in *Hawkins* were made prior to the marriage and were given in the form of testimony in a related court proceeding. In *Couture*, there was evidence that the accused and his spouse were in a valid and subsisting marriage at the time of trial; therefore, Darlene Couture was neither competent nor compellable to testify for the Crown. To permit the Crown to rely on her statements would result in changes being made to the rule against spousal competence, which the Court was not prepared to do.

### Discussion Question

The rationale behind the traditional common law spousal competence rule was to promote marital harmony and to avoid the natural repugnance of testifying against one's spouse (or common law partner, based on the decision in *Hall*). Is this rule still applicable in society today, or should it be struck down by Parliament? Should the sanctity of relationships have any place in the criminal justice system?

---

## Compellability

**compellability**
whether a witness may
be forced to testify

All witnesses are compellable to give evidence. The only exception to **compellability** is for spouses. A wife or a husband may not be compelled to disclose any communications made during the marriage, pursuant to section 4(3) of the CEA. For criminal offences, spouses are not compellable, meaning that they cannot be forced to testify for the prosecution. However, the CEA makes exceptions for particular offences or attempts, including the following:

- any sexual offence involving a child;
- failing to provide necessities;
- abandoning a child;
- abduction of a child under the age of 16;
- bigamy;
- polygamy;
- unlawful solemnization of marriage;

- procuring;
- sexual assault;
- sexual assault with a weapon or causing bodily harm; or
- aggravated sexual assault (section 4(2) of the CEA).

Furthermore, for the following offences, where the complainant or the victim is under the age of 14, a spouse is compellable for the prosecution, pursuant to section 4(4) of the CEA:

- assault;
- aggravated assault;
- assault with a weapon or causing bodily harm;
- unlawfully causing bodily harm;
- criminal negligence causing bodily harm;
- criminal negligence causing death;
- infanticide;
- manslaughter;
- murder;
- attempt murder; or
- accessory to murder.

# Compelling Attendance to Court

## Subpoena

Part XXII of the *Criminal Code* deals with procuring the attendance of a witness to court. Section 698 of the *Criminal Code* allows a witness to be issued a **subpoena** to attend court when the witness is likely to give material evidence. For a summary conviction trial, a subpoena issued for a witness who resides within the province must be issued by a provincial court judge or justice. If the witness resides outside of the province, the subpoena must be issued by a provincial court judge.

**subpoena**
formal court-ordered document ordering a witness to attend a hearing

Pursuant to section 700(1) of the *Criminal Code*, the contents of a subpoena must include the date, time, and place that the witness is to attend, along with an indication to bring anything that he or she has in his or her "possession or control relating to the subject matter of the proceedings." A witness who is served with a subpoena must remain in attendance until he or she is excused by the presiding judge or justice. A template for a subpoena can be found as Form 16 of the *Criminal Code* and is included as Appendix K.

A subpoena must be served by a peace officer, as defined under section 2 of the *Criminal Code*, or by someone who is qualified to serve civil process in the province. The method of service is personal service or by leaving it with someone at the witness's usual place of abode with someone who appears to be at least 16 years of age. Proof of service of the subpoena is satisfied with affidavit evidence. A subpoena issued by a provincial court judge is effective throughout Canada, while a subpoena issued by a justice is effective throughout the province in which it was issued.

### Material Witness Warrant

When it is apparent that a witness who is likely to give material evidence is either evading service of a subpoena or will not attend court even if served with a subpoena, a justice or provincial court judge may issue a warrant for the witness's arrest, pursuant to section 698(2) of the *Criminal Code*. A warrant issued under this section requires the police to bring the witness to a specified court. A template for a material witness warrant can be found as Form 17 of the *Criminal Code* and is included as Appendix L.

In some cases, a witness may be bound by a recognizance to attend court and give evidence. If a justice is satisfied that the witness either has absconded or is about to abscond, a warrant of arrest may be issued for the absconding witness.

If a witness fails to appear at the proceeding for which he or she has been subpoenaed, or fails to remain at the proceeding, the presiding provincial court judge or justice may issue a warrant for the witness, as long as the subpoena was properly served and the witness has material evidence to give.

A witness who is arrested pursuant to a warrant may be detained in custody by a provincial court judge or justice, or may be released on a recognizance—either with or without sureties—to appear in court and give evidence. However, according to section 707(1), the maximum period of detention for a witness is no longer than 30 days unless the witness is brought before a provincial court judge for a hearing. If the judge is satisfied that further detention of the witness is warranted, the witness may be detained in custody for no more than 90 days. If less onerous methods of ensuring attendance are adequate, such as release on a recognizance with conditions, then the witness should not be detained in custody.

A witness may also be found guilty of contempt of court for failing to attend or remain in court for the purpose of giving evidence. The penalty for contempt of court, under section 708(2) of the *Criminal Code*, is a fine of no more than $100 and/or no more than 90 days' imprisonment.

# Special Provisions for Witnesses

Pursuant to section 486.1(1) of the *Criminal Code*, a witness who is under the age of 18 or who has a disability may have a support person present while he or she is testifying. This provision is also available to other witnesses over the age of 18 when the judge is of the opinion that having a support person present would assist the witness in providing a full and candid account, pursuant to section 486.1(2) of the *Criminal Code*. The Crown must make an application under this section before the judge makes an order, and the judge will consider factors such as the age of the witness, any mental or physical disability, the type of offence, the relationship between the accused and the witness, and other relevant circumstances. However, a support person may be prohibited from communicating with the witness during testimony.

A witness under the age of 18 may also testify outside of court or behind a screen, which is sometimes referred to as **obstructed view testimony**, in order to avoid having to see the accused, pursuant to section 486.2(1) of the *Criminal Code*. A witness over the age of 18 may also be permitted to testify behind a screen or outside of court when the judge believes that this is necessary in order for the witness to make a full and candid account. In making the order, the judge may consider the factors mentioned above. However, if the witness is permitted to testify outside of court, arrangements must be made for the judge, the jury, and the accused to watch the testimony of the witness via closed-circuit television.

An accused person is not permitted to personally cross-examine a witness under the age of 18 unless the presiding judge is of the opinion that this is necessary for the proper administration of justice. Pursuant to section 486.3(1), when the accused person is self-represented, the judge shall appoint counsel to conduct the cross-examination of the witness. The same protection is available for witnesses over the age of 18 when the judge is satisfied that the accused should not be permitted to cross-examine the witness in order for the witness to be able to provide a full and candid account. The judge may take into account the same factors mentioned above.

The issue of whether the use of obstructed view or out-of-court testimony infringes an accused person's right to life, liberty, and security interests under section 7 of the Charter has been raised before the courts. In the case of *R v JZS*, 2008 BCCA 401, affirmed 2010 SCC 1, the British Columbia Court of Appeal held that although the use of testimonial aids engages the accused's liberty and security interests, the accused's inability to confront a witness does not offend any principle of fundamental justice. The Court of Appeal held that there are enough safeguards to ensure trial fairness, such as the right of the accused to cross-examine the witness, and that the use of a screen does not undermine the presumption of innocence. A similar issue in balancing the accused's right to face the complainant against the complainant's religious beliefs was considered by the Supreme Court of Canada (see Case in Point: *R v NS*).

For any sexual offences, or other offences upon application by the Crown, the judge may impose an order directing that any information identifying a victim or witness shall not be published in any way, pursuant to sections 486.4 and 486.5 of the *Criminal Code*. The order is mandatory for sexual offences upon application by the Crown or by any victim or witness. For non-sexual offences, factors that the judge may consider in determining whether to make a non-publication order include:

- the right to a fair and public hearing;
- whether there is a real and substantial risk that the victim or witness would suffer significant harm if his or her identity were disclosed;
- whether the victim or witness needs the order for his or her security or for protection from intimidation or retaliation;
- society's interest in encouraging victims and witnesses to report crimes and participate in the process;
- whether effective alternatives are available to protect the identity of victims or witnesses;
- the salutary and deleterious effects of the proposed order;

**obstructed view testimony**
use of a device in court so that the witness does not have to see the accused, but the accused can see the witness

- the impact of the proposed order on the freedom of expression; and
- any other factor that the judge considers relevant.

Breaching a non-publication order is punishable as a summary conviction offence, pursuant to section 486.6(1) of the *Criminal Code*.

## CASE IN POINT

# Balancing the Accused's Right to a Fair Trial with a Witness's Right to Freedom of Religion

*R v NS*, 2012 SCC 72

### Facts

Two accused persons were charged with sexually assaulting N.S. The accused persons were relatives of N.S. At the preliminary inquiry, N.S. wished to testify wearing a niqab, which is a cloth that covers the face with just the eyes visible and is worn by Muslim women for religious purposes. The preliminary inquiry judge ordered N.S. to remove her niqab.

The Ontario Court of Appeal ruled that if the accused's right to a fair trial and the witness's right to freedom of religion under the Charter are both engaged and cannot be reconciled, the witness may be ordered to remove the niqab. The Court of Appeal referred the matter back to the preliminary inquiry judge. N.S. appealed to the Supreme Court of Canada.

### Decision

The Supreme Court of Canada ruled that a witness will be required to remove a niqab while testifying if:

1. it is necessary to prevent a serious risk to the fairness of the trial; and
2. the salutary effects of requiring the witness to remove the niqab outweigh the deleterious effects.

The Supreme Court indicated that four factors would need to be considered in this analysis:

- the sincerity (and not the strength) of the witness's religious beliefs;
- the nature of the evidence provided by the witness and the risk to trial fairness;
- alternative ways to accommodate both the rights of the accused and the witness; and
- weighing of the salutary effects of requiring the witness to remove the niqab (accused's right to a fair trial and safeguarding the repute of the administration of justice) against the deleterious effects of doing so (harm done by limiting the witness's religious practice).

The Supreme Court ruled that each case will have to be considered on its own merits rather than imposing a strict rule for all situations. In the N.S. case, the matter was sent back to the preliminary inquiry judge.

### Discussion Question

The accused persons in this case were of the same religious faith as N.S. Should this have been a consideration in the Supreme Court of Canada's decision?

# Interviewing Witnesses

There is a common saying that there is no property in witnesses, meaning that any party may speak to a potential witness, whether that witness will be favourable to the party or not. This is true in criminal law, with the only exception being that when a witness is represented by a lawyer or paralegal, the counsel for the opposing side must obtain the consent of the witness's legal representative before speaking to the witness, pursuant to rule 7.02 of the Rules.

According to rule 4.02(1) of the Rules, a paralegal may interview a witness whether that witness is under subpoena or not. However, according to guideline 12, section 12 of the *Paralegal Professional Conduct Guidelines*, the paralegal must disclose his or her interest, along with the name of the client he or she is representing and the stage of proceedings the matter is in. The paralegal should also take great care in not suppressing any evidence or not procuring the witness in staying out of the way.

---

**PRACTICE TIP**

When interviewing a witness who may potentially become adverse or hostile at trial, it is best to have a third party present during the interview to avoid any allegations of improper influence. The third party may be advised to take detailed notes during the interview.

It may also be beneficial for the paralegal to record the interview; however, the witness should be notified if the interview is being recorded.

The paralegal should also consider whether to produce a written summary or statement of what the witness has said during the interview and have the witness review and sign the statement. This may provide a safeguard against the witness later attempting to change his or her version of events. A written statement may also be used to impeach and cross-examine the witness should he or she give contrary evidence at trial. The paralegal should also obtain the contact information of the witness should the paralegal wish to subpoena the witness for trial.

During all dealings with witnesses, the paralegal should abide by rule 4.01 of the Rules, which deals with the duties of the paralegal as an advocate before the court.

---

# Communicating with Witnesses Giving Evidence

Rule 4.03 of the Rules describes the various circumstances in which a paralegal may or may not speak to a witness who is giving evidence in court. These situations are best illustrated in Figures 5.1 and 5.2. It should be noted that a **sympathetic witness** to the defence is not necessarily the defence paralegal's witness and an **unsympathetic witness** to the defence is not necessarily the Crown's witness. The situations are listed in the order that they occur in a criminal trial.

**sympathetic witness** witness whose testimony supports a party, even though the party may not be calling the witness to testify

**unsympathetic witness** witness whose testimony supports the opposing party, even though the witness is not necessarily being called by the opposing party

**Figure 5.1**

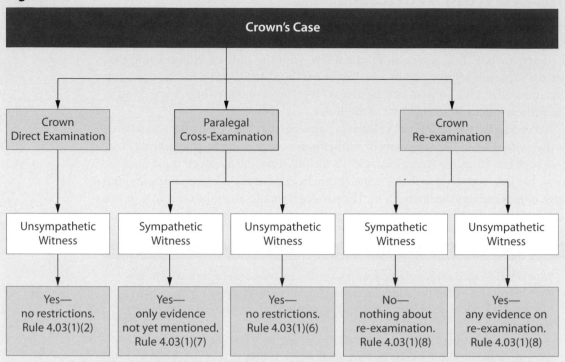

**Figure 5.2**

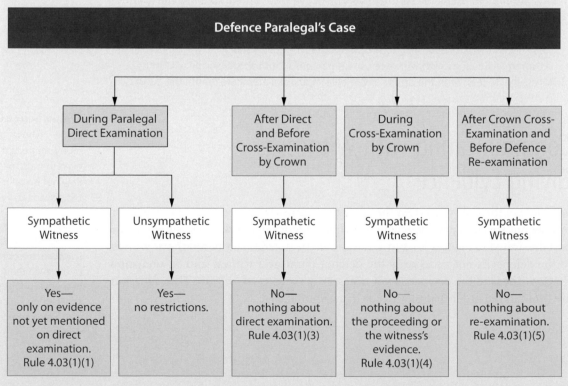

# CHAPTER SUMMARY

Witnesses are competent if they are able to testify and give evidence in court. Witnesses must swear an oath or make a solemn affirmation before they can testify. All witnesses may be compellable, meaning that they can be forced to testify, with the exception of spouses. Spouses are neither competent nor compellable for the prosecution, except for certain criminal offences.

A subpoena is issued in order to procure a witness's attendance in court. Evading the service of a subpoena or failing to attend court after being served with a subpoena may result in a material witness warrant being issued. A witness who is arrested on a warrant may be held in custody for up to 30 days.

Having a support person present, testifying behind a screen or from outside the courtroom, and non-publication orders are some of the special provisions available for witnesses under the age of 18 or for witnesses with special circumstances. These provisions allow for the witness to be able to give a full and candid account to the court.

The Rules outline ethical considerations in interviewing witnesses. When a witness is represented by a lawyer or licensee, the permission of the lawyer or licensee is required before the defence paralegal may interview the witness.

The Rules also apply to a defence paralegal who wishes to communicate with a witness who is giving testimony in court. Whether the defence paralegal may speak to a witness is dependent on the stage of the proceeding, which party is questioning the witness, and the nature of the witness.

## KEY TERMS

balance of probabilities, 78
compellability, 80
competence, 78
obstructed view testimony, 83
spousal privilege, 79
subpoena, 81
sympathetic witness, 85
unsympathetic witness, 85

## REVIEW QUESTIONS

### Short Answer

1. When interviewing a Crown witness or complainant, what must you advise them of first?

2. What must a party establish before a justice or provincial court judge will issue a warrant for a witness's arrest?

3. What *Criminal Code* provisions exist to encourage witnesses to provide full and candid testimony before the court?

## Apply Your Knowledge

1. With reference to the specific sections of the Rules that apply, decide whether the following statements are true or false:

   a. You may interview any Crown witness without the consent of the Crown prosecutor.

   b. You may interview any witness represented by another paralegal or lawyer without the consent of such paralegal or lawyer.

   c. During a short break after the Crown's cross-examination of your witness, you want to ask the witness a question in order to determine whether you will need to re-examine her. This is permissible.

   d. You ask for a break during your direct examination of a witness so that you can gather your thoughts. You walk over to get a coffee and the witness is in line in front of you. He asks you if you have change for a $20 bill. You are not able to speak to him at all since you are in the middle of your direct examination of this witness.

e. The Crown is conducting a re-examination of a Crown witness who has given favourable testimony to your client. The judge calls a short recess and leaves the courtroom. The Crown has also left the courtroom. The witness approaches you to tell you that she is nervous about a particular area of testimony that the Crown will ask her about. You can speak to her about this since she is a Crown witness.

2. George and Gina have been married for two years. While they were engaged, George told Gina about his elaborate plan to rob a jewellery store. One week after their wedding, George and his best friend, Robert, carry out the robbery. The Crown wants to call Gina as a witness in George's trial and in Robert's trial, as they want to ask her about what George said to her about his plans to rob the jewellery store. Is Gina competent and/or compellable as a witness? Which legal principles would apply?

# Disclosure and Pre-Trial Conferences

# 6

## LEARNING OUTCOMES

After reading this chapter, you should be able to:

- Outline the Crown's disclosure obligation to the accused

- Explain what occurs at a Crown pre-trial conference

- Explain what occurs at a judicial pre-trial conference

# Introduction

Before a criminal charge is set for trial, there are a number of pre-trial considerations to take into account. From settlement to trial management, there are numerous issues that must be considered by the defence paralegal prior to a trial. These issues are negotiated between the Crown and the defence at a Crown pre-trial and sometimes at a judicial pre-trial conference. However, before any meaningful discussions can take place, the defence must have full knowledge of the Crown's case against the client.

# Disclosure

## Right to Disclosure

One of the fundamental principles of our justice system is that the accused is entitled to make full answer and defence, pursuant to the common law and pursuant to section 7 of the Charter. Before an accused person can make any meaningful decisions about how to plead to a charge, he or she must fully understand and appreciate the extent of the Crown's case. The accused must be able to properly defend himself or herself against the charges that have been laid.

Historically, the element of surprise was a tactical strategy that one party would use against the other in criminal or civil proceedings. In criminal proceedings, the Crown would voluntarily provide **disclosure** to the defence, but there were no laws or procedural rules requiring the Crown to do so. In the *Criminal Code*, the accused's right to disclosure is mentioned in section 603, which states that an accused is entitled to inspect the indictment or the information, his or her statement, and a copy of the evidence. However, the disclosure obligation of the Crown is not limited to these items. The common law is more specific as to the exact nature of the Crown's obligation to disclose information. In the landmark case of *R v Stinchcombe*, [1991] 3 SCR 326, 83 Alta LR (2d) 193 [*Stinchcombe*], the Supreme Court of Canada highlighted the duty of the Crown to disclose any relevant information to the defence.

The Court stated that:

1. Materials that are in the Crown's possession are not the property of the Crown for the purpose of securing a conviction but are the public's property to ensure that justice is done.

2. All relevant information must be disclosed, regardless of whether or not the Crown intends to rely on it as evidence at the trial. This means that the information must be disclosed, whether it is **inculpatory evidence** or **exculpatory evidence**.

Furthermore, the Crown's discretion in determining whether the information is relevant or irrelevant is reviewable by the trial judge. The test for relevance is not an onerous one—relevance in this context means a reasonable possibility that information will be useful to the accused in making full answer and defence. The duty to disclose is an ongoing one, meaning that the Crown must continue to disclose any information that comes to light leading up to the trial, and if the accused is convicted, leading up to sentencing.

**disclosure**
the constitutional right of an accused person to obtain all information in the possession of the Crown that is relevant to establishing the guilt or innocence of the accused

**inculpatory evidence**
evidence that tends to establish the guilt or blameworthiness of the accused

**exculpatory evidence**
evidence that tends to exonerate or clear the accused

The defence paralegal must diligently pursue disclosure. The paralegal cannot remain silent about missing disclosure and then bring an application to seek an adjournment or a judicial stay of proceedings, claiming that disclosure has not been made. Remedies for the Crown's failure to disclose are discussed in Chapter 7.

## Exceptions to Disclosure

There are exceptions to disclosure. If the material is clearly irrelevant, then the Crown does not have to disclose it. If the material is protected by **privilege**, then the party claiming privilege must satisfy the court that it extends to the disclosure material. Finally, the timing of disclosure may be delayed due to an ongoing investigation or for the safety of witnesses.

> **PRACTICE TIP**
>
> Requests for disclosure should always be in writing so that the paralegal has a record of them on file. It is prudent to keep track of what was requested, the date it was requested, and to whom the request was sent. It will also ensure that there is proof of the request, should a pre-trial application be brought by the defence in the future. All requests should be sent by facsimile in order to generate a confirmation of receipt, which can also form part of the record.

**privilege**
an evidentiary rule that excludes certain confidential communications from being admissible as evidence in court

> **EXAMPLE**
>
> **Informant Privilege and Disclosure**
>
> Vinod has been charged with possession of stolen goods obtained by crime based on a tip that police received from a confidential informant. The police are aware of the identity of the confidential informant, but neither the Crown nor the defence know this information. Vinod's paralegal asks the Crown for disclosure of the name of this person. The police refuse to disclose the name on the basis of informant privilege. The matter must now be heard before a judge.

Any information or material that is in the possession of the police is considered to be under the Crown's control, and so if it is relevant, it must be disclosed to the defence. If the material is not in the Crown's possession but in the possession of a third party, such as a complainant or a witness, the accused must make an application before the court for disclosure of third party records. A recent exception to this rule has come up in the context of police disciplinary records, as seen in the case of *R v McNeil* (see Case in Point: *R v McNeil*).

**CASE IN POINT**

# Disclosure of Police Disciplinary Records

*R v McNeil*, 2009 SCC 3, [2009] 1 SCR 66

### Facts

The accused, Lawrence McNeil, was arrested and charged with possession of marijuana and cocaine for the purpose of trafficking. McNeil was convicted at trial, but prior to sentencing, he discovered that one of the investigating officers, Constable Rodney Hackett, had been involved in drug-related misconduct, which had resulted in criminal charges as well as disciplinary charges under the *Police Services Act*, RSO 1990, c P.15. McNeil brought a motion before the Ontario Court of Appeal seeking production of all documents relating to Constable Hackett's criminal and internal misconduct. The Court of Appeal ordered the criminal investigation files relating to Constable Hackett to be disclosed, concluding that no reasonable expectation of privacy attached to such records. However, the Court of Appeal did not definitively rule as to whether the internal *Police Services*

*Act* disciplinary records should likewise be disclosed. The Court of Appeal set aside McNeil's conviction, and the Crown appealed to the Supreme Court of Canada.

### Decision

In allowing the appeal, the Supreme Court of Canada held that no blanket ruling could be made regarding the privacy interests at stake in either criminal or police disciplinary records, but rather that a fact-based inquiry that considers the contents of the records is necessary. Further, the Court held that just as the Crown has a duty under *Stinchcombe* to disclose all relevant information in its possession, the police have a corresponding obligation to disclose to the Crown all material pertaining to their investigation of the accused. The Court held that this may include internal disciplinary records of an involved officer if they are relevant to the accused's case. Therefore, when there has been police misconduct that relates to the investigation of the accused, or when the actual finding of police misconduct could affect the accused's case, the records are said to be relevant and must be disclosed to the Crown, who in turn, must disclose the information to the accused. Not every finding of police misconduct will be relevant to the accused's case; however, if the credibility or reliability of the officer's evidence is at issue, then the test for relevance will likely be met.

### Discussion Question

Should *any* police misconduct on the part of the investigating officers be sufficient to justify disclosure of disciplinary records, given that police officers have a duty to uphold the law?

## Timing and Nature of Crown Disclosure

A disclosure package is typically provided by the Crown at the accused's first court appearance. If the accused is being detained in custody, then disclosure may be provided prior to the bail application, but in skeletal form. For an accused person in custody, a synopsis of the incident, along with the accused's criminal record, is available in order for the defence to prepare for a bail hearing. If the accused is not in custody, the disclosure is provided to the accused or his or her counsel at the first court appearance.

The items typically included as part of initial disclosure include:

- copy of the information;
- police report or narrative of the incident;
- statements of any victims and witnesses;
- accused's statement, if any;
- notes of investigating officers;
- criminal record of the accused;
- any videotaped statements;
- copies of photographs or images taken by the police; and
- copies of any court orders binding the accused.

Not all materials may be available to the defence at the first appearance. Certain items may be forthcoming at a subsequent court appearance. Additional disclosure items that may become available include:

- expert witness reports;
- forensic reports;
- use of force reports;

- copies of search warrants and informations to obtain search warrants (ITO);
- identification evidence;
- printed logs of any recordings (such as a 911 call);
- computer print-outs of any police database searches;
- notes of professionals such as doctors, paramedics, or firefighters;
- witness criminal records, if relevant; and
- police disciplinary records, if relevant.

As mentioned earlier, the accused must bring an application for the production of any records that may be in the possession of third parties. The accused also has a right to examine any exhibits that may be used at trial. This will typically be arranged with the Crown and the police.

> **EXAMPLE**
>
> **Viewing Exhibits to be Used at Trial**
>
> Alex has been charged with selling forged artwork. The police have seized pieces of artwork from Alex's house that are alleged to be forgeries. Alex is entitled to examine the pieces of artwork prior to his trial.

Some materials may be redacted to protect a confidential police source, police investigative techniques, advice covered by solicitor–client privilege, or information identifying the address of a witness. In the case of *Wood v Schaeffer*, 2013 SCC 71, [2013] 3 SCR 1053, the Supreme Court of Canada stated that police officers have a duty to prepare accurate, detailed, and comprehensive notes as soon as practicable after an incident. Police officers may be cross-examined on any discrepancies or gaps between their notes and their **viva voce** testimony. If a police officer has not taken any notes, the defence paralegal should request a **"will say" statement**. If a police officer is involved in any way in an investigation, *Stinchcombe* stands for the proposition that the officer must generate information even when none exists.

**viva voce**
a Latin term that means "with living voice"

**"will say" statement**
statement summarizing what a person will testify to in court

## Charge Screening Form

As part of a disclosure package, the Crown usually provides a Crown screening form or **charge screening form**. A charge screening form contains information as to how the Crown will be proceeding on the charge (by summary conviction or indictment), although the Crown is not required to make a formal election on the record until prior to a plea being entered. Additional information on the charge screening form may include:

- an early resolution position or any concessions that the Crown is prepared to make on an early guilty plea;
- the Crown position on sentencing on an early guilty plea;
- the Crown position on sentencing once a trial date has been set;

**charge screening form**
form, typically included as part of a disclosure package, that contains information on how the Crown is proceeding and the Crown's position on sentencing on a guilty plea and after trial

- whether the matter may be sent to a diversion program to deal with it outside of the court process;
- any conditions attached to disclosure or to the use of disclosure materials;
- instructions as to how to request additional disclosure; and
- instructions as to how to apply for legal aid.

The charge screening form is also signed and dated by the Crown attorney who prepared it. In order to expedite disclosure, the defence paralegal should send an initial disclosure request letter to the Crown prior to the first court appearance that confirms the identity of the client, the next court date, and that the paralegal is acting for the client.

## Requesting Additional Disclosure

The initial disclosure package should be promptly reviewed in order to ascertain what additional disclosure may be outstanding. At this initial stage, the Crown may not be aware of any missing items. Therefore, it is important for the accused's representative to be vigilant about checking the file to ensure that full disclosure has been provided. Failure to take this step may result in delay of the proceedings and prejudice to the client.

Once the initial disclosure has been reviewed carefully, a request for additional disclosure should be sent to the Crown with the date, time, and location of the next court appearance indicated on the request. Consideration should be given to whether any pre-trial applications will be brought before the court (see Chapter 7) and to whether any specific defences may be brought at trial based on the initial disclosure. Any additional requests should be followed up on in order to ensure that they have been responded to well in advance of the trial date.

It is also important for the paralegal to assess whether a request for additional disclosure will harm the client's case. For example, a client charged with theft from a convenience store discloses to the paralegal that a surveillance tape of the incident may be available from the store. If the paralegal requests a copy of the tape, then the Crown will become aware of its existence. If the tape contains incriminating evidence, this will obviously jeopardize the client's case. On the other hand, if the paralegal does not request the tape, the Crown and the police may not be aware of its existence at all. Of course, prior to making a decision as to whether to request this additional material, the paralegal should thoroughly interview the client about the details of the case and the evidence, as well as speak to other witnesses. The paralegal should also determine whether it is possible to obtain the additional evidence without bringing it to the attention of the Crown.

Once disclosure is received, it should be organized for easy referral and access within the client's file. Witness statements should be clearly marked and filed in one section, police notes should be separated by officer and involvement in the case, and reports should be placed near the top of the file for quick accessibility. The next step is to contact the Crown's office to schedule a Crown pre-trial conference.

**PRACTICE TIP**

It is important to identify all investigating officers involved in the criminal matter in order to determine whether all police notes and reports have been disclosed. When there is a verbal indication that a particular police officer did not take any notes, the paralegal should endeavour to obtain confirmation in writing from the officer that no notes were indeed taken. This will avoid any surprises at trial.

# Crown Pre-Trial Conference

A **Crown pre-trial conference** is a meeting between the Crown and the defence paralegal. Prior to the Crown pre-trial conference, the paralegal should take the following preparatory steps:

- assess the strengths and weaknesses of the crown's case;
- identify the legal issues;
- identify pre-trial applications that may be brought by the crown;
- identify pre-trial applications that may be brought by the defence;
- identify potential defences and their merits;
- determine whether an interpreter is required, either for the accused or for any defence witnesses;
- assess which witnesses will be called by the defence;
- determine whether any expert evidence is required; and
- estimate the amount of time required at trial for the client's case.

Prior to the Crown pre-trial conference, the paralegal should meet with the client to review the charges. The client should be advised of the strengths and weaknesses of the Crown's case and of any possible defences that could be raised based on the disclosure received to date. The client should be asked if he or she has any additional information that may lead to a defence. All options should be investigated by the paralegal, and the client should be advised of the pros and cons of each option. Any mitigating factors available to the client should be investigated fully, such as the client's background, supports in the community, reasons for offending, family situation and dependants, and employment status. The paralegal should be prepared to recommend a course of action to the client and obtain written instructions from the client as to how to proceed. Finally, the paralegal should consider creating a checklist to ensure that all matters that need to be discussed with the Crown are raised at the Crown pre-trial conference.

The Crown pre-trial conference is an informal meeting between the Crown and the defence paralegal. The client is not present at this conference. The paralegal should bring the client's file and be prepared to take notes during the meeting. The attending Crown's name, the date of the meeting, and the charges that are the subject of the pre-trial meeting should be recorded for future reference. The Crown will likely indicate how it will be proceeding against the accused—either by summary conviction or by indictment—as well as the penalty that the Crown will be seeking, either on a guilty plea and/or after trial.

The defence is not required to advise the Crown as to the names of the defence witnesses who will be called at trial. However, if the defence will be calling an alibi witness, the defence should identify this witness so that the Crown may investigate the alibi. If this is not disclosed, the Crown may successfully request an adjournment at trial.

If the defence wishes to call an expert witness at trial, the Crown must be provided with the *curriculum vitae* of the expert so that the Crown may investigate the

**Crown pre-trial conference**
meeting between the Crown and defence to discuss the evidence, the position of the parties, plea negotiations, or other issues related to a charge

expert's qualifications. Again, failure to do this may result in the Crown successfully obtaining an adjournment at trial.

The defence paralegal should be prepared to discuss any matters that are not in dispute and that may be proven by way of an agreed statement of facts or formal admissions. Of course, before making any agreements, the client must be informed and provide written instructions as to what facts are agreed upon.

If the Crown offers a position on resolution, it must be conveyed to the client first. The paralegal should also clearly record the Crown's position on sentencing. The Crown may suggest that a joint recommendation as to sentencing between the Crown and defence be offered to the court, or the Crown may wish to leave it as an open sentencing submission. Another option for a joint recommendation is to read in an agreed statement of facts between Crown counsel and the defence. In either case, the paralegal must advise the client that the judge is not compelled to accept a joint recommendation as to sentencing, nor is he or she bound by the suggestions of either side.

After the Crown pre-trial conference, a follow-up letter should be sent to the Crown confirming any concessions made at the conference and requesting any outstanding disclosure items. The paralegal should meet with the client to review the outcomes of the Crown pre-trial conference and get further instructions from the client in writing.

# Judicial Pre-Trial Conference

**judicial pre-trial conference**
meeting between a judge who will not be presiding at the trial, the Crown, and the defence to discuss matters related to the trial such as disclosure, applications, witnesses, or other legal issues

Section 625.1(1) of the *Criminal Code* deals with a pre-hearing or **judicial pre-trial conference** and stipulates that either the Crown or the accused may request the conference. Typically, when the trial is expected to take more than one full day, a judicial pre-trial conference is mandatory. Rule 4.2 of the *Criminal Rules of the Ontario Court of Justice* deals with judicial pre-trial conferences. Rule 4.2 requires the Crown to provide the judge with a copy of the synopsis of the allegations prior to the pre-trial conference. If the defence wishes to submit any materials, it must be provided at least three days prior to the pre-trial conference.

Some of the issues that may be discussed at the judicial pre-trial conference include confirming the estimate of time required for trial; setting timelines for the hearing of applications or the completion of disclosure; the possibility of resolution of the matter; and setting another judicial pre-trial conference, if required. Any agreements or admissions made by the Crown or defence at the pre-trial conference are recorded, transcribed, and attached to the information for the trial judge. The full text of rule 4.2 is set out in Appendix M.

Prior to the judicial pre-trial conference, the paralegal should meet with the client again to discuss the disclosure material, which should be more substantive at this stage. The paralegal should review the strengths and weaknesses of the Crown's case, as well as the options available to the client and the implications of each option. If the client is considering a guilty plea or attempting to persuade the Crown to withdraw the charge, then it is helpful to obtain letters of support. Of course, the client's written instructions should be obtained as to how the client wishes to proceed.

Pursuant to rule 4.2, the judicial pre-trial conference provides an opportunity for the defence paralegal to discuss whether there is a reasonable prospect of conviction, raise any mitigating facts on behalf of the defendant, mention case law that is beneficial to the client at sentencing, and provide copies of reference letters from the client's employer and community supports.

The judge who is assigned to the pre-trial conference will not be the trial judge. This is to ensure that the Crown and defence are able to discuss the evidence and the strengths and weaknesses of the case freely. The judicial pre-trial should be viewed as another opportunity to advocate on behalf of the client. If there are any issues that may be agreed upon at trial, they should be raised before the judge.

Issues that may or may not have been discussed at the Crown pre-trial conference relating to a plea agreement, a sentencing recommendation, the witness list for the Crown, estimated trial time for Crown and defence, any pre-trial applications, and any outstanding disclosure should be discussed at the judicial pre-trial conference. By the time of the judicial pre-trial conference, full disclosure should have taken place in order to ensure a meaningful discussion of the issues. Matters that are specific to the trial, such as the admissibility of evidence gathered by the police and the voluntariness of any statements given by the accused, should be raised as well so that sufficient time is scheduled for the hearing. The defence paralegal should indicate which police witnesses the defence wishes to have available at the trial in case they are not under subpoena by the Crown.

After the judicial pre-trial conference, the paralegal should draft a memorandum setting out the issues discussed and the position of the Crown and pre-trial conference judge. A letter should be sent to the Crown to confirm its position on various issues and the possible sentence. Another meeting with the client should be scheduled to review the position of the Crown and the pre-trial conference judge, and to get the client's final instructions as to whether the matter will be proceeding to trial.

In the next chapter, we will take a look at various pre-trial applications that may be brought before the trial and the procedure for preparing an application pursuant to the Criminal Rules.

# CHAPTER SUMMARY

The accused's right to full disclosure ties in with the right to make full answer and defence under the common law and the Charter. The Crown has an obligation to disclose all relevant information and materials to the accused, whether it is inculpatory or exculpatory. The defence must review the disclosure and act vigilantly in requesting any additional disclosure. While initial disclosure may be given at a first appearance, additional materials may need to be specifically requested. The defence must bring a special application for production of information that is in the possession of third parties.

The Crown and defence will meet to discuss the charges at a Crown pre-trial conference. The Crown will indicate how it is proceeding as well as provide a position on the sentence,

both on a guilty plea and after the matter is set for trial. Evidentiary issues and matters pertaining to the trial will be discussed, including the number of witnesses to be called by each side, an estimate of time required for the hearing, and whether any experts will be called to testify.

At a judicial pre-trial conference, matters that are specific to the trial will be discussed to ensure that the trial proceeds smoothly and efficiently. It is also an opportunity to determine whether any pre-trial applications will need to be brought before the trial. The strengths and weaknesses of the case will be discussed before the pre-trial judge, and any admissions or agreements made by the Crown or the defence will be recorded and transcribed for the benefit of the trial judge.

# KEY TERMS

charge screening form, 93
Crown pre-trial conference, 95
disclosure, 90
exculpatory evidence, 90
inculpatory evidence, 90
judicial pre-trial conference, 96
privilege, 91
*viva voce*, 93
"will say" statement, 93

# REVIEW QUESTIONS

## Short Answer

1. Why is disclosure important to an accused person in a criminal proceeding?

2. List five items that should be part of an initial disclosure package from the Crown on any criminal charge.

3. Identify three steps that a defence paralegal should take to prepare for a Crown pre-trial conference.

# Apply Your Knowledge

1. Your client is charged with two counts of theft that relate to two separate incidents. At the first appearance, you received a disclosure package from the Crown. Upon reviewing the material, you realize that several police officer's names are mentioned in the police report, but you only have the police notes of some of the officers. You have sent a request for "additional police notes of all the investigating officers." Two weeks later, you receive further disclosure from the Crown, including the police notes of all the officers mentioned on the file, except for two officers. There is a copy of a faxed response from the police sergeant at the district office where these officers are employed indicating that the request has been complied with. Do you need to take any further steps?

2. Nita Nath represents Jillian Jones on two counts of fraud. At the judicial pre-trial conference, the Crown provides a position on sentencing if Jillian were to plead guilty to one count of fraud. Nita believes that her client would be amenable to this offer from the Crown. The pre-trial judge asks Nita if she is prepared to accept the Crown's offer. What must Nita do?

# Pre-Trial Applications

## LEARNING OUTCOMES

After reading this chapter, you should be able to:

- Name and describe various *Criminal Code* pre-trial applications that can be brought by the defence in a criminal matter

- Name and describe various Charter pre-trial applications that can be brought by the defence in a criminal matter

- Name and describe other pre-trial applications that can be brought by the defence in a criminal matter

- Identify and distinguish between various remedies available for applications before the court

- Explain what is involved in drafting an application

- Outline the timelines for the serving, filing, and hearing of a pre-trial application

# Introduction

The best advice for a paralegal representing a client with a criminal charge is to prepare. A well-prepared paralegal defence agent will anticipate whether a pre-trial **application** will need to be brought in the case. As such, he or she must be aware of the requirements in the *Criminal Rules of the Ontario Court of Justice* for preparing an application, as well as the guidelines for filing and serving the application on the Crown. There are numerous pre-trial and trial applications that may be brought by the defence; this chapter will review the most common ones, along with a discussion of the applicable remedies.

# Criminal Code Applications

There are five *Criminal Code* pre-trial applications that will be discussed in this section: severance of counts, severance of accused persons, orders excluding the public and restricting publication, release of exhibits for testing, and amendment of the information.

## Severance of Counts

As mentioned in Chapter 2, an accused person may be charged with numerous counts in the same information, provided that the counts arise from the same transaction. Counts from the same transaction are included in one information in order to avoid multiple proceedings involving the same event and same witnesses. However, the accused may bring an application to sever the counts on the basis of potential prejudice to the accused at trial. The burden of proof will be on the accused to show why the counts should be severed. When the accused wants to testify on some of the counts but not all, he or she may be successful in bringing such an application.

Severance may also be granted by the court when there is no factual connection between two counts and the evidence on one count may be prejudicial to the accused on another count, since they are both on the same information and are being heard at the same time. Other reasons to grant severance include the complexity of the evidence, whether similar fact evidence will be used by the Crown, and the length of the trial with respect to the evidence (*R v Last*, 2009 SCC 45, [2009] 3 SCR 146). The court must weigh the prejudice to the accused against the public interest in avoiding multiple proceedings, including expense and inconvenience to witnesses. If the court does grant the accused's application, then the severed count will require a separate trial.

Section 591(3)(a) of the *Criminal Code* provides that when it is in the interests of justice to do so, the court may order the accused to be tried separately on one or more of the counts. Severance applications are more likely to be granted when the trial will be before a jury, since the jury may not heed any instructions given by the judge regarding the limited application and use of the evidence in the proceedings.

## Severance of Accused Persons

Two or more accused persons may be charged in one information and tried together as co-accused, as long as there is some link between the accused persons and the alleged offences. The Crown prefers to have accused persons tried together when there are allegations of a joint enterprise. Section 591(3)(b) of the *Criminal Code* permits the court to sever one or more accused and hold separate trials for each when it is in the interests of justice to do so.

Severance of accused should not be granted lightly, since separate trials may result in inconsistent verdicts. Furthermore, if each accused places responsibility on a co-accused who is being tried separately, both may be acquitted. However, when two or more co-accused have antagonistic defences—when one points the finger at another, when an accused wishes to call a co-accused at trial, or where evidence is admissible against one accused but inadmissible against another—then the court should consider this in an application to sever. Once again, the potential prejudice to the accused will be weighed against the public interest in wanting to conduct trials in a timely and efficient manner.

## Orders Excluding the Public and Restricting Publication

Typically, any criminal proceedings against accused persons are held in open court. However, section 486(1) of the *Criminal Code* allows a judge to order the exclusion of any or all members of the public from the courtroom when the judge is satisfied that such an order is in the interests of public morals, the maintenance of order, or the proper administration of justice, or if it is necessary for national defence or security. Consideration of the proper administration of justice includes protecting the interests of witnesses under the age of 18 years and other justice system participants.

For any sexual offences, section 486(3) indicates that either the Crown or the accused may apply for an order excluding the public from the courtroom, and if the judge does not make such an order, he or she must provide the reasons for not doing so. For any sexual offences, upon an application by the Crown, a complainant, or a witness, the judge must also make an order restricting the publication of any information that may identify the complainant or a witness under the age of 18 years, pursuant to section 486.4(2) of the *Criminal Code*. The order is discretionary for any witness over the age of 18 years for a sexual offence, under section 486.4(1) of the *Criminal Code*. The publication component includes broadcasting or any other transmission of information that could identify a complainant or a witness.

Sections 486.5(1) and (2) of the *Criminal Code* allow a judge to make an order restricting the publication of information that would identify any victim, witness, or justice system participant in any type of criminal matter if such an order is necessary for the proper administration of justice. An order under this section requires a written application to be made, with notice given to the Crown, the accused, and any other person affected by the order (see section 486.5(4)). Furthermore, under section 485.5(6), the judge may hold a hearing in private to determine whether such an order should be made. The factors that the judge would take into account when making such an order are set out in section 486.5(7) and include:

- the right to a fair and public hearing;
- whether there would be a real and substantial risk of significant harm to the victim, witness, or justice system participant if their identity were disclosed;
- whether the order is necessary to protect the victim, witness, or justice system participant from intimidation or retaliation;
- the importance of encouraging victims and witnesses to report offences and participate in the criminal justice system;
- whether other alternatives exist to protect the identities of victims, witnesses, and justice system participants;
- the beneficial or harmful effects of the proposed order;
- the impact of the order on the freedom of expression of people affected by the order; and
- any other relevant factors.

## Release of Exhibits for Testing

Section 605(1) of the *Criminal Code* deals with the release of an exhibit for the purpose of scientific or other testing on application by either the Crown or the defence. Under this section, three days' notice must be given to the accused or the Crown, depending on which party is bringing the application. The judge may place conditions on the order of release in order to safeguard and preserve the exhibit for trial. Failure to abide by the conditions of the order is punishable by contempt of court, pursuant to section 605(2) of the *Criminal Code*.

This provision may be used by the defence in order to have a piece of evidence tested by the defence's own expert. In certain situations, the police may have failed to test the evidence, or the defence may wish to obtain a second opinion from an independent expert. Occasionally, the Crown may agree to allow the defence expert to examine the evidence. However, when the Crown is not in agreement, the defence paralegal may rely on this section to make an application before the court.

The Crown may also place stipulations on the release of the exhibit, such as waiver of continuity of the exhibit at trial, a description of where the testing will take place, the length of time the item will be required, and whether a representative of the Crown or a police officer will be permitted to be present during the procedures. See Case in Point: *R v Hay* for an example of an application by the defence to have an exhibit released for testing after the conclusion of the trial.

## CASE IN POINT

# Forensic Testing of Exhibits Post-Trial

*R v Hay*, 2010 SCC 54, [2010] 3 SCR 206; *R v Hay*, 2013 SCC 61, [2013] 3 SCR 694

## Facts

On July 6, 2002, Collin Moore and his brother, Roger Moore, were hosting a charity dance at the HHMS nightclub in Toronto. In the early morning hours, two men came in and shot Collin and Roger. Roger was injured, but Collin died. The accused, Leighton Hay, and co-accused, Gary Eunick, were both charged with first degree murder. There was substantial evidence against Gary Eunick, who was Hay's sister's boyfriend and lived at Hay's mother's residence. There was evidence that shortly before the murder, Gary Eunick and his brother, along with one or two other individuals, had attempted to enter the club without paying the $10 cover charge. A fight broke out between the Eunick brothers and the Moore brothers. Eventually, the Eunick brothers and the individuals they were with left the club.

The Crown's theory of the case was that Gary Eunick and Leighton Hay returned and shot Collin and Roger Moore. An eyewitness saw a green Honda Civic leaving the scene with Eunick in the rear passenger side. The witness called 911 and gave police the licence plate number, which was later found to belong to Hay's mother. When the police attended to Hay's mother's residence, both Leighton Hay and his sister, Lisa Hay, along with the co-accused, Eunick, were inside. Eunick and Lisa Hay indicated that Leighton Hay had been sleeping at home during the incident. They also denied their own involvement in the shooting but admitted to being at the club prior to the shooting. There was an eyewitness who selected Leighton Hay from a photo line-up as the second shooter and described him as having short dreadlocks on top of his head.

Police officers seized a number of items from the house, including an electric razor and a crumpled piece of newspaper from a trash can with short curly hairs. Neither the Crown nor the defence submitted the hair for forensic testing, but the Crown argued that Hay shaved his head to change his appearance after the shooting. Both Hay and Eunick were convicted at trial and appealed their convictions.

The Court of Appeal upheld the convictions, and Hay appealed to the Supreme Court of Canada. Ancillary to the application, Hay also brought a motion for the hair samples to be released for testing to determine if they were scalp or facial hairs. This was a rare application for release of exhibits post-conviction. Further, it appeared that neither the defence nor Crown were aware that forensic testing could distinguish between scalp and facial hairs, so this type of testing was not previously requested by either party.

## Decision

The Supreme Court of Canada allowed the defence appeal, granted the motion to adduce fresh evidence, and ordered a new trial, holding that the fresh evidence about the hair clippings could have affected the jury's verdict. Furthermore, the Crown relied heavily on the evidence pertaining to the length of the accused's hair. The fresh evidence consisted of two forensic expert opinions as to the percentage of hair from the scalp as opposed to the face or trunk of the accused. The Court stipulated that it was in the interests of justice to consider this evidence, given the nature of the charge that the accused was facing.

## Discussion Question

Should the defence be entitled to have their own expert examine the exhibits as of right without having to bring an application before the court?

## Amendment of the Information

As mentioned in the previous chapter, a defence paralegal should review the disclosure carefully. If there is an apparent defect in the information, the accused may bring a motion to **quash** the information, pursuant to section 601(1) of the *Criminal Code*. A motion to quash may be brought at any time before a plea is entered and only with leave of the court after a plea is entered. The court may order the count to be amended to cure the defect instead of granting the motion to quash.

**quash**
a ruling by the court that nullifies a proceeding, a document, or an order

At any stage of the proceedings, the court must amend any defects of form, or reference to a wrong statute, or other defects as disclosed by the evidence at trial. When there is evidence at trial that would support an amendment to an essential element of a charge or a defect as to substance, the court must amend the count. Section 601(4.1) of the *Criminal Code* also provides that when there is a variation between the evidence and the time of the offence, it is not a material defect as long as the information was laid within the limitation period. Similarly, if there is any variation between the evidence and the location indicated on the information, it is not a material defect as long as the location is within the territorial jurisdiction of the court.

In determining whether an amendment should be made to a count in the information, section 601(4) provides that the court must take into account:

- the matters disclosed by the evidence taken at the preliminary inquiry;
- the evidence taken at trial;
- the circumstances of the case;
- whether the accused has been misled or prejudiced in his or her defence by any variance, error, or omission; and
- with regard to the merits of the case, whether an amendment may be made without injustice occurring.

Under section 601(5) of the *Criminal Code*, if the court is of the view that the accused has been misled or prejudiced by the amendment, the accused may be entitled to an adjournment of the proceeding.

> **EXAMPLE**
>
> **Amendment of a Count During the Trial**
>
> Ying is charged with assault, pursuant to section 265(1)(a) of the *Criminal Code*. In the middle of the Crown's case, the Crown realizes that Ying should have been charged under section 265(1)(b) for threatening to hit the complainant by way of a gesture. The Crown argues that the count should be amended. Ying's paralegal argues that allowing the count to be amended would cause serious prejudice to Ying, as her entire defence is based on the actual application of direct force, pursuant to section 265(1)(a), as cited in the information.

# Charter Applications

There are three Charter pre-trial and trial applications that will be discussed in this section: disclosure, trial delay, and exclusion of evidence.

## Disclosure

As discussed in Chapter 6, the Crown has a duty to disclose all information that is relevant, whether it is inculpatory or exculpatory to the accused. The defence paralegal must act diligently to obtain disclosure, but once it is requested, the Crown's duty to provide disclosure is an ongoing one. There may be situations in which the Crown does not agree that the items being sought are relevant and will refuse to provide disclosure. On other occasions, the request may have been buried and not complied with. Regardless of the reason for non-disclosure, once the defence has made requests in writing and the Crown has failed to comply with the requests, the defence must file a formal application in order to obtain a remedy for non-disclosure.

In the application, the defence should set out a factual basis to establish relevance, clearly identify what materials are being sought, outline the previous requests made for the disclosure, and state that the materials have not been provided by the Crown. The letters sent to the Crown requesting disclosure should be attached in chronological order as exhibits to the application.

The remedies available for a disclosure application will be discussed below. Section 7 of the Charter provides for the right to life, liberty, and security of the person, and section 11(d) of the Charter provides for the right to a fair hearing. Therefore, the accused must have full disclosure in order to appreciate and respond to the Crown's case.

> **PRACTICE TIP**
>
> The defence paralegal should follow-up any requests made at the Crown or judicial pre-trial conference with a written letter. Not only will this assist the defence in organization and preparation for trial, but it will also provide written documentation that may be attached to a pre-trial application.

## Trial Delay

Section 11(b) of the Charter provides for the right of an accused to be tried within a reasonable time. When there is an unreasonable delay, the accused is entitled to bring an application for a stay of proceedings. Typically, when considering delay, time runs from when the information is laid until the trial is concluded, and in some cases, until sentencing.

In the landmark case of *R v Askov*, [1990] 2 SCR 1199, 74 DLR (4th) 355 [*Askov*], the Supreme Court of Canada came up with a four-part test for determining when the delay is unreasonable:

- length of the delay;
- explanation for the delay;
- waiver of the accused's rights by the accused; and
- prejudice to the accused.

### Reasons for Delay

Delay is scrutinized for reasons attributable to the Crown, which includes systemic or institutional delay, and for reasons attributable to the accused, as well as the inherent time requirements of the case.

Factors that are attributable to the Crown may include delayed disclosure, workload pressures, changes in the Crown attorney assigned to a case, the conduct of the Crown and police officers, and unavailable police witnesses. Systemic or institutional delays are also attributable to the Crown, such as a lack of resources, including the availability of Crown attorneys, judges, courtrooms, or even court interpreters.

Factors that are attributable to the accused include situations in which the accused directly contributed to the delay or when the accused's actions were deliberate or calculated tactics meant to postpone the proceedings. The burden is on the Crown to prove that the accused's actions were deliberate or calculated, unless an inference can be drawn from the actions. The length of the delay that is attributable to the accused is deducted from the overall length of the delay in determining whether or not it is reasonable. This is to prevent the accused from using delay as a means to escape trial.

### Length of the Delay

The inherent time requirements of a case refer to the time taken to get to the point at which both parties are ready to set a trial date. Therefore, the time taken to retain counsel, proceed to a bail hearing, obtain disclosure, attend a judicial pre-trial conference, and resolve legal issues is considered to be neutral when calculating the delay, unless either the Crown or the defence acted in bad faith. A more complicated case may justify a longer period of time to deal with the steps of the trial process.

When considering the length of time in a delay application, the court will allocate the time period to each of the categories as outlined above. Obviously, the longer the delay, the more difficult it will be to justify it as being reasonable. There may be an appropriate range for delay; however, there is no set length that is deemed to be reasonable or unreasonable. Rather, delay is determined on a case-by-case basis according to the test outlined in *Askov*.

### Morin Guidelines

In the case of *R v Morin*, [1992] 1 SCR 771, 71 CCC (3d) 1 [*Morin*], the Supreme Court of Canada suggested guidelines that may be used to assess what constitutes an acceptable period of time in calculating delay. The Court stated that these guidelines are not fixed; rather, they are benchmarks and should be adjusted according to special circumstances and issues specific to each region.

The *Morin* guidelines suggest that a range of eight to ten months' institutional delay in provincial courts and a range of six to eight months' delay in superior courts is appropriate. It should be kept in mind that the greater the prejudice to the accused, the shorter the acceptable period of institutional delay. Conversely, the longer the delay, the more likely that prejudice will be inferred. In the case of *R v Lahiry*, 2011 ONSC 6780, Justice Code stated that institutional delay only starts to run from the point in time when both parties are *ready* for trial, not necessarily from the date that the trial is set.

### Prejudice to the Accused

Prejudice to the accused stems from two different avenues: actual prejudice and inferred prejudice. Actual prejudice may result from factors such as onerous bail conditions, having the burden of criminal proceedings hanging over oneself, or witnesses no longer being available at the time of trial. Prejudice may also be inferred or presumed from a very long and unreasonable delay. The Crown may prove that no actual prejudice has resulted to the accused. For these reasons, it is important to set out the procedural history of the case in sufficient detail, which is usually done by way of providing transcripts from each court appearance.

The defence paralegal must be careful if he or she intends to submit an affidavit from the client about any economic, familial, or emotional hardship that has resulted from the delay, since the Crown has the right to cross-examine the affiant. If the defence paralegal wishes to argue that abiding by extensive bail conditions has posed a hardship to the accused, then a copy of the recognizance should be attached as an exhibit to the application without the necessity of an affidavit. Affidavits may also be presented from family members or the accused's employer.

### Waiver

In order for the accused to have waived his or her right to trial within a reasonable time, the waiver must be clear and unequivocal. For example, if an accused is offered a number of early trial dates and asks for dates that are delayed even though his representative is available on earlier dates, it may be argued that he has waived his rights. Waiver may also be implicit, in that the actions of the accused show that he or she waives his or her right to a trial within a reasonable time.

## Exclusion of Evidence

An application to exclude unconstitutionally obtained evidence is very common in criminal law. If the accused is alleging that police breached his or her Charter rights in the course of obtaining evidence, then an application may be brought asking the court to exclude evidence as a result of the breach. In Ontario, rule 2.5(2)(a)(iii) of the Criminal Rules indicates that an application to exclude evidence pursuant to the Charter should be heard by the trial judge either at the start of the trial, in advance of hearing the evidence, or as part of a *voir dire* during the trial. In other words, an application to exclude evidence is a trial application, not a pre-trial application; however, notice must be given to the Crown prior to the hearing.

Section 24(2) of the Charter provides that if a court "concludes that evidence was obtained in a manner that infringed or denied any rights or freedoms guaranteed by this Charter, the evidence shall be excluded if it is established that, having regard to all the circumstances, the admission of it in the proceedings would bring the administration of justice into disrepute." Bringing the administration of justice into disrepute refers to the overall reputation of the justice system from a societal point of view, should the evidence be admitted. This means maintaining the integrity of and public confidence in the justice system.

The test for exclusion of evidence was refined by the Supreme Court of Canada in the case of *R v Grant*, 2009 SCC 32, [2009] 2 SCR 353 [*Grant*], in which the Court set out a three-part test (see Figure 7.1).

> **PRACTICE TIP**
>
> The Ontario Court of Justice has developed a Justice on Target strategy to address delay in criminal courts. Justice on Target has come up with benchmarks to determine the number of court appearances or length of time that it takes to bring a criminal charge or charges to completion. The benchmarks were created by an advisory group consisting of the judiciary, Crown attorneys, the defence bar, Legal Aid Ontario, corrections staff, and court services staff. The benchmarks serve as guidelines and are not meant to be used as rigid rules. For more information on Justice on Target, see the Ontario Ministry of the Attorney General website at <http://www.attorneygeneral.jus.gov.on.ca/english/jot/>.

**Figure 7.1**

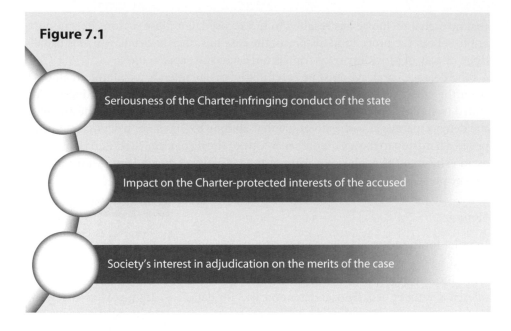

Seriousness of the Charter-infringing conduct of the state

Impact on the Charter-protected interests of the accused

Society's interest in adjudication on the merits of the case

## Test for Exclusion of Evidence

The court must assess the effect of admitting the evidence on the public's confidence in the justice system using the following factors:

1. The seriousness of the Charter-infringing conduct of the state, which focuses on the severity of the conduct leading to the Charter breach. This involves looking at whether the breach was deliberate or wilful and whether the police were acting in good faith.

2. The impact on the Charter-protected interests of the accused. This involves looking at how the accused was affected by the breach. Examples of impact on the accused's Charter-protected interests include intrusion into the accused person's privacy, the right not to be compelled to provide self-incriminatory evidence, and the effect on the accused person's dignity. These are not exhaustive—there may be other factors that affect the accused's Charter rights. The more serious the impact on the accused's Charter rights, the greater the risk that admission of the evidence would bring the administration of justice into disrepute.

3. Society's interest in adjudication on the merits of the case, meaning all of the circumstances of the case. This inquiry involves consideration of the negative impact of admitting the evidence, as well as the repercussions of failing to admit the evidence. This includes looking at factors such as the public's interest in getting to the truth, the reliability of the evidence, and the importance of the evidence to the Crown's case in light of the nature of the Charter breach.

Where the exclusion of evidence would bring the administration of justice into disrepute, the court must balance this against the severity of the Charter breach.

# Other Applications

Three applications will be discussed in this section: adjournment of trial, withdrawal of counsel, and application for third party records. These applications are not mentioned in the *Criminal Code* and are not brought pursuant to the Charter, but they are common applications nonetheless.

## Adjournment of Trial

There are many situations that may result in either the accused or the Crown having to request an adjournment of the trial. Usually, an adjournment request is brought because a witness is not available or a witness or an accused is ill. Occasionally, there may be a change in the accused's representation, and the new defence paralegal acting for the accused may not be available on the trial date that was set by the former agent.

Ideally, adjournment applications should be brought as far in advance of the trial date as possible so as to avoid wasting valuable court time or resources. When the application is brought in advance of the trial date, it should be served and filed pursuant to the Criminal Rules (see Drafting the Application later in this chapter). However, the defence paralegal may not be aware of the unavailability of a witness until the day of trial. In this situation, an adjournment request will need to be sought before the trial judge, and the defence will have to ask the court to dispense with the formal requirements for a supporting application and affidavit. The court should still be provided with as much information as possible as to the nature of the illness and the likelihood of the witness attending a later trial date if the adjournment is granted.

> **EXAMPLE**
>
> **Adjournment Request Due to Illness of Witness**
>
> On the morning of her trial date, Monica receives a call from her friend Judy, who is scheduled to testify in court on Monica's behalf. Unfortunately, Judy is very ill with the flu and cannot attend court. Monica informs her paralegal immediately, and the request for the adjournment is made as soon as court commences. As part of her request for an adjournment, Monica's paralegal advises the court of the conversation between Monica and Judy and clarifies to the judge that should the adjournment request be granted, Judy will return to testify on the rescheduled trial date.

Trial judges have wide latitude in deciding whether or not to grant a request for an adjournment. Unless the accused is needlessly attempting to delay the proceedings, most judges will grant a defence request for an adjournment when it is necessary for the accused to make full answer and defence. When the Crown is seeking an adjournment of the trial, the judge may accede to the Crown's request, but the accused should consider whether to bring a delay application down the road, especially if the trial is postponed for a long period of time. The defence paralegal should also consider whether to ask for certain bail conditions to be lifted on the form of release, particularly if they are too onerous for the client to abide by while awaiting the trial.

## Withdrawal of Counsel

Withdrawal of counsel is discussed in Chapter 1. The timing of and reasons for withdrawal are key considerations for the court as well as for the paralegal, pursuant to his or her professional obligations under the *Paralegal Rules of Conduct*. As mentioned in Chapter 1, in the case of *R v Cunningham*, the Supreme Court of Canada outlined a number of factors that the court should take into account in deciding whether to grant the request of counsel to withdraw, including:

- whether it is feasible for the accused to represent himself or herself;
- other means of obtaining representation;
- the impact on the accused from the delay in proceedings, particularly if the accused is in custody;
- conduct of counsel, such as if counsel gave reasonable notice to the accused to allow the accused to seek other means of representation, or if counsel sought leave of the court to withdraw at the earliest possible time;
- the impact on the Crown and any co-accused;
- the impact on complainants, witnesses, and jurors;
- fairness to defence counsel, including consideration of the expected length and complexity of the proceedings; and
- the history of the proceedings, such as whether the accused has changed counsel repeatedly.

As with other pre-trial applications, it is best to bring an application to withdraw as far in advance of the trial date as possible. However, there will be circumstances in which the adjournment request can only be brought on the day of trial.

## Third Party Records

**third party records**
records that are in the possession of parties other than the Crown and the defence

**Third party records** are records that are beyond the possession or control of the Crown. Sections 278.1 to 278.91 of the *Criminal Code* contain statutory guidelines for bringing applications for third party records for sexual offences. Since sexual offences are beyond the scope of practice for paralegals as of the date of this publication, these sections will not be discussed in this chapter.

For non-sexual offences, third party records may still be important to the accused in making full answer and defence. Examples of these third party records include medical records of a complainant or witness, cellphone or other electronic communication records, records that are created by service providers, and any other records that may affect the credibility of a witness or complainant in the proceedings. It should be noted that acts of police misconduct that are relevant to the investigation at hand now form part of the Crown's general disclosure obligation to the defence (see discussion in Chapter 6).

The application for third party records is referred to as an *O'Connor* application, after the case of *R v O'Connor*, [1995] 4 SCR 411, 130 DLR (4th) 235 [*O'Connor*]. *O'Connor* dealt with the counselling, medical, and school records of a complainant in a case in which the accused was charged with a number of sexual offences. The *O'Connor* test for disclosure of third party records was revised by the Supreme Court of Canada in the case of *R v McNeil*, in which the Court set out the following two-step procedure regarding the production of third party records:

1. The person seeking production of the records must satisfy the court that the records are "likely relevant" to the proceedings, meaning that there is a reasonable possibility that the records are logically probative to an issue at trial or to the credibility or competence of a witness. The "likely relevant" test is a significant but not onerous threshold to meet. The requirement that likely relevance be established first avoids the potential for "fishing expeditions" for irrelevant information. If likely relevance is established, then the third party record holder will be ordered to produce the records to the court for inspection to determine whether production should be ordered.

2. The court must balance the interests of the accused in being able to make full answer and defence with any residual privacy interest held by third parties in the records. Essentially, the inquiry involves asking if there would be any basis for not disclosing the records to the accused if the third party records were in the Crown's possession. The court may exercise discretion in ordering production of the records and may make stipulations that redactions be made or that conditions be attached to production.

Therefore, if the defence paralegal is contemplating an application for third party records, the record-holder must be served with a subpoena for the hearing of the application, along with enough detail to identify the records that are the subject of the proceeding. Rule 2.5(2)(c) of the Criminal Rules indicates that an application for third party records is a trial application brought before the trial judge in advance of evidence being called.

# Remedies

In any pre-trial application, in addition to serving and filing the correct application forms, it is also essential that the accused seek the appropriate **remedy**. Remedies may vary depending on the stage of the proceedings and the nature of the application. Not all remedies are available for all applications; therefore, it is important for the defence paralegal to be familiar with the various remedies available in criminal law. Remedies may be found in the legislation (*Criminal Code* or Charter) or pursuant to the common law. Four remedies will be discussed in this section: judicial stay of proceedings, quashing the charge, exclusion of evidence, and dismissal of the charge.

**remedy**
legal redress for harm or injury

## Judicial Stay of Proceedings

A **judicial stay of proceedings** stems from the common law, traditionally applicable when forcing the accused to stand trial would amount to an abuse of process. This remedy has now been superseded by the Charter. A judicial stay of proceedings is a

**judicial stay of proceedings**
ruling by the court that halts further legal process in a matter

remedy of last resort, granted only in situations in which no other remedy would be just. It is a remedy granted only in the "clearest of cases" (*R v Regan*, 2002 SCC 12, [2002] 1 SCR 297 at paragraph 53; *O'Connor*, *supra*, at paragraph 68).

The court's authority to grant a judicial stay of proceedings is found under section 24(1) of the Charter, which guarantees that "anyone whose rights or freedoms have been infringed or denied may apply to a court of competent jurisdiction to obtain such remedy as the court considers appropriate and just in the circumstances." Although section 24(1) does not expressly mention a judicial stay of proceedings, it is a remedy that is granted pursuant to this section.

A judicial stay of proceedings may be granted at a pre-trial application or at trial. Once a judicial stay of proceedings has been entered by the court, the court may not ever adjudicate the matter again—it is an ultimate remedy. A judicial stay of proceedings is granted when a successful delay application is brought, pursuant to section 11(b) of the Charter, or in situations in which evidence is lost or police misconduct is so egregious that no other remedy would be appropriate.

A judicial stay of proceedings must be distinguished from the Crown deciding to stay a charge, which is in the Crown's unfettered discretion and is not reviewable by the court. When the Crown stays a charge, it reserves the right to reinstate the charge within a specific time limit.

## Quashing the Information

The remedy of quashing of the charge or the information is sought when there is a lack of jurisdiction evident or a defect apparent on the face of an information. For example, if a charge is laid outside of the limitation period, the appropriate remedy is an application to quash the information. Similarly, if there is a material defect in the information, such as a person other than the accused being named, the appropriate remedy would be an application to quash. This remedy may also be sought to quash a subpoena when it contains a material defect.

A remedy to quash a charge may only be brought on a pre-trial basis. Even when the defence is successful, the Crown has the option to proceed with the remaining charges or to re-lay a new information, as long as it is within the limitation period. Quashing of the charge may be done at common law or pursuant to section 601(1) of the *Criminal Code*.

## Exclusion of Evidence

As discussed above, exclusion of evidence is a Charter remedy, pursuant to section 24(2). The remedy of exclusion of evidence is granted when the admission of it in the proceedings would bring the administration of justice into disrepute. While section 24(1) of the Charter is the section that grants the court jurisdiction to impose a remedy that is "appropriate and just in the circumstances," once the applicant has established a Charter violation, section 24(2) specifically gives power to the court to exclude evidence once the test is met (see *Grant*).

Exclusion of evidence is a remedy granted after a *voir dire* application in the course of a trial. Typically, the items that the defence seeks to exclude are incriminatory, such as statements made by the accused, bodily samples, or other physical evidence obtained by the police. If the defence is successful in obtaining this remedy, the Crown may not have sufficient evidence to proceed any further against the accused, or the Crown may decide to proceed with the remaining evidence.

## Dismissal of the Charge

A **dismissal** of the charge is only granted by the court once a trial has commenced, and it is based on the merits of the case. A dismissal is typically granted when there is not enough evidence against the accused. This should be contrasted with a situation in which the Crown and defence have both called evidence at trial and the court decides to enter an **acquittal** against the accused based on the burden of proof not being met by the Crown. A dismissal is not available as a pre-trial remedy.

**dismissal**
decision of the court that terminates proceedings against an accused once the trial has commenced

**acquittal**
formal judicial finding that the accused is not guilty of the offence(s) charged

> **EXAMPLE**
>
> **The Runaway Witness**
>
> In the middle of John's shoplifting trial, one of the Crown's key witnesses—a store security officer—leaves the courtroom and does not return. Despite repeated attempts to page the witness to the courtroom, the witness does not respond. The trial judge dismisses the matter.

# Drafting the Application

In Ontario, the *Criminal Rules of the Ontario Court of Justice* govern procedures in all criminal proceedings in the Ontario Court of Justice. The new version of the Criminal Rules became effective on July 1, 2012, simplifying the procedures for bringing an application before the court. The new Criminal Rules also recognize the role of licensed paralegals in criminal law. The Criminal Rules include three forms: application, response, and consent. The main objective of the Criminal Rules is to deal with proceedings justly and efficiently, with wide discretion given to judges to excuse compliance with the Criminal Rules in order to achieve this objective. The Criminal Rules may be found on the Ontario Court of Justice website at <http://www.ontariocourts.ca/ocj/criminal-rules/>. A copy of the Criminal Rules can be found in Appendix M.

Rule 2 of the Criminal Rules deals with applications. Rule 2.1(1) indicates that an application is commenced by serving an application in Form 1 on the opposing parties and filing it with proof of service. A template for Form 1 can be found in Appendix N.

An application in Form 1 must contain detailed information about the application itself. In addition to the region of the court and the court file number, the hearing date and location of the hearing must be filled out. The criminal charges with the next appearance and the date and type of court appearance must be listed in Form 1, as well as the name of the applicant and the name and contact information of the applicant's legal representative.

A concise statement of the subject of the application must be set out. In other words, this means clearly stating what the application is for and the remedy being sought. An itemized list of the grounds to be argued in support of the application must be included. This should be followed by a detailed statement of the specific facts that support the basis for the application.

The final section of the form provides a list of materials or evidence that the applicant is relying upon in the application. Examples of materials or evidence include transcripts of earlier proceedings, a brief statement of legal argument in support of the application, affidavits, case law or legislation, an agreed-upon statement of facts, and oral testimony of witnesses. It is important for the defence paralegal to give thought to which items of evidence will support the application. For example, in a delay application pursuant to section 11(b) of the Charter, transcripts of earlier court appearances in which the defence paralegal has repeatedly requested disclosure on the record but has been denied timely disclosure would be vital to the argument of the applicant. If the application is for the quashing of the information due to a material defect, then a copy of the information should be attached to the application.

Form 1 must be dated and signed by the legal representative, with the name and contact information of the respondent set out. For applications in criminal law in which the applicant is the accused, the respondent would obviously be the Crown. When there is an application for third party records, the application must be served on the third party as well. Form 1 should be filled out accurately in order to assist the court in understanding the nature of the application being brought and the remedy being sought by the applicant.

Rule 2.2(1) states that a party responding to an application shall serve and file a response in Form 2 on the applicant. It contains a detailed statement of the party's reasons for responding to the application, a response to the grounds listed in the application, and a detailed statement of the facts supporting the respondent's position. Other materials and evidence may also be attached to Form 2, such as legal arguments, affidavits, transcripts, and case law. A template for Form 2 can be found in Appendix O.

When both parties consent to the application and are represented by counsel or licensed paralegals, a consent in Form 3 may be filed without the need for a hearing, pursuant to rule 2.7(1) of the Criminal Rules. A template for Form 3 can be found in Appendix P.

# Timing, Service, and Filing of the Application

According to rule 2.4(1) of the Criminal Rules, a pre-trial application must be heard at least 60 days before the trial. Examples of pre-trial applications are listed under rule 2.4(2). Examples of trial applications are listed under rule 2.5(2).

Rule 3 of the Criminal Rules deals with the service of the application and response. Pursuant to rule 3.1(1), an application in Form 1 must be served and filed with proof of service at least 30 days before the hearing date of the application. Pursuant to rule 3.1(2), a response in Form 2 shall be served and filed with proof of service at least 15 days before the hearing date of the application. However, the court may shorten or lengthen these time periods.

In accordance with rule 3.3(1) of the Criminal Rules, service may be in person, by facsimile, or by email, with hard copies of the documents to be filed with the court. Rule 3.3(2) indicates that when electronic filing technology is available and authorized by the local region, documents may be served and filed electronically without any hard copies required.

---

### PRACTICE TIP

There are tactical considerations that should be taken into account from the defence paralegal's perspective when drafting the application. If the application contains too much detail, there is an opportunity for a Crown witness to augment his or her testimony in order to address any deficiencies in the Crown's case. Therefore, the application should specify the grounds to be argued but not provide the specifics of the argument to be made at the actual hearing.

# CHAPTER SUMMARY

Several pre-trial and trial applications may be brought, depending on the nature of the relief being sought by the applicant. *Criminal Code* applications include severance of counts, severance of accused persons, orders to exclude the public and restrict publication, release of the exhibits for testing, and amendment of the information.

Severance of counts and severance of accused persons refer to the application to split counts from an information or to split two or more accused persons from being tried together. Orders to exclude the public and restrict publication are based on the proper administration of justice and other factors set out in the *Criminal Code*. The defence may bring an application for release of exhibits for testing when they wish to have the evidence examined by their own expert. If an information contains a defect, depending on the nature of the defect, either the Crown or the defence may bring an application to amend it.

Common Charter applications include disclosure, trial delay, and exclusion of evidence. When the defence has requested disclosure from the Crown and is of the opinion that the Crown has not complied with the request, the defence may bring an application before the court. When there is unreasonable delay in the proceedings, the defence may bring a delay application. When evidence is alleged to have been obtained as a result of a Charter violation, the defence may bring an application seeking exclusion of the evidence.

Other applications include an adjournment of the trial, withdrawal of representation, and applications for third party records.

Identifying the appropriate remedy is an essential aspect of an application. Remedies vary depending on the stage of the proceedings and the nature of the application being brought before the court. Common remedies include a judicial stay of proceedings, quashing of the charge, dismissal of the charge, and exclusion of evidence.

An application in Form 1 of the Criminal Rules must contain sufficient detail as to the subject of the application; the grounds, facts, and evidence in support of it; and the remedy being sought.

A pre-trial application must be heard at least 60 days before the trial. The application must be served and filed at least 30 days before the hearing date of the application, and a response must be served and filed at least 15 days before the hearing date of the application.

# KEY TERMS

acquittal, 113
application, 100
dismissal, 113
judicial stay of proceedings, 111
quash, 103
remedy, 111
third party records, 110

# REVIEW QUESTIONS

## Short Answer

1. What is a pre-trial application?

2. Under what circumstances will the court amend a defect in the information as opposed to quashing it?

3. Name three possible remedies that may be available to an accused person bringing a pre-trial application before the court.

4. Where would a defence paralegal find the procedural requirements for filing and serving an application?

5. How many days before the trial must the pre-trial application be heard?

## Apply Your Knowledge

1. Leslie was charged with shoplifting on April 20, 2011. She retained a criminal defence paralegal to represent her within two weeks of her first court appearance in June 2011. Her trial date has been adjourned three times. The first trial date had to be rescheduled because the store security guard was ill. The second trial date was adjourned because one of the police officers did not attend court. The third trial date was adjourned because there was not enough time scheduled for the trial. On Leslie's last court appearance, a trial date was set for September 4, 2014. What type of application should be brought on Leslie's behalf? What is the appropriate remedy?

2. Jacques was arrested for assaulting his neighbour. He was released on a promise to appear, promising to attend court on May 15, 2014. When he attended court, he received a disclosure package from the Crown. When Jacques met with his paralegal and gave him the disclosure package, the paralegal discovered that the information contained one count of uttering threats. All of the disclosure materials identify an offence of assault. What application should be brought before the court? What remedy should the paralegal seek?

3. Suri was arrested by the police for mischief under $5,000. She was taken to the police station by one set of police officers. When another set of police officers came into the interview room, they did not provide her with the right to contact counsel. Suri gave these officers a written statement admitting to the offence. What application may be brought on Suri's behalf? What remedy should her paralegal request?

4. Nav has been charged with making harassing phone calls to his former place of employment. Nav wants records from the Workplace Safety and Insurance Board showing that his employer is guilty of unsafe work practices. The Crown does not have these records in their possession. What application would Nav's paralegal bring before the court?

# The Trial

## LEARNING OUTCOMES

After reading this chapter, you should be able to:

- Explain how a diversion program works

- Describe the arraignment process and the possible pleas available to a defendant

- Outline the paralegal's professional obligations to the client regarding the entering of a plea

- Identify the steps in a trial

- Evaluate some of the common defences available to an accused person in a criminal trial

- Explain the significance of a verdict in a criminal trial

- Discuss when a section 810 recognizance may be entered into by the defendant

# Introduction

We will begin this chapter with a brief look at diversion programs, followed by a discussion of entering pleas. The ethical and procedural aspects of having a client enter a plea will be reviewed. The steps of a trial will be outlined with respect to the Crown's case and the defence's case, with a discussion of various possible defences available to an accused. Finally, the provisions and availability of a peace bond will be explained.

# Diversion Programs

**diversion program**
alternative to a criminal proceeding; typically available to an accused person who does not have a criminal record and who is charged with a less serious offence

**Diversion programs** are an alternative to prosecution. The rationale behind diversion is that not all criminal charges need to be dealt with through the court process and a criminal prosecution. The Crown determines which cases are eligible for diversion, since it is up to the Crown to make decisions regarding the prosecution of a case. Diversion is usually considered when an accused person has a minimal or no criminal record and the offence is very minor in nature.

Cases may be pre-approved for diversion by the Crown even before the information is laid. In other situations, the charge screening form may indicate that the case has been pre-approved for diversion.

Agreeing to diversion does not involve an admission of guilt regarding the offence. However, there are consequences that stem from it. An accused person must accept responsibility for the charge and must be willing to comply with the terms of the program. Each courthouse or jurisdiction may offer slightly different programs, depending on the location and their availability. Examples of diversion programs include community service work, counselling sessions for anger management or addictions, or making a charitable donation to a non-profit organization.

Some courthouses have direct accountability programs, which are available to adults with limited or no prior involvement in the criminal justice system and who have been charged with a minor criminal offence. Direct accountability programs involve a **community justice worker**, who assists the accused in setting up counselling sessions or finding a suitable placement for community service hours. The community justice worker also verifies with the Crown when the conditions of diversion have been satisfied.

It is important to follow through with the terms of diversion, since the Crown has the discretion of withdrawing the offer to divert if the accused is delaying the completion of the program or not complying with the conditions. If there are legitimate reasons for the delay in finishing the program, the defence paralegal should provide an update to the Crown. Once the conditions have been satisfied, the Crown may stay or withdraw the charge. If the charge is stayed or withdrawn, it does not result in a criminal conviction on the accused's record. Therefore, participating in and completing a diversion program is beneficial to the accused.

It is important to note the difference between a charge that is stayed and a charge that is withdrawn. If a charge is withdrawn, it may not be brought back before the

> **PRACTICE TIP**
>
> When the Crown does not offer diversion, but the defence paralegal is of the opinion that the case may be appropriate for it, he or she should raise this with the Crown. It may have been overlooked, or circumstances may have changed that now make it appropriate for the matter to be diverted.

**community justice worker**
person who attends court on a regular basis, receives referrals from the Crown for diversion, and assists the accused in registering in and fulfilling the conditions of a diversion program

court—the prosecution of that charge has finished. If a charge is stayed, it may be brought back before the court within one year from the date that it is stayed. While it is rare for the Crown to reinstitute proceedings on a charge that has been stayed, it is still an available option. For example, if an accused person provided a letter from a charitable organization confirming that he or she made a charitable donation and the Crown stayed the charge as a result, but it later came to light that the accused submitted a fraudulent letter (meaning that no such donation was actually made), the Crown could reinstitute the charge within one year of entering the stay.

In the next section, we will look at what happens prior to the start of a trial.

# Arraignment and Entering Pleas

When the defendant appears for trial, the charges set out in the information are formally read by the clerk of the court, and the defendant is asked whether he or she will plead guilty or not guilty. This is referred to as the **arraignment**. Section 801(1) of the *Criminal Code* describes the arraignment process for a summary conviction matter. Although this section states that the "substance" of the information shall be read to the defendant, in practice, the wording of the charge is read out in its entirety. The defendant is then asked how he or she wishes to plead, pursuant to section 801(1)(a) of the *Criminal Code*. The plea is then recorded by the clerk of the court.

**arraignment**
formal reading of the charge or charges against the accused, in which the accused is asked to enter a plea

## Types of Pleas

Pursuant to section 606(1) of the *Criminal Code*, there are only two types of common pleas that may be entered by the defendant: guilty or not guilty. If a plea of not guilty is entered, then the matter proceeds to trial. If the defendant enters a guilty plea, then a conviction is entered, and the matter proceeds to sentencing. During the sentencing, the Crown reads in a summary of the facts of the offence, provides the court with details of the defendant's criminal record, and puts forth a position on sentence. The criminal record must be acknowledged by the defendant or proven by the Crown.

The defence is also entitled to put forth the defendant's version of events and make submissions as to the appropriate sentence. If the defence's version of the facts varies too substantially from the Crown's version, or if it calls into question one of the elements of the offence, then the guilty plea will not be accepted by the court. In this situation, the Crown would have to call evidence to prove the contested allegations beyond a reasonable doubt. Upon the hearing of the facts or calling of evidence, it is then up to the judge to pronounce sentence. The judge may pronounce sentence immediately after the submissions of Crown and defence, or the judge may reserve his or her decision on sentence.

*autrefois acquit*
a special plea available to a defendant when he or she has previously been tried and acquitted of the same offence and therefore cannot be tried for it again

*autrefois convict*
a special plea available to a defendant when he or she has previously been tried and convicted of the same offence and therefore cannot be tried for it again

**pardon**
a special plea available to a defendant when he or she has previously been pardoned for the same offence and therefore cannot be tried for it again

## Special Pleas

Pursuant to section 607(1) of the *Criminal Code*, three special pleas are available to the accused: ***autrefois acquit***, ***autrefois convict***, and **pardon**. If the accused enters a special plea, it is sufficient that he or she states that there has been a lawful acquittal, conviction, or pardon of the offence charged in the count to which the plea relates and that he or she indicates the time and place of that acquittal, conviction, or pardon.

These special pleas are available for a summary conviction offence since they relate to the "double jeopardy" principle that an accused person cannot be tried twice for an offence for which he or she has already been acquitted or convicted. If the identity of the former charge is admitted as evidence, the court will discharge the accused. If the accused is unsuccessful in establishing the identity of the former charge, then he or she will be called upon to enter a plea of guilty or not guilty.

# Advice to Clients Before Entering a Guilty Plea

Pursuant to rule 4.01(8) of the *Paralegal Rules of Conduct*, at any point before or after a charge is laid, a paralegal may discuss the possible resolution of the matter with the Crown, unless the client provides instructions not to do so. However, prior to entering into any plea agreement with the Crown, the paralegal must do the following to ensure compliance with rule 4.01(9) of the Rules:

1. advise the client about the prospects of an acquittal or finding of guilt;
2. advise the client of the implications and possible consequences of a guilty plea, including the fact that the court is not bound to accept any agreements as to sentencing;
3. confirm that the client is prepared to voluntarily admit the factual and mental elements of the offence charged; and
4. obtain the client's instructions in writing about entering a guilty plea.

In addition to rule 4.01(9) of the Rules, the defence paralegal must also advise his or her client of the provisions of section 606(1.1) of the *Criminal Code*. According to section 606(1.1), a court may only accept a guilty plea if it is satisfied that the accused:

1. is making the plea voluntarily;
2. understands that the plea is an admission of the essential elements of the offence;
3. understands the nature and consequences of the plea; and
4. understands that the court is not bound by any agreement between the Crown and the defence.

If the court is not satisfied that the conditions of section 606(1.1) are met, then the court has the discretion to allow the guilty plea to be withdrawn. Even when the defendant has been advised of the implications of a guilty plea and voluntarily wishes to enter a plea of guilty, problems may arise once the plea is entered. The defendant may not agree with the facts read by the Crown or may not admit to essential elements of the offence.

Occasionally, even when the court is satisfied that the defendant understands the nature and consequences of a guilty plea and admits the essential elements of the offence, the defendant may still indicate a desire to change the plea to not guilty. In this situation, a withdrawal of guilty plea hearing may need to take place in order to determine whether the plea was valid and should remain or whether the defendant should be allowed to change his or her plea, either because the plea was invalid or because there has been a miscarriage of justice. The burden is on the accused to establish that the plea was invalid. The defence paralegal may or may not be able to continue to represent the client if the court withdraws the guilty plea, depending on whether the continued representation will lead to a breach of the Rules. However, any admissions made to the previous paralegal will be protected by solicitor–client privilege.

**rebuttal**
refuting or contradicting the evidence put forth

**verdict**
formal decision made by the judge or jury at the end of a trial

# Steps in the Trial

Once the accused is arraigned and enters a plea of not guilty, the trial begins. The following steps are involved in the trial process:

## Steps in the Trial Process

1. Start of Crown's case—Crown conducts direct examination of Crown's first witness

2. Defence conducts cross-examination of Crown's first witness

3. Crown may conduct re-examination of first witness on new issues raised during cross-examination by defence only

4. Crown calls second and subsequent witnesses; the same procedure occurs with each witness

5. Close of Crown's case

6. After calling all of its witnesses, if Crown has not established a *prima facie* case, the defence may bring a motion for directed verdict of acquittal

7. If Crown has established a *prima facie* case, defence must decide whether to call evidence (by calling the accused or other witnesses)

8. Start of defence's case—defence conducts direct examination of defence's first witness

9. Crown cross-examines defence's first witness

10. Defence may conduct re-examination of first witness (only on new issues raised during cross-examination by Crown)

11. Defence calls second and subsequent witnesses and same procedure occurs with each witness

12. After calling all of its witnesses, defence rests

13. Crown may call reply or **rebuttal** evidence, which is limited to circumstances in which the defence has raised a new matter or defence that the Crown could not reasonably have anticipated (for example, alibi evidence)

14. Closing submissions by defence, based on the evidence called at trial and inferences that may be drawn

15. Closing submissions by Crown, based on the evidence called at trial and inferences that may be drawn

16. **Verdict** delivered by trial judge

17. If defendant found guilty, sentencing may proceed at this time, or matter may be adjourned for sentencing to take place at a later date

## The Crown's Case

In lengthy or complex trials, or in trials on indictable matters, both the Crown and defence may deliver opening statements prior to witnesses being called. However, opening statements are not usually given in summary conviction trials.

As discussed earlier in Chapter 3, if the Crown is relying on a statement given by the accused, the Crown must first prove the voluntariness of the statement in a *voir dire*. A *voir dire* may also be held to determine the admissibility of evidence obtained by the police, to determine whether hearsay evidence is admissible, and to qualify an expert. The Crown may wish to begin its case with the *voir dire* and then ask to have the evidence—if it is determined to be admissible—apply to the trial. Alternatively, the Crown may enter into a *voir dire* when the evidentiary issue comes up as the trial proceeds.

The Crown must establish a *prima facie* case before the defence is obligated to call any evidence. This means that the Crown must establish some evidence for all of the elements of the offence. If the Crown fails to make a *prima facie* case, the defence may bring a motion for a directed verdict of acquittal. The effect of a directed verdict of acquittal is that the accused is acquitted, or found to be not guilty of the offence, and the case is dismissed. In order to successfully bring this motion, the defence paralegal must be aware of what the elements of the offence are and be prepared to argue which specific element the Crown has failed to prove on a *prima facie* basis.

If the Crown has proven its case on a *prima facie* basis, the defence must decide whether or not it wishes to call evidence, and in particular, whether or not to call the accused to give evidence. If the defence is calling other witnesses as part of the case, the accused may not need to testify. On the other hand, if the Crown's case is very compelling, or if the accused has a good legal defence, then perhaps it is better trial strategy to call the accused to testify. These are options that the paralegal must discuss with the accused well in advance of the trial, but the ultimate decision is up to the accused. It is important to note that it is the accused's constitutional right to remain silent throughout the entire criminal trial process. Accordingly, if the accused exercises his or her Charter-protected right to not testify, this choice cannot be used by the trier of fact as proof of the accused's guilt.

## The Defence's Case

**air of reality test**
threshold test in which the trial judge considers the totality of the evidence in order to determine whether there is an evidentiary foundation for a particular defence

Whether or not the accused chooses to testify, the goal of the defence is to raise a reasonable doubt. This may be done by thorough cross-examination of the Crown witnesses, or there may be a viable defence based on the disclosure materials and evidence adduced at trial. The **air of reality test** dictates that when an accused wishes to rely on a specific defence, he or she must first establish an evidentiary foundation for it. In other words, the judge must first determine whether there is some evidence before the court that would lend an air of reality to the defence. The air of reality test is more applicable when there is a trial before a jury, since it ensures that jurors do not consider ridiculous defences that are not supported by the evidence and that only serve to complicate and detract from the issues at hand. Conversely, the trial judge is required to advise the jury of any defences that would meet the air of reality test, even though they may not have been raised by the defence.

# Common Defences

There are several defences that may be relied upon by the accused in a criminal matter. Some of the more familiar ones will be discussed in this section, including:

- *de minimis non curat lex*,
- consent,
- self-defence,
- necessity,
- duress,
- automatism, and
- mistake of fact.

## De Minimis Non Curat Lex

**De minimis non curat lex** is a Latin expression meaning that the law does not concern itself with trivial matters. This is a common law defence based on the proposition that the judicial system should not be plagued with offences that merely meet the technical requirements of a crime. This defence also protects accused persons from being branded with the stigma of a criminal conviction for conduct that is trifling in nature.

There is not a lot of case law on the use of *de minimus non curat lex* as a legal defence, likely because the Crown exercises discretion in the types of cases that it proceeds with. Nonetheless, the Supreme Court of Canada has made comments indicating that this defence is available in criminal law (*R v Hinchey*, [1996] 3 SCR 1128, 147 Nfld & PEIR 1; *Canadian Foundation for Children, Youth and the Law v Canada*, 2004 SCC 4, [2004] 1 SCR 76).

*de minimis non curat lex*
a defence that arises when the criminal conduct of the accused is so trivial that it is not worthy of the attention of the law

> ### EXAMPLE
>
> #### Defence of *De Minimis Non Curat Lex*
>
> Vinh and Stacey are in a class together and take opposite points of view on any discussion. One day, Stacey is upset with Vinh and pokes him in the arm after class. If Vinh were to call the police to make a complaint against her, Stacey may be able to rely on the defence of *de minimis non curat lex*, as it is so trifling in nature.

## Consent

**Consent**, or the accused's honest but mistaken belief in consent, is a common defence to the offences of assault and sexual assault. Since sexual assault is outside of the scope of practice for paralegals, the defence of consent as it pertains to sexual offences will not be discussed in this section. The offence of assault, pursuant to section 265(1)(a) of the *Criminal Code*, is defined as the application of intentional force to another person—either directly or indirectly—without the other person's consent. Therefore, it is a defence to assault that the accused had an honest yet mistaken belief that the complainant or victim consented to the application of force.

**consent**
a defence that arises when the accused has an honest yet mistaken belief in the complainant's consent to an action

If the victim does not resist or submits to the assault, then the accused may rely on the defence of consent. However, the defence is limited by section 265(3) of the *Criminal Code*, which indicates that no consent is obtained when the complainant does not resist or submits to the assault because of the application of force to the complainant or another person, or because of threats made to the complainant or another person, or by reason of fraud or the exercise of authority. Additionally, consent may be apprehended, meaning that as long as there is some evidence that the defendant held an honest belief that the victim consented, he or she may rely on the defence of consent.

It should be noted that the defence of consent does not apply to assault resulting in bodily harm or aggravated assault. In the case of *R v Jobidon*, [1991] 2 SCR 714, 66 CCC (3d) 454, the accused and the victim got into a consensual bar fight. The accused struck the victim once and the victim was knocked unconscious. The accused continued to strike the victim even after he became unconscious, and the victim died as a result of his injuries. The Supreme Court of Canada ruled that consent is not a defence when bodily harm results or when excessive force is used.

In these situations, consent is vitiated due to the application of force being intended to cause harm to the complainant.

---

> **EXAMPLE**
>
> **Defence of Consent**
>
> Sarah and Kavita play on opposite teams during college hockey practice games. All of the players impliedly consent to some bodily contact. However, in one of the practice games, Kavita goes out of her way to trip Sarah with her hockey stick and then kicks at her with her skate in order to get control of the puck. Sarah suffers from a sprained ankle as a result of the assault. Due to Kavita's use of excessive violence, consent is vitiated, as it is not implied that Sarah would agree to such bodily harm.

## Self-Defence

**self-defence**
a defence that applies when the accused must use reasonable force to defend himself or herself or another person

**Self-defence** is a statutory defence found in section 34 of the *Criminal Code*. If a person has reasonable grounds to believe that force or a threat of force is being used against him or her or another person, he or she may commit an act to defend or protect him or herself or the other person, as long as the act is reasonable under the circumstances. Pursuant to section 34(2), there are a number of factors that shall be considered by the court in determining whether the act is reasonable, including:

- the nature of the force or threat;
- whether the use of force was imminent or whether there were other options available;
- the person's role in the incident;
- whether any party to the incident used or threatened to use a weapon;
- the size, age, gender, and physical capabilities of the parties;

- the nature, duration, and history of the relationship between the parties, including any prior use of force and the nature of that threat or force;
- any history of interaction or communication between the parties;
- the nature and the proportionality of the person's response to the use of or threat of force; and
- whether the act committed was in response to a use of threat of force that the person knew was lawful.

All of these factors apply to a three-part test to self-defence, pursuant to section 34(1) of the *Criminal Code*:

1.  Did the accused have a reasonable belief that force was being used or was threatened against him or her or another person? It is not a requirement that the other person be someone under the accused's protection. It is also not a requirement that the accused believe that the force will result in death or bodily harm.

2.  What was the accused's purpose in committing the act? Was it to protect or defend himself or herself or another person from the actual or threatened force, or was it to exact retribution or revenge on someone?

3.  Were the defendant's actions reasonable under the circumstances? An objective test is applied to this criterion.

A similar provision permits an accused to protect his or her property if he or she is in peaceable possession of it and someone else is either about to enter the property, is entering the property, or has already entered the property without being entitled by law to do so. This provision also applies if someone is about to take property, is taking property, has already taken property, or is about to damage or destroy property. Under these circumstances, the accused may be found not guilty of committing an act to protect the property in order to prevent someone from coming in, taking, or damaging the property. Finally, in order for the defence to apply, the conduct must be reasonable under the circumstances. Defence of property is a statutory defence pursuant to section 35 of the *Criminal Code*.

The use of excessive force is prohibited under section 26 of the *Criminal Code*, even when the person is authorized by law to use force. Section 25(1) of the *Criminal Code* specifies that if a police officer acts on reasonable grounds to administer or enforce the law, he or she may use as much force as is necessary for that purpose. This is limited to a reasonable use of force.

However, force that is intended or is likely to cause death or grievous bodily harm may be justified when the suspect is fleeing from police, when the police are attempting to arrest the suspect, and when force is necessary for the safety of the officer or others (see Case in Point: *R v Nasogaluak*). The use of excessive force on the part of law enforcement authorities may result in criminal charges, as well as disciplinary proceedings under the *Police Services Act*. Furthermore, when the accused believes on reasonable grounds that a police officer is acting unlawfully, he or she may act in self-defence, pursuant to section 34(3) of the *Criminal Code*.

## CASE IN POINT

# Police Use of Excessive Force

*R v Nasogaluak*, 2010 SCC 6, [2010] 1 SCR 206

### Facts

The RCMP received a tip about an intoxicated driver and were involved in a high speed pursuit of the accused, Lyle Nasogaluak. When the accused came to a stop, officers had to use force to remove him from his vehicle. He resisted, and one officer punched him twice in the head while wrestling him out of the car. Nasogaluak continued to resist and the officer yelled at him to stop resisting before punching him in the head again. The accused was then pinned face down on the ground with one officer straddling his back and another officer kneeling on his thigh. Nasogaluak refused to put his hands up to be handcuffed, so a second officer punched him twice in the back, breaking his ribs. This ultimately resulted in the accused suffering from a punctured lung.

While at the RCMP detachment, the accused provided breath samples that placed him over the legal blood alcohol limit. As he did not have any obvious signs of injury and did not request any medical assistance, no attempts were made to get him any medical attention. Nasogaluak told an officer that he was hurt and could not breathe, and he was also observed to be crying, leaning over, and moaning. When he was released the next morning, the accused went to the hospital. He was diagnosed as having broken ribs and a collapsed lung that required emergency surgery.

The officers did not report the force that they had used during the arrest and provided very little information about the circumstances leading up to the arrest. The accused pled guilty to charges of impaired driving and flight from police officers. During the sentencing, the judge found that the officers used excessive force during the arrest and breached the accused's rights under section 7 of the Charter. The judge reduced the accused's sentence to a 12-month conditional discharge on each count, even though there is a statutorily mandated minimum fine for a first offence of impaired driving.

The Court of Appeal agreed that there was sufficient evidence to support the trial judge's finding as to the excessive force used by the officers but set aside the conditional discharge on the impaired driving offence and imposed the mandatory minimum fine. They did not interfere with the sentence imposed for the flight from police offence. Both the Crown and the accused appealed to the Supreme Court of Canada.

### Decision

The appeal and cross-appeal were dismissed. The Supreme Court of Canada stated that the conduct of the RCMP officers was a substantial interference with the accused's physical and psychological integrity and security of the person, and it was a clear breach of section 7 of the Charter. Section 25(1) of the *Criminal Code* permits use of force to effect an arrest, but only to the extent that it is reasonably necessary. Under section 25(3), force intended or likely to cause death or grievous bodily harm is prohibited unless the officer has reason to believe that the amount of force used is necessary to protect himself or herself or another person. The allowable degree of force is constrained by the principles of proportionality, necessity, and reasonableness.

However, the Court went on to say that the sentencing judge's discretion in crafting the appropriate sentence is limited by case law and statute. A sentencing judge cannot reduce a sentence below a statutorily mandated minimum unless the provision is unconstitutional. There was no need for the sentencing judge to turn to section 24(1) of the Charter in order to reduce the sentence. Sentencing provisions in the *Criminal Code* provide adequate remedial protections to accused persons whose rights have been infringed, whether these rights are Charter-related or not.

### Discussion Question

Should sentencing judges have residual discretion to override otherwise constitutional mandatory minimum sentences in situations in which police officers use excessive force? Conversely, when an accused person pleads guilty to an offence, how much weight should the court place on a breach of a Charter right in crafting an appropriate sentence?

# Necessity

**Necessity** is a common law defence that recognizes that when faced with imminent danger, a person may be forced to break the law. The Supreme Court of Canada refined the test for necessity in *R v Latimer*, 2001 SCC 1, [2001] 1 SCR 3, stating that there are three elements to the defence:

1. imminent peril or danger;
2. no reasonable legal alternative to the course of action that the defendant undertakes; and
3. proportionality between the harm inflicted and the harm avoided.

The danger or peril must be immediate and unavoidable, making compliance with the law nearly impossible. The harm avoided must be at least comparable to the harm inflicted. The proportionality of the harm is assessed on the basis of an objective test—that is, what a reasonable person would do. The first two criteria are assessed on a modified objective standard, taking into account the situation and characteristics of the accused.

**necessity**
a defence that applies when the accused is forced to break the law in order to avoid a greater harm

> **EXAMPLE**
>
> ### Defence of Necessity
>
> Dragana is driving home at 2 a.m. after an evening out. While she is waiting at a traffic stop, a masked man opens the passenger side door of her vehicle and orders her to drive to the nearest automated teller machine. The masked man holds a knife to Dragana and tells her to run the red light. Dragana does as she is told but hits another vehicle in the process. The man flees from the scene and Dragana is eventually charged with driving carelessly for causing the collision. Dragana can rely on the defence of necessity, as she felt that had she not listened to the masked man, he would have hurt her.

# Duress

**Duress**, which is similar to necessity, is a statutory defence arising under section 17 of the *Criminal Code*. The defence of duress may be used when the accused is under compulsion to commit an offence by way of threats of death or bodily harm. Section 17 provides that the threat must be of immediate death or bodily harm and that the person threatening the accused must be present when the offence is committed. However, the "immediate" and "present" requirements of the defence have been struck down as unconstitutional (see *R v Ruzic*, 2001 SCC 24, [2001] 1 SCR 687 [*Ruzic*]). Therefore, in practice, for the defence of duress to be successful, the threat must be of present or future death or bodily harm directed at the accused or a third party, and the accused must reasonably believe that the threat will be carried out. There remains a close temporal connection required between the threat and the harm threatened, but it need not be immediate (see Case in Point: *R v Ryan*).

**duress**
a defence both available under common law and statute that applies when an accused person is compelled to commit an offence by way of threats of death or bodily harm

This defence does not apply to serious and violent offences, which are detailed under section 17, nor to parties to an offence. However, parties to an offence may still rely on the common law defence of duress, which likewise does not require the strict criterion of immediacy of the threat but rather a close temporal connection between the threat and the harm threatened. The common law defence of duress is similar to necessity in that there must be no legal way out of the situation the accused is facing. The trier of fact should apply an objective–subjective test when determining whether there was a clear, safe avenue of escape, meaning that the unique circumstances in which the accused is situated are examined, as well as the accused's perception of the events. Once the accused raises the defence of duress and provides some supporting evidence, the burden shifts to the Crown to prove beyond a reasonable doubt that the accused was not under duress when he or she committed the offence.

## CASE IN POINT

# Duress as a Defence When the Accused Has Been Subjected to Domestic Abuse

*R v Ryan*, 2013 SCC 3, [2013] 1 SCR 14

### Facts

The accused, Nicole Ryan, had been the victim in an abusive marriage. She was fearful that her husband would cause either serious bodily harm or death to herself and her daughter. According to the accused, her husband had threatened to kill her on many occasions if she ever left him. In September 2007, Ryan started planning to have her husband killed, and she spoke to at least three people about carrying out this plan. She paid one man $25,000 to commit the murder, but he refused, asking for more money.

One day, unbeknownst to Ryan, she was contacted by an undercover RCMP officer posing as a "hit man." She met with this officer and agreed to pay him $25,000 to kill her husband. Details of the plan were discussed, including when the killing would take place. The accused also paid the officer $2,000 as a deposit. Later that evening, she provided the undercover officer with her husband's photograph and address. She was arrested shortly thereafter and charged with counselling the commission of an offence not yet committed (murder).

At trial, the Crown relied on audio and videotaped recorded conversations between the accused and the undercover officer, as well as the accused's statement after her arrest. The accused conceded that the Crown had proven a *prima facie* case but relied on the common law defence of duress. Even though the accused's husband did not testify, the trial judge accepted the accused's evidence regarding the violent and threatening behaviour of her husband. The trial judge also found that Ryan's only reason for her actions arose from this violence toward herself and her daughter, as she reasonably believed that there was no other safe alternative. Therefore, the trial judge found that the common law defence of duress applied, and Ryan was acquitted.

The Crown appealed to the Court of Appeal, but the Court of Appeal upheld the verdict of acquittal. The Crown further appealed to the Supreme Court of Canada, arguing that duress would only apply if the accused was forced by threats to commit an offence against a third party.

### Decision

The Supreme Court of Canada noted that the defences of necessity, duress, and self-defence applied in similar situations to excuse the conduct of the accused when the accused acted criminally in response to an external threat. However, unlike situations of self-defence, the victim in a situation of duress or necessity is generally an innocent third party. Motivation for the attack or threats is irrelevant in self-defence, whereas in cases of duress, the purpose of the threat is to force the accused to commit an offence.

The Supreme Court also noted that self-defence is completely codified under the *Criminal Code*, but the defence of duress is partly codified and partly based on the common law. The rationale behind duress is moral involuntariness, meaning that there is no legal way out. The act is criminal but should not be punished because the accused had no choice. Self-defence, on the other hand, is a justification to act in a certain way—to meet force with force.

The Court went on to say that self-defence should be more readily available than the defence of duress. Duress is only applicable in situations in which the accused is compelled to commit an offence as a result of being threatened with death or bodily harm.

The Supreme Court of Canada allowed the Crown's appeal. However, the Court entered a judicial stay of proceedings based on the lack of clarity behind the defence of duress and the resulting strategic decisions made by Ryan's defence to conduct the trial in a certain manner based on the existing law. The Court also took note of the abuse that the accused suffered at the hands of her husband.

### Discussion Question

Does the Supreme Court of Canada's decision in this case create a legal void for people who suffer domestic abuse?

## Automatism

**Automatism** is a legal defence in which a person performs an illegal act unconsciously or involuntarily. Voluntariness is part of the *actus reus* of an offence. The *Criminal Code* refers to a defence of mental disorder, or insane automatism, which arises from a disease of the mind. However, the type of automatism that will be discussed in this section is non-mental disorder automatism or non-insane automatism, which arises when a person commits an involuntary action but that action does not stem from a disease of the mind; this entitles the accused to an acquittal.

The test for non-mental disorder automatism was set out by the Supreme Court of Canada in the case of *R v Stone*, [1999] 2 SCR 290, 173 DLR (4th) 66. The Supreme Court of Canada stated that the defendant must first set a proper foundation for the defence by asserting that his or her actions were involuntary. The accused is then required to introduce psychiatric evidence to confirm the involuntariness of his or her actions. The trial judge must determine whether there is evidence upon which a properly instructed jury could find, on a balance of probabilities, that the accused acted involuntarily. In arriving at this determination, the trial judge may consider other relevant factors, such as:

- the severity of the triggering stimulus that brings on the automatistic state;
- corroborating evidence of bystanders;
- corroborating medical history of automatistic-like dissociative states;
- the presence or absence of motive; and
- the relationship between the alleged trigger of the automatism and the victim of the automatistic violence.

None of the above factors is determinative on its own, and the Supreme Court noted that as medicine advances, additional types of evidence that demonstrate involuntariness may become available.

Non-mental disorder has only been used rarely in Canada.

**automatism**
a defence that applies when the accused's physical actions are involuntary as a result of either a disease of the mind or a non-mental disorder

## Mistake of Fact

**Mistake of fact** is a common law defence that operates to negate the defendant's fault in committing the offence. It only applies if one of the essential elements of the offence requires subjective *mens rea* on the accused's part, which involves asking whether the accused knowingly or intentionally committed an offence.

Generally, section 19 of the *Criminal Code* indicates that ignorance of the law by someone who commits an offence is not an excuse. However, when the subjective *mens rea* of the accused with respect to the law is an essential element that the Crown must prove, then a reasonable mistake made by the accused would result in *mens rea* not being established by the Crown.

Mistakes of law must be distinguished from mistakes of fact. While a mistake of fact may provide a valid defence to a charge, a mistake of law does not. An example of a mistake of law would be a person who samples candies from the bulk foods section of a grocery store and is then arrested for theft under $5,000. If the person claims that he or she did not believe that sampling candies from the store constitutes theft, then he or she is operating under a mistake of law. Section 19 of the *Criminal Code* would indicate that this is not a valid defence to the charge of theft.

> **EXAMPLE**
>
> **Defence of Mistake of Fact**
>
> Raina brings her backpack with her to the library. After doing some research for her class, Raina leaves with what she believes is her backpack, but it actually belongs to someone else. Raina has made a mistake of fact—she thought that the backpack belonged to her. Raina's intention was not to deprive the rightful owner of his or her backpack, which is an essential element of theft. Therefore, she has a valid defence to the charge of theft.

In order for mistake of fact to be a valid defence, the mistake must be an honest one, and the situation must be such that no offence would have been committed had the circumstances been as the accused believed them to be. In the example above, if Raina had left the library with someone's cellphone with the intention of stealing it but discovered that she had actually taken an mp3 player instead, she could not rely on the defence of mistake of fact. While her intention was to steal a cellphone, even according to her version of events, she has committed an offence. Her error does not negate her *mens rea*.

# The Verdict

After the Crown and defence have finished calling evidence and have provided closing statements, the judge must then consider and weigh the evidence before rendering a decision or verdict in the trial. Usually, in simple trials, the judge may take a short time to deliberate before providing his or her verdict. For more complex or lengthier trials, the judge may need several weeks before providing his or her decision and reasons for the decision.

Regardless of whether the accused is acquitted or convicted, the verdict must be recorded. If the accused is found not guilty of an offence, the judge must cause an order under Form 37 to be drawn up, pursuant to section 570(2) of the *Criminal Code*. If the accused is found guilty of an offence, then pursuant to section 570(1) of the *Criminal Code*, the judge must endorse the information, and upon request by either the Crown or defence, cause a conviction in Form 35 or an order in Form 36 to be drawn up. A memorandum of the conviction or order must also be made by the summary conviction court, pursuant to section 806(1) of the *Criminal Code*. If there is a conviction, then sentencing may proceed immediately or may be adjourned to a later date.

The defence paralegal should be cognizant of the rule against multiple convictions, known as the ***Kienapple* principle**, after the Supreme Court of Canada's decision in *Kienapple v R*, [1975] 1 SCR 729. The *Kienapple* principle holds that when an accused is found guilty of two or more offences arising out of the same transaction, and the elements of the offences are substantially the same, the accused should only be convicted of the most serious offence. The other charges should be stayed by the court.

In order for this principle to apply, there must be a factual and a legal connection between the charges. A factual connection means that the charges arise from the same transaction. A legal connection means that the offences are made out from one wrongful act. However, the *Kienapple* principle is a common law one and can be overridden by Parliament if it expressly provides for multiple convictions to arise out of a single event or transaction. In this case, the provision would likely be subject to a Charter challenge.

> **EXAMPLE**
>
> **The *Kienapple* Principle: Impaired Driving and Driving over 0.08%**
>
> One night, Roger was pulled over by the police for driving erratically. He was charged with two offences: driving impaired and driving over 0.08 of blood-alcohol concentration. It is common for the police to charge an accused with both offences, as a person can be impaired at a much lower level than 0.08 and not be able to operate their motor vehicle. Therefore, if there is a problem with the Breathalyzer instrument or the breath samples obtained by the police, Roger may still be convicted of driving impaired but acquitted of driving over 0.08. However, if the Crown establishes its case beyond a reasonable doubt on both counts, the *Kienapple* principle would take effect, and the court would only enter a conviction against Roger on one of the counts. Typically, the Crown asks for a conviction to be entered on driving over 0.08, as it indicates that the accused was driving with a higher blood-alcohol concentration than if the accused were convicted of driving impaired.

# Section 810 Recognizance Orders

A section 810 recognizance order is commonly known as a **peace bond**. Section 810(1) of the *Criminal Code* provides that when any person fears that another person will cause personal injury to himself or herself, or to his or her spouse, common law partner, or child, or will damage his or her property, the person may lay an information before a justice.

*Kienapple* **principle**
principle of law that states that when the accused is found guilty of more than one offence arising out of the same transaction, and the elements of the offences are substantially the same, the accused ought to be convicted of only the most serious offence, and the other offences should be stayed by the court

**peace bond**
recognizance order with conditions that the court orders an accused person to abide by when the complainant has reason to fear the accused

Section 810(2) provides that when a justice receives this information, he or she must cause the parties to appear before the court, and an adjudication of the matter must take place. The judge must be satisfied that the person who has brought the information before the court has reasonable grounds for his or her fears based on the evidence adduced at the hearing.

Under section 810(3)(a), the court may order the defendant to enter into a recognizance, either with or without sureties, with conditions that the defendant:

- keep the peace and be of good behaviour;
- abide by a weapons prohibition;
- surrender any weapons and authorizations, licenses, and registrations pertaining to the weapons;
- not have any direct or indirect contact or communication with the complainant, his or her spouse, or children; and
- not attend at or within a specified distance of where the complainant or his or her spouse or children may be found.

The maximum duration of a recognizance under this section is a period of 12 months. If the defendant refuses to enter into the recognizance, he or she may be committed into custody for a period not exceeding 12 months, under Form 23. Although the procedure for determining whether the defendant should be ordered to enter into a peace bond is similar to a trial, the burden of proof is much less. The complainant must only be able to show that he or she has reasonable grounds to fear the defendant. An application to have the accused enter into a peace bond may also be brought by someone on behalf of the complainant.

A trial judge has the power to have an accused person enter into a section 810 recognizance when the Crown has not proven its case beyond a reasonable doubt but when there is sufficient evidence that the complainant has reasonable grounds to fear the accused. An order requiring the accused to enter into a peace bond is not a conviction. Although the details of the recognizance are available to the police on the Canadian Police Information Centre (CPIC), it does not form a conviction on a record.

Section 810(4.1) of the *Criminal Code* permits an accused person to apply to have the conditions of the recognizance modified. A breach of the section 810 recognizance is treated as a *Criminal Code* charge of breaching a court order and is punishable as a hybrid offence. Therefore, a conviction for breach of a peace bond will result in a criminal conviction.

There is no jurisdiction for a court to order a youth to enter into a section 810 recognizance.

> **PRACTICE TIP**
>
> A peace bond may be an appropriate way to dispose of a charge under the *Criminal Code* for an accused person who does not have a prior criminal record. If an accused is charged with uttering threats or assault, and the incident is relatively minor in nature, the defence paralegal may attempt to convince the Crown to have the accused enter into a section 810 recognizance order in exchange for the charge to be withdrawn. This may be a perfectly acceptable resolution to a situation in which the complainant and the accused do not know each other and have no reason to have any future contact.

# CHAPTER SUMMARY

When an accused person has a minimal or no criminal record, he or she may be eligible to have his or her charge dealt with by way of a diversion program. If the accused fulfils the terms of the program, the Crown will either withdraw or stay the charge, and the accused will not have a criminal record.

Prior to the start of a trial, the charges are read to the accused; this is the arraignment process. A plea of guilty or not guilty is entered, and the plea is recorded by the clerk of the court.

However, before a plea is entered, the paralegal must discuss the prospects of an acquittal or a finding of guilt, as well as the implications and consequences of a guilty plea. The paralegal must obtain the client's instructions regarding a plea, the plea must be entered into voluntarily, and the accused must understand the nature and consequences of the plea.

At the trial, the Crown must present its case first. The Crown's witnesses are cross-examined by the defence. If the Crown has not established a *prima facie* case, the defence may bring a motion for a directed verdict of acquittal. If the Crown has established a *prima facie* case, the defence must decide whether or not to call evidence.

Some of the defences available to an accused include *de minimis non curat lex*, consent, self-defence, necessity, duress, automatism, and mistake of fact.

At the end of a trial, the judge renders a verdict. The *Kienapple* principle is the rule against multiple convictions and holds that when an accused faces two or more charges that arise out of the same transaction, have the same elements, and are the result of one unlawful act, the accused should only be convicted of the most serious offence.

Finally, section 810 of the *Criminal Code* allows a complainant to bring an information against a defendant when the complainant has reasonable grounds to fear the defendant. If the judge is satisfied that the reasonable grounds are established, the judge may order the defendant to enter into a recognizance to keep the peace and abide by other conditions. The recognizance is valid for one year, and breach of it may result in a charge against the defendant.

## KEY TERMS

air of reality test, 124
arraignment, 121
automatism, 131
*autrefois acquit*, 121
*autrefois convict*, 121
community justice worker, 120
consent, 125
*de minimis non curat lex*, 125
diversion program, 120
duress, 129
*Kienapple* principle, 133
mistake of fact, 132
necessity, 129
pardon, 121
peace bond, 133
rebuttal, 123
self-defence, 126
verdict, 123

## REVIEW QUESTIONS

### Short Answer

1. What is a diversion program?
2. Name the five possible pleas available to a defendant after the reading of the charge or charges.
3. What two things must a court be satisfied of before accepting the accused's guilty plea?
4. Under what circumstances would the accused enter into a section 810 recognizance order?

## Apply Your Knowledge

1. Anna has a sleep disorder that causes her to wake up to find herself in strange places with no memory of how she got there. Early one morning, Anna hears loud voices around her. When she opens her eyes, she finds a police officer and other people standing in front of her. The officer tells her that she is under arrest for mischief for causing damage to property. She has a can of spray paint in her hand and the wall in front of her is covered with graffiti. Several witnesses have observed her spray paint the wall, but Anna has no memory of this. Which defence would you consider bringing on Anna's behalf?

2. Barinder is annoyed at the woman standing in the "10 items or less" line at the grocery store. The woman has at least 20 items in her cart. Barinder tries to politely tell the woman that she should go to another line when the woman abruptly turns away from him. Barinder reaches out to touch the woman's shoulder. The woman uses her cell phone to call the police, and Barinder is charged with assault. Which defence would you bring on Barinder's behalf?

3. Carlos plays travel hockey. In a game against another team, Carlos cross-checks one of his opposing team members. Although his opponent has the puck, Carlos hits him a bit harder than required to get control of the puck. After the game, the other player calls the police and Carlos is charged with assault. Which defence would you consider in this situation?

4. Don is walking home from the bar at 2 a.m. He is walking along a dimly lit street and senses that someone is following him. Looking behind him, he sees a figure wearing a balaclava. As Don starts walking faster, the figure continues following him. Don looks back again to see that the person has pulled out a switchblade. Don runs to the nearest building and breaks the window, hoping that an alarm will ring and will scare the assailant. Don is successful—the assailant takes off in the other direction. However, the police arrive within minutes and charge Don with mischief for breaking the glass. Which defence would apply in this situation?

5. Eduard is at a grocery store on a busy Saturday morning. His cart is filled with groceries, and Eduard slowly makes his way to pay for the items. As Eduard is leaving, store security arrests him for shoplifting. At the bottom of Eduard's cart is a box of meat that he forgot to place on the conveyor belt. Is there a defence you could bring on behalf of Eduard?

6. Fatima has newly immigrated to Canada. All of her family members live in Cairo. A drug dealer in Cairo has threatened to kill Fatima's parents unless she helps the drug dealer and his cartel to import drugs into Canada. Fatima grudgingly cooperates, as she is fearful for her parents' safety. After the first shipment, Fatima is arrested for trafficking. Which defence could Fatima raise?

7. Gerald is sleeping one night when he hears the sound of breaking glass coming from his kitchen. He quickly grabs a baseball bat and runs into his kitchen. He finds two young males attempting to open the back door through the broken window panel. He shouts at them and hits one of the males on the shoulder with his bat. The two males take off running. The next day, police arrive at Gerald's house and arrest him for assault for hitting one of the males with the bat. Is there a defence that could apply in this situation?

# Sentencing and Appeals

# 9

## LEARNING OUTCOMES

After reading this chapter, you should be able to:

- Explain the steps that must take place prior to and at a sentencing hearing

- Outline the fundamental purpose and objectives of sentencing

- Discuss the various types of sentence that the court may impose on an offender

- Describe how criminal records are maintained in Canada

- Identify what may be appealed by a defendant in a summary conviction matter

# Introduction

In this chapter, we will take a detailed look at the sentencing process, which occurs after the offender enters a guilty plea or is convicted after a trial. The fundamental purpose and principles of sentencing under the *Criminal Code* will be examined, as well as the various types of sentences available to the court. The chapter concludes with a look at how criminal records are maintained in Canada and a brief discussion on summary conviction appeals.

# Sentencing Procedure

Section 720(1) of the *Criminal Code* indicates that as soon as practicable after a finding of guilt, the court must determine the appropriate sentence to be imposed. However, under section 720(2), sentencing may be delayed with the consent of the Crown and the defence in order to permit the offender to attend a treatment program. Examples of treatment programs include counselling for anger management, domestic violence, gambling, or substance abuse. Any treatment program must be provincially approved and judicially supervised. Sentencing may also be delayed for other reasons, such as to allow for victim input pursuant to section 722.2(2), or to allow the Crown or defence to call evidence at the hearing.

> **PRACTICE TIP**
>
> When the defence paralegal has instructions from the client to have the client enter a guilty plea to the charge or charges, and when from the facts of the case it appears that client would benefit from counselling, the paralegal should canvass whether the client would be willing to enroll in an approved treatment program prior to sentencing. Attending counselling of the client's own volition, as opposed to being ordered by the court to do so, may be viewed as a mitigating factor during sentencing.

At a sentencing hearing, both the Crown and the offender have an opportunity to make submissions with respect to the facts, pursuant to section 723 of the *Criminal Code*. The rules of evidence are somewhat relaxed at a sentencing hearing, in which any relevant evidence is admissible, subject to the judge's overriding discretion to require evidence and subject to the objections of the Crown or the defence. It should be noted that hearsay evidence is permitted during sentencing.

The court may also require production of evidence on any issue it deems to be necessary in determining the appropriate sentence. The court may compel any witness to appear in order to give evidence or assist the court in determining the appropriate sentence. When the facts are in dispute during sentencing, a **Gardiner hearing** would take place (see *R v Gardiner*, [1982] 2 SCR 368, 140 DLR (3d) 612). The party wishing to rely on a relevant fact has the burden of proving it, and each party has the ability to cross-examine a witness called by the opposing party. The provisions of a *Gardiner* hearing have been codified under section 724(3) of the *Criminal Code*.

It is also permissible for the Crown and the defence to proceed on an **agreed statement of facts** when the facts are not in dispute. If the Crown is relying on an aggravating fact, it must be proved beyond a reasonable doubt. The Crown is entitled to read in the offender's previous criminal record containing convictions and the sentences for those convictions, upon proof of the criminal record or acknowledgment by the offender.

*Gardiner* **hearing**
hearing to establish facts in dispute during a sentencing

**agreed statement of facts**
circumstances of the offence that are agreed upon by the Crown and the defence and are submitted before the court

## Pre-Sentence Report

Pursuant to section 721(1) of the *Criminal Code*, the sentencing court, the Crown, or the defence may request that a report be prepared by a probation officer to assist the court in imposing an appropriate sentence. This is referred to as a **pre-sentence report**. A pre-sentence report usually contains information on:

- the offender's age, character, attitude towards the offence, and degree of acceptance of responsibility;
- the offender's previous criminal record;
- any history of alternative measures used to deal with the offender; and
- any other information requested by the court.

> **pre-sentence report**
> report prepared by a probation officer after interviewing the accused and other sources for use in sentencing

The probation officer who prepares a pre-sentence report may interview the offender's supports in the community, including family members, teachers, or employers. The pre-sentence report does not include offences respecting the offender that are pending. The purpose of the pre-sentence report is to provide the court with a detailed background of the offender. It may be beneficial for the defence to request one when the Crown is seeking a period of incarceration and the defence is seeking a non-custodial sentence. Although the probation officer may express an opinion as to a suitable sentence, the court is not bound by the probation officer's recommendation. Once the report is complete, copies are sent to the Crown, the defence, and the court prior to the sentencing hearing. The court may require the probation officer to be in attendance in order to answer any questions posed by the parties.

## Victim Impact Statement

Section 722(1) allows for a **victim impact statement** to be completed and filed at the sentencing. For the purposes of this section, a victim is defined under section 722(4) as "a person to whom harm was done or who suffered physical or emotional loss as a result of the commission of the offence." When a victim is deceased, ill, or incapacitated, a person such as the spouse, common law partner, dependant, or relative of the victim may provide a victim impact statement on behalf of the victim. Under section 722.2(1), the court must inquire as to whether the victim of the offence has been advised of the opportunity to prepare a victim impact statement. The sentencing hearing may be adjourned to allow a victim to prepare a statement as long as the adjournment will not interfere with the administration of justice.

> **victim impact statement**
> written statement describing the harm or loss suffered by someone harmed by, or who has suffered physical or emotional loss as a result of, an offence

A victim impact statement is prepared in writing and is filed at the sentencing hearing. The victim may also read out the statement in court prior to it being filed. Even when a victim has not prepared a formal statement, he or she may be permitted to provide evidence to the court at sentencing. Although the statement may provide details as to the harm or loss suffered by the victim, the victim does not have any say in the actual sentence to be imposed on the offender. Copies of the victim impact statement must be provided to the Crown and to the defence.

## Joint Recommendations as to Sentence

**plea bargaining**
an agreement between the Crown and the defence in which the offender pleads guilty to a lesser charge, fewer charges, or in which the Crown proposes a reduced sentence

**joint submission**
a sentencing submission in which the Crown and defence recommend the same sentence for the judge's consideration

*quid pro quo*
a Latin term that stands for the proposition of something granted to a person in exchange for that person giving something up or doing something in return

As discussed in Chapter 6, the sentencing court is not bound by a joint recommendation as to sentence put forth by the Crown and the defence. However, **plea bargaining** is an essential aspect of the criminal justice system. Plea bargaining may result in a plea of guilty to a less serious charge, guilty pleas to certain charges with other charges withdrawn by the Crown, or the Crown and defence making a **joint submission** to the court as to what the appropriate sentence should be.

A plea bargain ensures that a finding of guilt is entered against the defendant and saves the victim or complainant from having to go through a trial. A plea bargain may also be offered by the Crown when there are weaknesses in the Crown's case and the Crown does not wish to take the risk of proceeding with a trial. Usually, the Crown makes some sort of concession in terms of the penalty that it is seeking against the offender as a form of *quid pro quo*. Without plea bargains in the criminal justice system, there would be significant delays in proceeding with matters before the court.

The sentencing judge typically gives more weight to a joint recommendation put forth by both parties when there is a substantial *quid pro quo* (*R v Wolonciej*, 2011 MBCA 91). An example of this may be when the Crown and defence provide a joint submission for the court to consider with a lenient proposed sentence in light of weaknesses in the Crown's case. Another example is when one of the Crown witnesses is unavailable to testify, and rather than attempting to adjourn the trial to another hearing date, the Crown and defence attempt to resolve the matter by proposing a joint submission as to sentence.

---

**EXAMPLE**

**A Joint Submission as to Sentence**

On the morning of Raoul's trial date, the Crown informs Raoul's defence paralegal that one of the Crown witnesses is in the hospital due to an injury and that the Crown will be seeking an adjournment of the trial date. Since Raoul is anxious to have the matter disposed of quickly, he tells his paralegal that he is willing to consider entering a guilty plea to the charge. The Crown's position on sentencing was originally a conditional sentence. However, in order to avoid having the matter adjourned again, both the Crown and defence decide to put forth a joint recommendation before the court for a fine plus probation.

---

In the examples above, the Crown would be willing to propose a more lenient sentence in light of the fact that there are problems with the case. In these circumstances, the sentencing court is less likely to stray from the joint submission unless the sentence is unfit, unreasonable, would bring the administration of justice into disrepute, or would be contrary to the public interest.

# Purpose and Principles of Sentencing

## Fundamental Purpose and Objectives

The fundamental purpose of sentencing is to promote respect for the law and the maintenance of a just, peaceful, and safe society, according to section 718 of the *Criminal Code*. This purpose is achieved through one or more of the following six objectives, as demonstrated in the figure below.

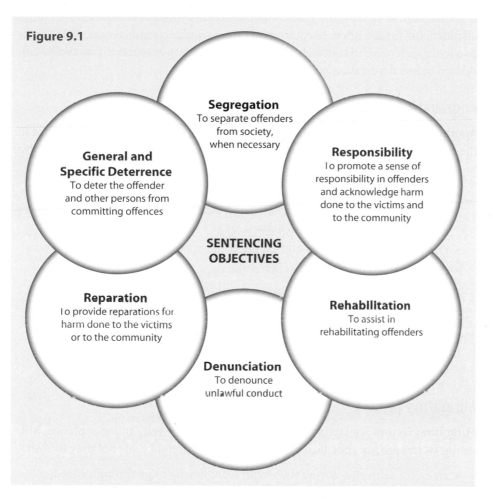

**Figure 9.1**

**Segregation**
To separate offenders from society, when necessary

**General and Specific Deterrence**
To deter the offender and other persons from committing offences

**Responsibility**
To promote a sense of responsibility in offenders and acknowledge harm done to the victims and to the community

**SENTENCING OBJECTIVES**

**Reparation**
To provide reparations for harm done to the victims or to the community

**Rehabilitation**
To assist in rehabilitating offenders

**Denunciation**
To denounce unlawful conduct

**general deterrence**
a sentencing principle aimed at discouraging the public from committing a similar offence

**specific deterrence**
a sentencing principle aimed at discouraging the particular offender from committing a similar offence

**segregation**
a sentencing principle aimed at separating offenders from society

**responsibility**
a sentencing principle aimed at holding offenders accountable for their actions

**rehabilitation**
a sentencing principle aimed at reforming offenders through treatment or programming

**denunciation**
a sentencing principle that is aimed at condemning or demonstrating disapproval of an offence committed or of the conduct of an offender

**reparation**
a sentencing principle aimed at having offenders make amends for harm or injury caused to a victim or to society

Although all of these sentencing objectives are of equal importance, the sentencing judge may give more weight to some objectives over others, depending on the circumstances of the case and of the offender. For certain categories of offences, such as offences against children or peace officers, the *Criminal Code* mandates that the court give primary consideration to the objectives of deterrence and denunciation, pursuant to sections 718.01 and 718.02.

## Fundamental Principle

The fundamental principle of sentencing, according to section 718.1 of the *Criminal Code*, is that the sentence must be proportionate to the seriousness of the offence and the degree of responsibility of the offender. In determining a proportionate sentence, the moral blameworthiness of the offender must be taken into account. A sentence must be individualized to the offender, even after parity is taken into account.

Section 718.2 of the *Criminal Code* outlines other sentencing principles to be taken into account, including a list of aggravating factors. Section 718.2(b) makes reference to parity, stating specifically that similar sentences should be imposed on similar offenders for similar offences committed under similar circumstances. This section also makes reference to restraint, noting that less restrictive sanctions should be considered before deprivation of liberty.

## Aggravating Factors

**aggravating factor**
circumstance that may increase the severity of the sentence imposed

**Aggravating factors** are factors that would increase the severity of the sentence for the offender. Aggravating factors specifically mentioned under section 718.2(a) include:

- evidence that the crime was motivated by bias, prejudice or hate based on race, national or ethnic origin, language, colour, religion, sex, age, mental or physical disability, sexual orientation, or any other similar factor;
- evidence that the offender abused his or her spouse or common-law partner;
- evidence of abuse of a person under the age of 18 years;
- evidence that the offender abused a position of trust or authority;
- evidence of the impact of the crime on the victim, with consideration of the victim's age, health, and financial situation;
- evidence of involvement with a criminal organization; or
- evidence that the offence was a terrorism offence.

## Mitigating Factors

**mitigating factor**
circumstance that may decrease the severity of the sentence imposed

**Mitigating factors** are factors that would reduce the severity of the sentence. Mitigating factors are not specifically listed under the *Criminal Code* but may include:

- an early guilty plea, saving the victim from having to go through a trial;
- remorse expressed by the offender;
- the offender's involvement in counselling or treatment;
- lack of criminal record;
- age of the offender;
- background of the offender, especially with respect to any mental or physical disability or hardship that contributed to the offence;
- formal apology made to the victim;
- restitution paid to the victim prior to sentencing; and
- the offender being gainfully employed.

It should be noted that substance abuse is not viewed as a mitigating factor (see *R v Ayorech*, 2012 ABCA 82).

## Aboriginal Offenders

Section 718.2(e) of the *Criminal Code* states that all available sanctions other than imprisonment should be considered, "with particular attention to the circumstances of aboriginal offenders." In the case of *R v Gladue*, [1999] 1 SCR 688, 171 DLR (4th) 385 [*Gladue*], the Supreme Court of Canada discussed the application of section 718.2(e), a provision created by Parliament to address the historical over-representation of Aboriginal offenders among those serving custodial sentences (see Case in Point: *R v Gladue*).

## CASE IN POINT

# Does Section 718.2(e) Apply to Aboriginal Offenders Who Do Not Reside in Aboriginal Communities?

*R v Gladue*, [1999] 1 SCR 688, 171 DLR (4th) 385

### Facts

Jamie Tanis Gladue was an Aboriginal woman who pled guilty to manslaughter for stabbing and killing her common law spouse. Gladue believed that the victim had been having an affair with her older sister. The accused had been drinking prior to the incident, and it was estimated that her blood alcohol content was between 155 and 165 milligrams of alcohol in 100 millilitres of blood. She was 19 years old and had a minimal criminal record. The victim had verbally provoked the accused prior to the attack.

The sentencing judge sentenced Gladue to three years of imprisonment, reasoning that although the offender was of Aboriginal status, she resided in an urban area off-reserve. The Court of Appeal dismissed Gladue's appeal, and she appealed to the Supreme Court of Canada.

### Decision

The Supreme Court took note of the fact that regardless of where the offender resides, the sentencing judge must be made aware of alternatives to incarceration. Even though Gladue did not live in a reserve, she could still avail herself of this section, because judges may take judicial notice of the broad systemic factors that affect Aboriginal people as a whole and of the importance that

Aboriginal cultures place on restorative justice. Accordingly, the Court stated that restorative justice principles must be considered alongside with traditional sentencing principles when dealing with Aboriginal offenders.

The Supreme Court of Canada outlined two issues for courts to consider when determining the sentence to impose upon an Aboriginal offender:

- the unique systemic or background factors that have played a part in bringing the offender before the court; and

- the appropriate types of sentencing procedures and sanctions because of the particular Aboriginal heritage or connection of the offender.

### Discussion Question

In *R v Ipeelee*, 2012 SCC 13, [2012] 1 SCR 433 [*Ipeelee*], a case in which the Supreme Court of Canada reaffirmed the principles in the *Gladue* decision, the only dissenting opinion was that of Justice Rothstein. Justice Rothstein stated that when an Aboriginal offender is a long-term offender and the safety of the public is at risk, the protection of the public is of paramount concern. When rehabilitation and segregation are both key objectives in sentencing, can these objectives be reconciled in any meaningful way?

In *Gladue*, the Supreme Court indicated that the guiding principles outlined were not meant to circumvent the traditional sentencing purposes and principles under the *Criminal Code*. The *Gladue* principle cannot be used to override a statutorily mandated sentence, such as a minimum period of incarceration set out for a particular offence. Unless the court is faced with a serious violent offence, a *Gladue* offender is more likely to receive a reduced sentence. The *Gladue* principle is considered by the sentencing court by ordering a pre-sentencing report, referred to as a "Gladue Report."

The Supreme Court of Canada confirmed the *Gladue* principles in *Ipeelee*, noting that courts have been hesitant to take judicial notice of the systemic and background factors affecting Aboriginal people in Canadian society.

# Types of Sentences

In this section, we will look at the various types of sentencing options that may be imposed for a summary conviction matter, ranging from the least severe to the most severe. These sentencing options include absolute and conditional discharges, suspended sentences/probation, fines, restitution, conditional sentences, and imprisonment.

## Absolute and Conditional Discharge

**absolute discharge**
when the accused is found guilty of an offence but is discharged without a probation order or conditions, and no conviction results

**conditional discharge**
when the accused is found guilty of an offence but is discharged with conditions placed on him or her, and no conviction results

**Absolute discharges** and **conditional discharges** are described in section 730 of the *Criminal Code*. For any offences that do not include a minimum punishment, or are not punishable by 14 years' imprisonment or by life imprisonment, the sentencing court may impose an absolute or conditional discharge if it is in the offender's best interests and not contrary to the public interest. A discharge is not equivalent to a conviction. Therefore, even though the offender has been found guilty of an offence or has entered a guilty plea to an offence, if he or she receives a discharge, no criminal conviction is entered on the record of the offender.

If the offender receives an absolute discharge, there are no conditions attached to it. This means that the offender is not placed on probation and does not have to do anything to satisfy any conditions.

If a conditional discharge is imposed, the offender is bound by a probation order and conditions are attached to the discharge. The conditions that may be ordered by the court are similar to those placed on a probation order (see discussion on Suspended Sentence/Probation). During the period of the conditional discharge (which may be up to a period of two years), if the offender is convicted of another offence, the discharge may be revoked and the offender may be convicted and sentenced on the original offence.

Once the duration of the conditional discharge has passed and the conditions have been followed successfully, the discharge becomes absolute. Even though a discharge is not a formal conviction, it does appear on a criminal record as a discharge. Typically, the court will only grant a discharge to an offender who is appearing before the court for the first time on an offence that is relatively minor in nature.

## Suspended Sentence/Probation

Probation is a sentencing option that may be imposed on its own by way of a **suspended sentence** or conditional discharge, or in combination with another penalty, such as a fine or a period of incarceration not exceeding two years. Section 731(1)(a) of the *Criminal Code* permits the sentencing judge to impose a suspended sentence with conditions as prescribed in the probation order when there is no minimum punishment attached to the offence.

The factors that are taken into account by the court are the age and character of the offender, and the nature of and circumstances surrounding the commission of the offence. If a suspended sentence is imposed, it is a stand-alone order, meaning that no other penalty may be imposed for the offence. A suspended sentence may be for a period not exceeding three years, after which point the court has discretion to re-sentence the accused, since a suspended sentence is not a final order. Probation is viewed as a rehabilitative measure as opposed to a punitive measure.

Section 732.1 refers to compulsory and optional conditions placed on a probation order. The compulsory conditions include:

- keeping the peace and being of good behaviour;
- appearing before the court when required to do so by the court; and
- notifying the court or the probation officer in advance of any change of name or address, and promptly notifying the court or probation officer of any change of employment or occupation.

The optional conditions of a probation order include:

- reporting to a probation officer within a specified time period and in the manner directed by the probation officer;
- remaining within the jurisdiction of the court unless written permission is obtained to leave the jurisdiction;
- abstaining from the consumption of alcohol, non-prescription drugs, or other intoxicants;
- abstaining from owning, possessing, or carrying a weapon;
- providing for the support or care of dependants;
- performing up to 240 hours of community service over an 18-month period;
- participating in a provincially approved treatment program (including the ignition interlock program and follow-up treatment as directed); and
- complying with other reasonable conditions as the court deems desirable.

The sentencing court is mandated to provide a copy of the probation order to the offender, explain the conditions of the order, explain the procedure for making changes to the optional conditions, and take reasonable steps to ensure that the offender understands the order. The probation order comes into effect on the date that it is made.

Either the Crown or the offender may bring an application to vary the conditions on a probation order. A probation order may also be transferred to another jurisdiction, such as when the offender moves to another province during the period of

**suspended sentence**
suspension of a jail sentence, in which the offender is placed on probation

probation. It should be noted that breaching a probation order is a hybrid offence under the *Criminal Code*. A template for a probation order is found in Form 46 of the *Criminal Code* and can be found in Appendix Q.

## Fines

Section 734 of the *Criminal Code* outlines the power of the sentencing court to impose a fine in addition to any other sanction that may be imposed. For summary conviction offences, section 787(1) of the *Criminal Code* dictates that the maximum fine is $5,000. For indictable offences, there is no upper limit on the amount of the fine. A fine may be imposed on its own or as part of a probation order. Typically, the Crown prefers that the fine be imposed as part of a probation order so that it is easier to enforce if the fine is not paid. If the fine is attached to a probation order, then the offender faces a breach of probation charge if the fine is not paid.

When an offender is fined, a term of imprisonment in default of the fine is calculated. For a summary conviction offence, the term of imprisonment in default is no more than six months, for obvious reasons. However, before the court will impose a fine, it must inquire into the offender's ability to pay the fine, pursuant to section 734(2) of the *Criminal Code*. Section 734.1 provides that a fine order must set out:

- the amount of the fine;
- the manner in which the fine is to be paid;
- the time by which the total fine or a portion of it is to be paid; and
- any other terms that the court deems to be appropriate.

An offender is deemed to be in default of the fine when it has not been paid in full by the date specified in the order. A copy of the fine order must be provided to the offender with the payment conditions explained by the court, as well as an explanation of the fine option program.

Provision for a fine option program is set out under section 736(1) of the *Criminal Code*, which states that the offender may earn credits toward the fine for work performed in a program established by the provincial government. The program must determine the rate at which credits are earned. Examples of government programs may include building habitats or other non-profit projects.

If an offender is in default of the fine, section 734.5 of the *Criminal Code* permits the province to refuse to renew a licence or a permit if part of the proceeds of the fine are to be paid to the province. Non-payment of a fine is also enforceable as a judgment in any civil court with jurisdiction. Under section 734.7 of the *Criminal Code*, the court may also issue a warrant of committal for an offender who is in default of payment.

## Restitution

**restitution**
financial compensation for injury or loss to a victim

For offences that cause a victim to suffer damages or loss, pursuant to section 738 of the *Criminal Code*, the court may order the offender to pay **restitution**, either upon request by the Crown or on its own motion. Restitution may be ordered as follows:

- for damage, loss, or destruction of property;
- for pecuniary damages, including loss of income or support, when there is bodily or psychological harm;
- for basic expenses to the offender's spouse and/or children, when the offence involves bodily or psychological harm to the spouse or children; and
- for costs to re-establish identification, credit history, and credit rating, when the offence involves identity theft.

Unpaid restitution orders may be entered as civil judgments.

## Victim Surcharge

A victim surcharge is payable in addition to any other punishment imposed on the offender, pursuant to section 737(1) of the *Criminal Code*. The surcharge amounts to 30 percent of any fine imposed on an offender, or if no fine is imposed, the surcharge amounts to $100 for a summary conviction offence. However, the court may increase the victim surcharge when the court considers it to be appropriate under the circumstances and when the court is satisfied that the accused is able to pay the higher amount. If the offender is able to establish that he or she would suffer undue hardship from having to pay the victim surcharge, the judge may exempt the offender from having to pay it. As with fines, the amount of the victim surcharge must be specified, along with the manner of payment, the time to pay, and the procedure for applying for a change in the terms of payment. The fine option program does not apply to the victim surcharge.

## Conditional Sentences

A **conditional sentence** is a sentence of imprisonment of two years or less that is served in the community. The offender must abide by conditions imposed by the court for the duration of the sentence and is closely monitored by a supervisor. The conditions are typically more restrictive than those in a probation order. For example, the offender may be bound by a condition that he or she shall not leave his or her residence without prior authorization from the supervisor—hence the commonly known term "house arrest."

A conditional sentence order is only handed out to offenders who do not pose a significant threat to the public. It is not available for offences for which there is a mandatory minimum period of incarceration or offences that are punishable by a maximum penalty of ten years or life imprisonment. As of November 2012, changes have been made to the *Criminal Code* to confine conditional sentences to less serious offences. Specifically, conditional sentences are not available for offences involving bodily harm, drugs, weapons, or any offences punishable by a minimum term of imprisonment (which covers all types of sexual offences involving children), as well as other categories of offences prosecuted by way of indictment.

As with probation orders, conditional sentence orders contain both compulsory conditions and optional conditions, pursuant to section 742.3 of the *Criminal Code*. Compulsory conditions include:

**conditional sentence**
jail sentence of no longer than two years that is served in the community

- keeping the peace and being of good behaviour;
- appearing before the court when required to do so by the court;
- reporting to a supervisor within two working days or as directed by the court, and thereafter as required and in the manner directed by the supervisor;
- remaining within the jurisdiction of the court unless written permission is obtained to leave the jurisdiction from the court or the supervisor; and
- notifying the court or the supervisor in advance of any change of name or address and promptly notifying the court or supervisor of any change of employment or occupation.

Optional conditions on a conditional sentence order may include:

- abstaining from the consumption of alcohol, non-prescription drugs, or other intoxicants;
- abstaining from owning, possessing, or carrying a weapon;
- providing for the support or care of dependants;
- performing up to 240 hours of community service over an 18-month period;
- participating in a provincially approved treatment program; and
- complying with reasonable conditions as directed by the court in order to secure the good conduct of the offender and to prevent a repetition of the same or other offences.

The court must explain the conditions and the procedure to apply to vary the optional conditions. The supervisor may also propose changes to the conditional sentence order, with written notification given to the offender, the Crown, and the court. If the changes are not agreed to by all parties, a hearing must take place before the original sentencing judge. A conditional sentence order may be transferred to another province, but only with the consent of the attorney general of the transferring province.

If the offender breaches a term of the conditional sentence, a hearing must take place within 30 days of the arrest or as soon as practicable. A written report from the offender's conditional sentence supervisor, along with written and signed witness statements, may form the evidence at the hearing, although the offender is entitled to seek leave to cross-examine the supervisor and witnesses. If the offender is in custody on a new charge, the conditional sentence is suspended during the period of imprisonment for the new offence.

For a breach of a conditional sentence order, the court has wide powers to take no action, change the optional conditions, suspend the conditional sentence and order the offender to serve a portion of the unexpired sentence in custody, or terminate the conditional sentence and order the offender to serve the remainder of the sentence in custody.

## Imprisonment

Imprisonment is the most severe sanction that can be imposed on an offender in Canada. Sentences of imprisonment that are two years or longer are served at federal penitentiaries, whereas sentences of two years less one day are served at provincial prisons. Since summary conviction matters are punishable by a maximum term of six months imprisonment, we will look at the different ways in which this jail term may be served.

Section 732(1) permits the court to impose an **intermittent sentence** when the sentence of imprisonment is for 90 days or less. An intermittent sentence requires the offender to serve the sentence during the dates and times specified in the order. An intermittent sentence may require the offender to report to the jail at 6 p.m. on a Friday night and serve the sentence until Monday morning at 6 a.m. for each weekend until the sentence is complete. During the time that the offender is not serving jail time, he or she is bound by a probation order.

**intermittent sentence**
sentence of incarceration of 90 days or less, to be served during days and times specified in the order

Factors that the court takes into account in determining whether or not to grant an intermittent sentence are the age and character of the offender, the nature and circumstances surrounding the commission of the offence, and the availability of accommodations to ensure that an intermittent sentence can be complied with. Typically, an intermittent sentence is granted to offenders who are employed and would lose their employment if they were to serve jail time on consecutive days. If the offender is a caregiver to family members, he or she may also be eligible for an intermittent sentence.

### Concurrent Versus Consecutive Sentences

If an offender is being sentenced on two or more offences, the court may decide whether to impose a **concurrent sentence** or a **consecutive sentence**. A concurrent sentence means that the offender is sentenced for two or more offences and serves the sentences at the same time.

**concurrent sentence**
sentence for two or more separate offences that are served at the same time

**consecutive sentence**
sentence for two or more separate offences that are served one after the other

---

**EXAMPLE**

**A Concurrent Sentence**

Harry is a habitual shoplifter and has numerous convictions on his criminal record for theft. Harry is being sentenced on one count of theft under $5,000 for shoplifting from a store and one count of mischief under $5,000 for scribbling graffiti on the store security officer's table after he was detained by the security officer. Harry receives a sentence of three months' jail on the theft charge and one month jail on the mischief charge, to be served concurrently. Therefore, the total length of time that Harry will serve is three months' jail.

---

A consecutive sentence means that the offender serves one sentence after the other one is complete. Using the above example, Harry would serve three months for the theft charge, then one month for the mischief charge, for a total of four months in jail. However, the totality principle, under section 718.2(c) of the *Criminal Code*, indicates that when consecutive sentences are imposed, the combined sentence should not be unduly long or harsh. If two or more offences were committed at the same time or were related, then the court may impose a concurrent sentence. On the other hand, if the offences were committed on separate occasions and are unrelated, the court may impose a consecutive sentence.

### Credit for Pre-Trial Custody

Prior to 2010, sentencing judges had the discretion to grant double credit for any time spent in custody on a pre-trial basis. In rare cases, judges had the discretion to grant triple credit for exceptional cases in which pre-trial detention conditions were proven to be difficult. The rationale behind giving two-for-one or three-for-one credit was based on the fact that remand facilities are harsher than prisons and penitentiaries. However, the federal government passed the *Truth in Sentencing Act*, SC 2009, c 29, which came into effect in February 2010 and is now legislated as section 719(3) of the *Criminal Code*. Section 719(3) indicates that the court may only grant credit for any time spent in pre-trial custody on a one-to-one basis. For example, if an offender has spent 30 days in jail prior to sentencing and receives a sentence of 60 days in jail, credit will be granted for the 30 days spent in jail before the sentencing. Therefore, the offender will only serve 30 additional days in jail. Before the *Truth in Sentencing Act* was passed, the offender would receive double credit for the 30 days of pre-trial custody and would therefore serve no additional time in jail.

Section 719(3.1) permits the court to rely on an exception if the circumstances warrant—to permit credit for one and one-half days for each day spent in pre-trial custody. The court must provide reasons on the record for any credit given to pre-trial custody. However, if the offender has a lengthy criminal record and has been denied bail as a result, or if the offender has breached conditions of bail, he or she may not be able to rely on this provision to gain one and one-half days' credit for the detention period. Since these are fairly new legislative changes under the *Criminal Code*, it remains to be seen how judges will exercise their discretion in the allocation of credit toward pre-trial custody.

### Earned Remission

Inmates serving sentences in prisons are permitted to accumulate a specific number of days of earned remission to reduce their time spent in custody. Typically, if an inmate is of good behaviour and abides by the rules and regulations of the institution, then he or she may be eligible for release after serving two thirds of the sentence. Participating in programming may count toward remission, whereas violations of regulations or negative behaviour may result in the loss of earned remission.

### Parole Eligibility

Offenders serving sentences of two years less one day imprisonment are governed by the Ontario Parole Board. Inmates who are serving sentences of more than six months are automatically considered for **parole**, or early release, after serving one third of their sentence. For offenders serving a sentence of less than six months, an application must be made in writing to be considered for parole.

**parole**
provisional release of a prisoner prior to the completion of the entire sentence

# Criminal Records

In Canada, criminal records are maintained by the Canadian Police Information Centre (CPIC). CPIC contains records of all convictions for which a pardon has not been granted, all charges regardless of disposition, outstanding warrants and charges, and all judicial orders. Although absolute and conditional discharges are not convictions, they are maintained on CPIC until after the discharge period has ended. Cases that have ended in an acquittal or cases in which charges have been withdrawn or stayed also remain in the system until they are purged after a set period of time.

Local police services have their own databases for keeping track of persons with whom they have come into contact. Information entered into a local police service's system cannot be accessed by another police service unless that information is also entered into the CPIC database. CPIC information may be viewed by all levels of law enforcement and some government departments and agencies, although there are varying degrees of access to the database.

People who have been convicted of a crime, have finished serving their sentence, and have demonstrated that they have not been re-involved with the criminal justice system may apply for a **record suspension** (formerly known as a pardon) under the *Criminal Records Act*, RSC 1985, c C-47. A record suspension sets aside the applicant's criminal record so that the person may apply for employment and educational opportunities without having to provide details about their conviction. A record suspension removes the conviction from CPIC, but it does not erase the conviction.

Not all offences are eligible for a record suspension, and under section 4(1) of the *Criminal Records Act*, there is a waiting period after conviction before an application may be made. For summary conviction offences, the waiting period is five years after the completion of the sentence. For indictable offences, the waiting period is ten years after the completion of the sentence. Applications are made to the Parole Board of Canada, and a fee is involved. Record suspensions may also be revoked by the Parole Board of Canada if the person is convicted of another offence or is found to have provided false information.

**record suspension**
status that allows people who have been convicted of an offence but have served their sentence and demonstrated their ability to abide by the law to have their criminal record kept separate and apart from other criminal records

## Summary Conviction Appeals

Summary conviction appeals are governed by section 813 of the *Criminal Code*. A defendant in a criminal matter may appeal from:

- a conviction or order;
- a sentence; or
- a verdict of unfit to stand trial or not criminally responsible on account of mental disorder.

The Crown may appeal from:

- an order staying proceedings or dismissing an information;
- a sentence passed on the defendant; or
- a verdict of not criminally responsible on account of mental disorder or unfit to stand trial.

A notice of appeal must be filed pursuant to the rules of the appellate court in that province. The time limit to file an appeal of a summary conviction matter is set out under section 830(3) of the *Criminal Code*, which indicates that the notice of appeal must be filed within 30 days of the conviction.

The powers of the appeal court are outlined under section 834(1). The appeal court may:

- either affirm, reverse, or modify the conviction, judgment, order, or verdict; or
- send the matter back to the summary conviction court with the appeal court's opinion.

The appeal court may also make any order that it considers proper.

**PRACTICE TIP**

Even though paralegals may not appear in Superior Court to deal with a summary conviction appeal, when a client clearly indicates that he or she wishes to appeal a conviction and/or sentence and is in the process of obtaining representation for the appeal, the paralegal should ensure that the trial or sentencing transcripts are ordered on a timely basis. When filing the notice of appeal, the appellant must include a certificate from the court reporter stating that copies of the transcript have been ordered.

# CHAPTER SUMMARY

Prior to sentencing, a pre-sentence report may be ordered by the Crown, by the defence, or by the court to assist the sentencing judge in determining the appropriate sentence. A victim impact statement is also completed by the victim and filed with the court. The Crown and defence may prepare an agreed statement of facts or propose a joint submission on sentence for the court's consideration.

The fundamental purpose of sentencing is to promote respect for the law and the maintenance of a just, peaceful, and safe society, which is accomplished through the objectives of denunciation, general and specific deterrence, segregation, rehabilitation, reparation, and acceptance of responsibility. The fundamental principle of sentencing is proportionality between the seriousness of the offence and the moral blameworthiness of the offender. The court may take into account both aggravating and mitigating factors in arriving at an appropriate sentence.

The various types of sentencing options available to the court include an absolute or conditional discharge, a suspended sentence, a fine, an order for restitution, a conditional sentence order, or a term of imprisonment. Both the defendant and the Crown may appeal from a conviction or an acquittal, a sentence, or a verdict of fitness to stand trial.

Criminal records are maintained by CPIC. Information pertaining to convictions, warrants, charges, and judicial orders are kept in the database. Various law enforcement and some government agencies have access to CPIC.

An accused person in a summary conviction matter may appeal a conviction, a sentence, or a verdict of unfit to stand trial or not criminally responsible on account of mental disorder. The Crown may appeal an acquittal, a sentence, or a verdict of unfit to stand trial or not criminally responsible on account of mental disorder. A notice of appeal must be filed within 30 days of the conviction.

# KEY TERMS

absolute discharge, 144
aggravating factor, 142
agreed statement of facts, 138
concurrent sentence, 149
conditional discharge, 144
conditional sentence, 147
consecutive sentence, 149
denunciation, 141
*Gardiner* hearing, 138
general deterrence, 141
intermittent sentence, 149
joint submission, 140
mitigating factor, 142
parole, 150
plea bargaining, 140
pre-sentence report, 139
*quid pro quo*, 140
record suspension, 151
rehabilitation, 141
reparation, 141
responsibility, 141
restitution, 146
segregation, 141
specific deterrence, 141
suspended sentence, 145
victim impact statement, 139

# REVIEW QUESTIONS

## Short Answer

1. Describe how aggravating and mitigating factors affect sentencing, and provide examples of each.

2. What information is included in a pre-sentence report?

3. What is the fundamental purpose of sentencing under the *Criminal Code*?

4. What is the fundamental principle of sentencing under the *Criminal Code*?

5. What are the six objectives of sentencing under the *Criminal Code*?

## Apply Your Knowledge

1. Hareem is a 20-year-old client who is charged with shoplifting. Her record is minimal—four years ago, she was arrested for joyriding. The charge was sent for diversion, as she was a youth. The circumstances surrounding this theft charge are as follows: Hareem took a loaf of bread and a package of lunch meat. Hareem tells you that she took the items in order to be able to feed her younger brother. Hareem ran away from home when she turned 18, and now she is responsible for supporting her younger brother, who lives with her. The items were recovered almost immediately by store security, so there was no loss involved. Hareem is very upset, as she has just been accepted to the two-year paralegal diploma program at a local college. Based on these facts, as Hareem's defence paralegal, what sentence would you propose to the court? Identify the objective(s) of sentencing that would be met by your proposal.

2. Ingrid is a 52-year-old client who has just been convicted of assault against her common law boyfriend. Her criminal record consists of recent convictions for uttering threats and prior assaults against the same victim. You are fairly certain that you will not be able to keep Ingrid out of jail this time. Ingrid's mother suffers from a visual impairment and lives with Ingrid. Ingrid tells you that she cannot afford to hire a caregiver to look after her mother if she has to go to jail. Based on these facts, as Ingrid's defence paralegal, what sentence would you propose to the court? Identify the objective(s) of sentencing that would be met by your proposal.

3. Jason is a 30-year-old client charged with fraud. He stole money from a petty cash fund at a car dealership where he used to work. He has since been fired. Jason tells you that he took the money in order to pay off a gambling debt. Jason does not have a previous criminal record, but given that he used his position at the dealership in order to cover up his tracks, you realize that this is a fairly serious incident. Jason has had a long-standing problem with gambling and has no savings as a result. Jason owes $3,000 to the dealership. Based on these facts, as Jason's paralegal, what sentence would you propose to the court? Identify the objective(s) that would be met by your proposal.

# Appendixes

# *Law Society Act*, RSO 1990, c L.8, By-law 4, Section 6(2)

A

## Scope of activities, Class P1, Activities authorized

6(2)  Subject to any terms, conditions, limitations or restrictions imposed on the class of licence or on the licensee and subject to any order made under the Act, a licensee who holds a Class P1 licence is authorized to do any of the following:

1. Give a party advice on his, her or its legal interests, rights or responsibilities with respect to a proceeding or the subject matter of a proceeding.
2. Represent a party before,
    i. in the case of a proceeding in the Small Claims Court, before the Small Claims Court,
    ii. in the case of a proceeding under the Provincial Offences Act, before the Ontario Court of Justice,
    iii. in the case of a proceeding under the Criminal Code, before a summary conviction court,
    iv. in the case of a proceeding before a tribunal established under an Act of the Legislature of Ontario or under an Act of Parliament, before the tribunal, and
    v. in the case of a proceeding before a person dealing with a claim or a matter related to a claim, before the person.
3. Anything mentioned in subsection 1(7) of the Act, provided the activity is required by the rules of procedure governing a proceeding.
4. Select, draft, complete or revise, or assist in the selection, drafting, completion or revision of, a document for use in a proceeding.
5. Negotiate a party's legal interests, rights or responsibilities with respect to a proceeding or the subject matter of a proceeding.
6. Select, draft, complete or revise, or assist in the selection, drafting, completion or revision of, a document that affects a party's legal interests, rights or responsibilities with respect to a proceeding or the subject matter of a proceeding.

# Template for Information,
# Form 2 of the *Criminal Code*

B

FORM 2

*(Sections 506 and 788)*

INFORMATION

Canada, Province of _____ , *(territorial division)*.

This is the information of C.D., of _____ , *(occupation)*, hereinafter called the informant.

The informant says that (*if the informant has no personal knowledge state that he believes on reasonable grounds and state the offence*).

Sworn before me this _____ day of

_____ , A.D. _____ , at .

_____
(*Signature of Informant*)

_____

A Justice of the Peace in and for _____

Note: The date of birth of the accused may be mentioned on the information or indictment.

Template for information,
Form 2 of the Criminal Code

# Canadian Charter of Rights and Freedoms, Sections 1, 7–14, and 24

C

## Constitution Act, 1982

Enacted as Schedule B to the *Canada Act 1982* (UK) 1982, c 11,
which came into force on April 17, 1982

### PART I
### CANADIAN CHARTER OF RIGHTS AND FREEDOMS

Whereas Canada is founded upon principles that recognize the supremacy of God and the rule of law:

### Guarantee of Rights and Freedoms

### Rights and freedoms in Canada

1. The *Canadian Charter of Rights and Freedoms* guarantees the rights and freedoms set out in it subject only to such reasonable limits prescribed by law as can be demonstrably justified in a free and democratic society.

• • •

### Legal Rights

### Life, liberty and security of person

7. Everyone has the right to life, liberty and security of the person and the right not to be deprived thereof except in accordance with the principles of fundamental justice.

### Search or seizure

8. Everyone has the right to be secure against unreasonable search or seizure.

### Detention or imprisonment

9. Everyone has the right not to be arbitrarily detained or imprisoned.

### Arrest or detention

10. Everyone has the right on arrest or detention
    (a) to be informed promptly of the reasons therefor;
    (b) to retain and instruct counsel without delay and to be informed of that right; and
    (c) to have the validity of the detention determined by way of *habeas corpus* and to be released if the detention is not lawful.

### Proceedings in criminal and penal matters

11. Any person charged with an offence has the right

(a) to be informed without unreasonable delay of the specific offence;

(b) to be tried within a reasonable time;

(c) not to be compelled to be a witness in proceedings against that person in respect of the offence;

(d) to be presumed innocent until proven guilty according to law in a fair and public hearing by an independent and impartial tribunal;

(e) not to be denied reasonable bail without just cause;

(f) except in the case of an offence under military law tried before a military tribunal, to the benefit of trial by jury where the maximum punishment for the offence is imprisonment for five years or a more severe punishment;

(g) not to be found guilty on account of any act or omission unless, at the time of the act or omission, it constituted an offence under Canadian or international law or was criminal according to the general principles of law recognized by the community of nations;

(h) if finally acquitted of the offence, not to be tried for it again and, if finally found guilty and punished for the offence, not to be tried or punished for it again; and

(i) if found guilty of the offence and if the punishment for the offence has been varied between the time of commission and the time of sentencing, to the benefit of the lesser punishment.

### Treatment or punishment

12. Everyone has the right not to be subjected to any cruel and unusual treatment or punishment.

### Self-crimination

13. A witness who testifies in any proceedings has the right not to have any incriminating evidence so given used to incriminate that witness in any other proceedings, except in a prosecution for perjury or for the giving of contradictory evidence.

### Interpreter

14. A party or witness in any proceedings who does not understand or speak the language in which the proceedings are conducted or who is deaf has the right to the assistance of an interpreter.

• • •

### Enforcement

### Enforcement of guaranteed rights and freedoms

24(1) Anyone whose rights or freedoms, as guaranteed by this Charter, have been infringed or denied may apply to a court of competent jurisdiction to obtain such remedy as the court considers appropriate and just in the circumstances.

**Exclusion of evidence bringing administration of justice into disrepute**

(2)  Where, in proceedings under subsection (1), a court concludes that evidence was obtained in a manner that infringed or denied any rights or freedoms guaranteed by this Charter, the evidence shall be excluded if it is established that, having regard to all the circumstances, the admission of it in the proceedings would bring the administration of justice into disrepute.

# Template for Information to Obtain a Search Warrant, Form 1 of the *Criminal Code*

D

FORM 1

*(Section 487)*

INFORMATION TO OBTAIN A SEARCH WARRANT

Canada, Province of _____ , *(territorial division)*.

This is the information of A.B., of _____ in the said *(territorial division)*, *(occupation)*, hereinafter called the informant, taken before me.

The informant says that *(describe things to be searched for and offence in respect of which search is to be made)*, and that he believes on reasonable grounds that the said things, or some part of them, are in the *(dwelling-house, etc.)* of C.D., of _____ , in the said *(territorial division)* *(Here add the grounds of belief, whatever they may be.)*

Wherefore the informant prays that a search warrant may be granted to search the said *(dwelling-house, etc.)* for the said things.

Sworn before me this _____ day of

_____ , A.D. _____ , at _____ .          _____

                                              *(Signature of Informant)*

_____

A Justice of the Peace in and for _____

# Template for Warrant to Search, Form 5 of the *Criminal Code*

E

FORM 5

*(Section 487)*

WARRANT TO SEARCH

Canada, Province of _____ _____ , *(territorial division)*.

To the peace officers in the said *(territorial division)* or to the *(named public officers)*:

Whereas it appears on the oath of A.B., of _____ that there are reasonable grounds for believing that *(describe things to be searched for and offence in respect of which search is to be made)* are in _____ at _____ , hereinafter called the premises;

This is, therefore, to authorize and require you between the hours of *(as the justice may direct)* to enter into the said premises and to search for the said things and to bring them before me or some other justice.

Dated this _____ day of _____ A.D. _____ , at _____ .

_____

A Justice of the Peace in and for _____

# Template for Appearance Notice Issued by a Peace Officer to a Person Not Yet Charged with an Offence, Form 9 of the *Criminal Code*

F

FORM 9

*(Section 493)*

APPEARANCE NOTICE ISSUED BY A PEACE OFFICER
TO A PERSON NOT YET CHARGED WITH AN OFFENCE

Canada, Province of _____ , (*territorial division*).

To A.B., of _____ , (*occupation*):

You are alleged to have committed (*set out substance of offence*).

1. You are required to attend court on _____ day, the _____ day of _____
A.D. _____ , at _____ o'clock in the _____ noon, in courtroom No.
_____ , at _____ court, in the municipality of _____ , and to attend
thereafter as required by the court, in order to be dealt with according to law.

2. You are also required to appear on _____ day, the _____ day of _____
A.D. _____ , at _____ o'clock in the _____ noon, at _____ (*police
station*), (*address*), for the purposes of the *Identification of Criminals Act*. (*Ignore if
not filled in.*)

You are warned that failure to attend court in accordance with this appearance notice is
an offence under subsection 145(5) of the *Criminal Code*.

Subsections 145(5) and (6) of the *Criminal Code* state as follows:

> "(5) Every person who is named in an appearance notice or promise to
> appear, or in a recognizance entered into before an officer in charge or
> another peace officer, that has been confirmed by a justice under section 508
> and who fails, without lawful excuse, the proof of which lies on the person, to
> appear at the time and place stated therein, if any, for the purposes of the
> *Identification of Criminals Act* or to attend court in accordance therewith, is
> guilty of

(*a*)  an indictable offence and liable to imprisonment for a term not exceeding two years; or

(*b*)  an offence punishable on summary conviction.

(6)  For the purposes of subsection (5), it is not a lawful excuse that an appearance notice, promise to appear or recognizance states defectively the substance of the alleged offence."

Section 502 of the *Criminal Code* states as follows:

"**502.**  Where an accused who is required by an appearance notice or promise to appear or by a recognizance entered into before an officer in charge or another peace officer to appear at a time and place stated therein for the purposes of the *Identification of Criminals Act* does not appear at that time and place, a justice may, where the appearance notice, promise to appear or recognizance has been confirmed by a justice under section 508, issue a warrant for the arrest of the accused for the offence with which the accused is charged."

Issued at _____ a.m./p.m. this _____ day of _____ A.D. _____ , at _____ .

_____
(*Signature of peace officer*)

_____
(*Signature of accused*)

# Template for Summons to a Person Charged with an Offence, Form 6 of the *Criminal Code*

# G

FORM 6

*(Sections 493, 508 and 512)*

SUMMONS TO A PERSON CHARGED WITH AN OFFENCE

Canada, Province of _____ , *(territorial division)*.

To A.B., of _____ , *(occupation)*:

Whereas you have this day been charged before me that *(set out briefly the offence in respect of which the accused is charged)*;

This is therefore to command you, in Her Majesty's name:

*(a)* to attend court on _____ , the _____ day of _____ A.D. _____ , at _____ o'clock in the _____ noon, at _____ or before any justice for the said *(territorial division)* who is there, and to attend thereafter as required by the court, in order to be dealt with according to law; and

*(b)* to appear on _____ , the _____ day of _____ A.D. _____ , at _____ o'clock in the _____ noon, at _____ , for the purposes of the *Identification of Criminals Act*. *(Ignore, if not filled in)*.

You are warned that failure without lawful excuse to attend court in accordance with this summons is an offence under subsection 145(4) of the *Criminal Code*.

Subsection 145(4) of the *Criminal Code* states as follows:

> "(4) Every one who is served with a summons and who fails, without lawful excuse, the proof of which lies on him, to appear at a time and place stated therein, if any, for the purposes of the *Identification of Criminals Act* or to attend court in accordance therewith, is guilty of

(*a*)  an indictable offence and is liable to imprisonment for a term not exceeding two years; or

(*b*)  an offence punishable on summary conviction."

Section 510 of the *Criminal Code* states as follows:

"**510.**  Where an accused who is required by a summons to appear at a time and place stated therein for the purposes of the *Identification of Criminals Act* does not appear at that time and place, a justice may issue a warrant for the arrest of the accused for the offence with which he is charged."

Dated this _____ day of _____ A.D. _____ , at _____ .


_____          _____

A Justice of the Peace in and for _____ *or* Judge

# Template for Promise to Appear, Form 10 of the *Criminal Code*

H

FORM 10

*(Section 493)*

PROMISE TO APPEAR

Canada, Province of _____ , *(territorial division)*.

I, A.B., of _____ , *(occupation)*, understand that it is alleged that I have committed *(set out substance of offence)*.

In order that I may be released from custody,

1.  I promise to attend court on _____ day, the _____ day of _____ A.D. _____ , at _____ o'clock in the _____ noon, in courtroom No. _____ , at _____ court, in the municipality of _____ , and to attend thereafter as required by the court, in order to be dealt with according to law.

2.  I also promise to appear on _____ day, the _____ day of _____ A.D. _____ , at _____ o'clock in the _____ noon, at _____ *(police station)*, *(address)*, for the purposes of the *Identification of Criminals Act*. *(Ignore if not filled in.)*

I understand that failure without lawful excuse to attend court in accordance with this promise to appear is an offence under subsection 145(5) of the *Criminal Code*.

Subsections 145(5) and (6) of the *Criminal Code* state as follows:

> "(5)  Every person who is named in an appearance notice or promise to appear, or in a recognizance entered into before an officer in charge or another peace officer, that has been confirmed by a justice under section 508 and who fails, without lawful excuse, the proof of which lies on the person, to appear at the time and place stated therein, if any, for the purposes of the *Identification of Criminals Act* or to attend court in accordance therewith, is guilty of

(*a*) an indictable offence and liable to imprisonment for a term not exceeding two years; or

(*b*) an offence punishable on summary conviction.

(6) For the purposes of subsection (5), it is not a lawful excuse that an appearance notice, promise to appear or recognizance states defectively the substance of the alleged offence."

Section 502 of the *Criminal Code* states as follows:

"**502.** Where an accused who is required by an appearance notice or promise to appear or by a recognizance entered into before an officer in charge or another peace officer to appear at a time and place stated therein for the purposes of the *Identification of Criminals Act* does not appear at that time and place, a justice may, where the appearance notice, promise to appear or recognizance has been confirmed by a justice under section 508, issue a warrant for the arrest of the accused for the offence with which the accused is charged."

Dated this _____ day of _____ A.D. _____ , at _____ .


_____

(*Signature of accused*)

# Template for Recognizance Entered into Before an Officer in Charge or Other Peace Officer, Form 11 of the *Criminal Code*

FORM 11

*(Section 493)*

RECOGNIZANCE ENTERED INTO BEFORE
AN OFFICER IN CHARGE OR OTHER PEACE OFFICER

Canada, Province of _____ , *(territorial division)*.

I, A.B., of _____ , *(occupation)*, understand that it is alleged that I have committed *(set out substance of offence)*.

In order that I may be released from custody, I hereby acknowledge that I owe $ *(not exceeding $500)* to Her Majesty the Queen to be levied on my real and personal property if I fail to attend court as hereinafter required.

*(or, for a person not ordinarily resident in the province in which the person is in custody or within two hundred kilometres of the place in which the person is in custody)*

In order that I may be released from custody, I hereby acknowledge that I owe $ *(not exceeding $500)* to Her Majesty the Queen and deposit herewith *(money or other valuable security not exceeding in amount or value $500)* to be forfeited if I fail to attend court as hereinafter required.

1. I acknowledge that I am required to attend court on _____ day, the _____ day of _____ A.D. _____ , at _____ o'clock in the noon, in courtroom No. _____ , at _____ court, in the municipality of _____ , and to attend thereafter as required by the court, in order to be dealt with according to law.

2. I acknowledge that I am also required to appear on _____ day, the _____ day of _____ A.D. _____ , at _____ o'clock in the _____ noon, at *(police station)*, *(address)*, for the purposes of the *Identification of Criminals Act*. *(Ignore if not filled in.)*

I understand that failure without lawful excuse to attend court in accordance with this recognizance to appear is an offence under subsection 145(5) of the *Criminal Code*.

Subsections 145(5) and (6) of the *Criminal Code* state as follows:

"(5)  Every person who is named in an appearance notice or promise to appear, or in a recognizance entered into before an officer in charge or another peace officer, that has been confirmed by a justice under section 508 and who fails, without lawful excuse, the proof of which lies on the person, to appear at the time and place stated therein, if any, for the purposes of the *Identification of Criminals Act* or to attend court in accordance therewith, is guilty of

(*a*)  an indictable offence and liable to imprisonment for a term not exceeding two years; or

(*b*)  an offence punishable on summary conviction.

(6)  For the purposes of subsection (5), it is not a lawful excuse that an appearance notice, promise to appear or recognizance states defectively the substance of the alleged offence."

Section 502 of the *Criminal Code* states as follows:

"**502.**  Where an accused who is required by an appearance notice or promise to appear or by a recognizance entered into before an officer in charge or another peace officer to appear at a time and place stated therein for the purposes of the *Identification of Criminals Act* does not appear at that time and place, a justice may, where the appearance notice, promise to appear or recognizance has been confirmed by a justice under section 508, issue a warrant for the arrest of the accused for the offence with which the accused is charged."

Dated this _____ day of _____ A.D. _____ , at _____ .


_____

(*Signature of accused*)

# Template for Undertaking Given to a Peace Officer or an Officer in Charge, Form 11.1 of the *Criminal Code*

J

FORM 11.1

*(Sections 493, 499 and 503)*

UNDERTAKING GIVEN TO A PEACE OFFICER
OR AN OFFICER IN CHARGE

Canada, Province of _____ , (*territorial division*).

I, A.B., of _____ , (*occupation*), understand that it is alleged that I have committed (*set out substance of the offence*).

In order that I may be released from custody by way of (a promise to appear *or* a recognizance), I undertake to (*insert any conditions that are directed*):

(*a*) remain within (*designated territorial jurisdiction*);

(*b*) notify (*name of peace officer or other person designated*) of any change in my address, employment or occupation;

(*c*) abstain from communicating, directly or indirectly, with (*identification of victim, witness or other person*) or from going to (*name or description of place*) except in accordance with the following conditions: (*as the peace officer or other person designated specifies*);

(*d*) deposit my passport with (*name of peace officer or other person designated*);

(*e*) to abstain from possessing a firearm and to surrender to (*name of peace officer or other person designated*) any firearm in my possession and any authorization, licence or registration certificate or other document enabling the acquisition or possession of a firearm;

(*f*) report at (*state times*) to (*name of peace officer or other person designated*);

(*g*) to abstain from

    (i) the consumption of alcohol or other intoxicating substances, or

    (ii) the consumption of drugs except in accordance with a medical prescription; and (*h*)  comply with any other conditions that the peace officer or officer in charge considers necessary to ensure the safety and security of any victim of or witness to the offence.

I understand that I am not required to give an undertaking to abide by the conditions specified above, but that if I do not, I may be kept in custody and brought before a justice so that the prosecutor may be given a reasonable opportunity to show cause why I should not be released on giving an undertaking without conditions.

I understand that if I give an undertaking to abide by the conditions specified above, then I may apply, at any time before I appear, or when I appear, before a justice pursuant to (a promise to appear *or* a recognizance entered into before an officer in charge or another peace officer), to have this undertaking vacated or varied and that my application will be considered as if I were before a justice pursuant to section 515 of the *Criminal Code*.

I also understand that this undertaking remains in effect until it is vacated or varied.

I also understand that failure without lawful excuse to abide by any of the conditions specified above is an offence under subsection 145(5.1) of the *Criminal Code*.

Subsection 145(5.1) of the *Criminal Code* states as follows:

> "(5.1)  Every person who, without lawful excuse, the proof of which lies on the person, fails to comply with any condition of an undertaking entered into pursuant to subsection 499(2) or 503(2.1)
>
> (*a*)  is guilty of an indictable offence and is liable to imprisonment for a term not exceeding two years; or
>
> (*b*)  is guilty of an offence punishable on summary conviction."

Dated this _____ day of _____ A.D. _____ , at _____ .

_____

(*Signature of accused*)

# Template for Subpoena to a Witness, Form 16 of the *Criminal Code*

K

FORM 16

*(Section 699)*

SUBPOENA TO A WITNESS

Canada, Province of _____ , (*territorial division*).

To E.F., of _____ , (*occupation*);

Whereas A.B. has been charged that (*state offence as in the information*), and it has been made to appear that you are likely to give material evidence for (the prosecution *or* the defence);

This is therefore to command you to attend before (*set out court or justice*), on the _____ day of _____ A.D. _____ , at _____ o'clock in the _____ noon at _____ to give evidence concerning the said charge.*

*\*Where a witness is required to produce anything, add the following:*

and to bring with you anything in your possession or under your control that relates to the said charge, and more particularly the following: (*specify any documents, objects or other things required*).

Dated this _____ day of _____ A.D. _____ , at _____ .

_____

A Judge, Justice *or* Clerk of the Court

(*Seal, if required*)

# Template for Warrant for Witness, Form 17 of the *Criminal Code*

FORM 17

*(Sections 698 and 705)*

WARRANT FOR WITNESS

Canada, Province of _____ , *(territorial division)*.

To the peace officers in the *(territorial division)*:

Whereas A.B. of _____ , has been charged that *(state offence as in the information)*;

And Whereas it has been made to appear that E.F. of _____ , hereinafter called the witness, is likely to give material evidence for (the prosecution *or* the defence) and that*

*Insert whichever of the following is appropriate*:

(*a*) the said E.F. will not attend unless compelled to do so;

(*b*) the said E.F. is evading service of a subpoena;

(*c*) the said E.F. was duly served with a subpoena and has neglected (to attend at the time and place appointed therein *or* to remain in attendance);

(*d*) the said E.F. was bound by a recognizance to attend and give evidence and has neglected (to attend *or* to remain in attendance).

This is therefore to command you, in Her Majesty's name, to arrest and bring the witness forthwith before *(set out court or justice)* to be dealt with in accordance with section 706 of the *Criminal Code*.

Dated this _____ day of _____ A.D. _____ , at _____ .

_____
A Justice *or* Clerk of the Court

*(Seal, if required)*

# Criminal Rules of the Ontario Court of Justice, SI/2012-30

M

### RULE 1—GENERAL

**Fundamental objective**

1.1(1) The fundamental objective of these rules is to ensure that proceedings in the Ontario Court of Justice are dealt with justly and efficiently.

(2) Dealing with proceedings justly and efficiently includes

(a) dealing with the prosecution and the defence fairly;

(b) recognizing the rights of the accused;

(c) recognizing the interests of witnesses; and

(d) scheduling court time and deciding other matters in ways that take into account

(i) the gravity of the alleged offence,

(ii) the complexity of what is in issue,

(iii) the severity of the consequences for the accused and for others affected, and

(iv) the requirements of other proceedings.

**Duty of counsel, paralegals, agents and litigants**

(3) In every proceeding, each counsel, paralegal, agent and litigant shall, while fulfilling all applicable professional obligations,

(a) act in accordance with the fundamental objective; and

(b) comply with

(i) these rules,

(ii) practice directions, and

(iii) orders made by the Court.

**Duty of Court**

(4) The Court shall take the fundamental objective into account when

(a) exercising any power under these rules; or

(b) applying or interpreting any rule or practice direction.

**Commentary**
Rule 1.1 reflects the crucial considerations that are to be borne in mind by the Court and the parties at each stage of the proceeding before the Ontario Court of Justice.

### Scope of rules

1.2  These rules apply to all proceedings before the Court.

#### Commentary

These rules apply to criminal proceedings in the Ontario Court of Justice, including those presided over by judges and justices of the peace. Examples of where these rules apply are where a judge hears a trial of an offence under the *Criminal Code* or *Controlled Drugs and Substances Act*, or where a judge or justice of the peace presides in a set date court for criminal charges, or hears a peace bond application or firearms application. These rules do not apply to provincial offences proceedings, such as where a judge or justice of the peace presides at a trial under the *Highway Traffic Act*.

### Definitions

1.3  In these rules,

"Charter" means the *Charter of Rights and Freedoms*;

"Code" means the *Criminal Code*;

"Court" means a judge of the Ontario Court of Justice, and includes a justice of the peace in a context where the Code allows a justice of the peace to act;

"proceeding" means a proceeding under the Code.

### RULE 2—APPLICATIONS

### Application

2.1(1)  An application shall be commenced by serving an application in Form 1 on the opposing parties and any other affected parties and filing it with proof of service.

### Contents of document

(2)  The application in Form 1 shall include
  (a)  a concise statement of the subject of the application;
  (b)  a statement of the grounds to be argued; and
  (c)  a detailed statement of the factual basis for the application, specific to the individual proceeding.

#### Commentary

The only document that the party who is bringing an application before the Court under these rules must use is a Form 1 application. It is important that the application in Form 1 is filled out completely, as this will assist the Court and the other parties in understanding the relief sought, and the reasons in support of the application.

### Transcripts

(3)  If determination of the application is likely to require a transcript, the applicant shall serve and file it with the application in Form 1.

### Commentary

Transcripts of court proceedings may be very important to the Court in deciding an application. For example, on an adjournment application the transcript may reveal that a previous adjournment was granted due to the absence of the Crown's witness, and on this occasion it is a defence witness who is unavailable. Transcripts are also important where a party seeks a stay of proceedings due to unreasonable delay under s. 11(b) of the Charter. Where a party requires a transcript, it is important that the procedures for ordering transcripts in the jurisdiction are followed, so that there is sufficient time for the court reporter to produce the transcript for the hearing of the application.

## Response

2.2(1)  A party responding to an application shall serve a response in Form 2 on the applicant and any other affected parties and file it with proof of service.

## Contents of document

(2)  The response in Form 2 shall include
    (a)  a concise statement of the party's reasons for responding to the application;
    (b)  a response to the applicant's grounds; and
    (c)  a detailed statement of the factual basis for the party's position, specific to the individual proceeding.

### Commentary

The adversary system requires the participation of two informed parties. A timely and detailed response by the responding party is essential. Otherwise, the appearance of fairly administered justice may be impaired. The only document that the party who is responding to an application before the Court under these rules must use is a Form 2 response. It is important that the response in Form 2 is filled out completely, as this will assist the Court and the other parties in understanding the relief sought, and the reasons in support of the response. The responding party must also include proof of service on the applicant and any other affected parties in its material.

## Additional material

2.3(1)  If the application in Form 1 complies with subrules 2.1(2) and (3), no additional material need be served and filed unless required by an order of a pre-trial or trial judge.

(2)  Applicants and responding parties may serve and file any additional factual and legal material that they consider appropriate and helpful to assist the Court, including
    (a)  a brief statement of the legal argument to be made;
    (b)  one or more affidavits;
    (c)  case law to be relied upon, other than well-known precedents; and
    (d)  an agreed statement of facts.

**Commentary**

Additional materials may be filed that will assist the Court to decide the application. These might include a copy of the information or charge document, an agreed statement of facts, affidavits, and written argument and case law, whereappropriate. It may also be necessary to have witnesses attend court (e.g., on an application for an adjournment of trial, a person who has firsthand knowledge of the reasons for the unavailability of the witness on the trial date). Where cases or legislation are filed, the relevant passage(s) should be indicated. There is no need to reproduce well known material, such as a section of the *Criminal Code*, or a well-known decision of the Supreme Court of Canada on unreasonable delay, such as *Askov*. Only materials that will be referred to by the parties in their submissions to the Court should be filed under this rule.

**Time for pre-trial applications**

2.4(1)  A pre-trial application shall be heard at least 60 days before trial, unless theCourt orders otherwise.

(2)  For the purposes of subrule (1), pre-trial applications include

(a)  procedural applications, such as applications for adjournments or withdrawal of counsel of record;

(b)  preparatory applications for matters that are necessary before proceeding to trial, such as disclosure, release of exhibits for testing or commission evidence;

(c)  applications for severance and for particulars;

(d)  applications for the appointment or removal of counsel; and

(e)  applications for a stay of proceedings for unreasonable delay under paragraph 11(b) of the Charter.

(3)  An application for a stay of proceedings for unreasonable delay under paragraph 11(b) of the Charter shall be brought before the assigned trial judge.

**Time for trial applications**

2.5(1)  A trial application shall be heard at the start of the trial or during the trial, unless the Court orders otherwise.

(2)  For the purposes of subrule (1), trial applications include

(a)  applications under the Charter, such as applications that

(i)  challenge the constitutionality of legislation,

(ii)  seek a stay of proceedings, except for unreasonable delay under paragraph 11(b) of the Charter, or

(iii)  seek the exclusion of evidence;

(b)  complex evidentiary applications, such as applications for the admission of

(i)  similar act evidence,

(ii)  evidence of a complainant's prior sexual activity, or

(iii)  hearsay evidence; and

(c)  applications for access to records held by persons who are not parties to the proceeding.

### Commentary

Trial applications can take many forms. For example, an application to exclude evidence at an impaired driving trial for a breach of the Charter is most commonly dealt with in a blended or combined Charter *voir dire* and trial. However, there are other trial motions which would benefit from being dealt with by the trial judge in advance of hearing the evidence at the trial. For example, an application for the admission of similar act evidence or for access to private records may be better heard in advance of the other evidence in the proceeding, as the outcome may require the parties to consider calling additional witnesses or affect a party's presentation of his or her case. Rule 2.5 is designed to balance the benefits of certainty as to how a complex issue should be addressed with flexibility to ensure that the fundamental objective set out in rule 1.1 is properly respected.

### Time for other applications

2.6  An application to which neither rule 2.4 nor rule 2.5 applies, such as an application made by a witness or by the media, shall be heard at least 30 days before the trial, unless the Court orders otherwise.

### Commentary

The applications described in rules 2.4, 2.5 and 2.6 relate to matters that must be dealt with in order to properly proceed with the trial, or will affect the complexity of the trial and the time needed to complete it. These applications involve issues that should be apparent to the applicant well in advance of the trial, where prior notice to the responding party and the Court would promote the fundamental objective set out in rule 1.1. In general, where the applicant knows before the trial begins that a voir dire or admissibility hearing will be needed to tender certain evidence, there should be compliance with rule 2.5, unless otherwise ordered by a pre-trial or trial judge. Such an application will not be necessary for the routine tendering of documents, such as those for the admissibility of breath testing or drug certificates.

### Applications on consent

2.7(1)  Subject to subrule (2), an application in which all the parties are represented by counsel or by licensed paralegals may be dealt with on consent, without a hearing, if a party files a consent in Form 3.

(2)  If the Court is of the opinion that the application requires a hearing, a hearing date shall be ordered.

(3)  An application in which a party is not represented by counsel or by a licensed paralegal may be dealt with on consent if

   (a)  a party files a consent in Form 3;
   (b)  the self-represented party appears before the Court; and
   (c)  the Court is satisfied that the party understands the nature of the consent and the consequences of giving it.

**Commentary**

Parties are encouraged to consent to applications in a timely way in appropriate cases.

## RULE 3—SERVICE

### Times for service

3.1(1)  An application in Form 1 shall be served and filed with proof of service at least30 days before the date of the hearing of the application.

(2)  A response in Form 2 shall be served and filed with proof of service at least 15 days before the date of the hearing of the application.

### Exceptions

(3)  Despite subrules (1) and (2), the time periods set out in those subrules may be shortened or lengthened

(a)  by a local practice direction;

(b)  by an order of the Court; or

(c)  with the consent of the parties, except as described in rule 3.2.

**Commentary**

Timely notice of applications that are being brought under these rules is essential to the efficient management of trial proceedings. By way of example, if a stay of proceedings is granted for unreasonable delay under s.11 (b) of the Charter, the trial will not proceed, and the time scheduled for the trial will no longer be required. Determination of the application well in advance of the trial date permits the court time to be used for other matters. The general rule is that applications must be served and filed no less than 30 days before the date set for hearing the applications. Subrule 3.1 (3) provides exceptions to this, such as an order of the Court authorizing a different time period.

### Application for adjournment or to be removed from record

3.2  On applications for adjournment and applications to be removed from the record, shortening the time periods set out in subrules 3.1(1) and (2) requires the approval of the Court, in addition to the consent of the parties.

**Commentary**

Rule 3.2 provides that in limited circumstances, and where all the parties agree, the time for service of an application for adjournment or where counsel of record applies to be removed from the record, may be reduced by the Court. It is recognized that there are occasions where unexpected developments take place, such as the illness of a witness shortly before the trial date, or a breakdown in the lawyer- client relationship, and it is not possible to give as much notice as the rules require. In such cases, the parties should not wait until the trial date to bring the application, but instead bring the application as soon as the matter comes to their attention, and request that the Court permit the matter to be heard on short notice, with the consent of the other party.

## Methods of service

3.3(1)  Service under these rules may be made in person, by fax or by email, and hard copies of the documents served shall be filed.

## Electronic filing technology

(2)  If electronic filing technology is available and a practice direction authorizes its use, the documents may be served electronically, filed electronically or both. When a document has been filed electronically, it is not necessary to file a hard copy, unless the Court orders otherwise.

## RULE 4—CASE MANAGEMENT

### Hearing and trial management

4.1  When conducting a hearing or trial, the Court has the power to make any order or direction in relation to the conduct of the proceeding that would assist in ensuring that it is conducted in accordance with the fundamental objective set out in rule 1.1.

> **Commentary**
> In light of the Law Society's *Rules of Professional Conduct*, the *Principles of Civility for Advocates* and decisions from the Supreme Court of Canada and Ontario Court of Appeal, trial judges possess, and are expected to exercise, trial management powers in order to ensure that the proceedings are conducted reasonably, fairly and in accordance with the interests of justice. A trial judge will not be a mere observer who must sit by passively allowing counsel to conduct the proceedings in any manner they choose. For our justice system to operate effectively, trial judges must have the ability to control the course of proceedings before them.

### Judicial pre-trial conference

4.2(1)  In this rule, "pre-trial" means a judicial pre-trial conference.
(2)  Before attending the pre-trial, it is desirable for the parties to
    (a)  meet in order to attempt to resolve issues; and
    (b)  review the file.
(3)  At the pre-trial, it is required that the parties have authority to make decisions on
    (a)  disclosure;
    (b)  applications, including Charter applications, that the parties will bring at trial;
    (c)  the number of witnesses each party intends to call at the preliminary inquiry or at trial;
    (d)  any admissions the parties are willing to make;
    (e)  any legal issues that the parties anticipate may arise in the proceeding;
    (f)  an estimate of the time needed to complete the proceeding; and
    (g)  resolution of the matter, if appropriate.

> **Commentary**
> Pre-trials are an important mechanism to provide the public with a speedy trial that focuses on the matters in issue. As such they are encouraged. A pre-trial held with Crown counsel should occur in advance of the judicial pre-trial, in order to focus agreements and admissions as well as the matters

in issue. For the convenience of the parties, a pre-trial may be conducted by telephone with the consent of the pre-trial judge. A pre-trial on the record is particularly helpful for parties not represented by a licensee as defined in the *Law Society Act*. The court procedures can then be explained, the position of the Crown counsel on the issues can be related, and the issues set out in subrule (3) above can be canvassed.

### Materials

(4)  At least three days before the pre-trial, the prosecutor shall give the pre-trial judge a copy of a synopsis of the allegations, unless a local practice direction provides otherwise.

(5)  If the defence gives the pre-trial judge additional material, it shall do so at least three days before the pre-trial, if possible.

### Communications technology

(6)  If the pre-trial judge agrees, the pre-trial may be held by telephone or by means of some other form of communications technology.

### Judicial directions

(7)  After hearing from the parties during the pre-trial, the pre-trial judge may take one or more of the following steps:

(a)  confirm or amend the estimates of the time required to hear the proceeding;

(b)  set timelines for the exchange of materials on applications to be heard, or for the completion of disclosure on matters to be set for trial or preliminary hearing;

(c)  set times for the hearing of applications; and

(d)  set a date for a further pre-trial, if required.

#### Commentary

The effective management of the proceeding requires the cooperation of all parties. Failure to properly advise the court of relevant issues at the judicial pre-trial or to provide proper notice of the matters under this rule has the effect of inconveniencing the public, the parties and the Court. As such, it is necessary to set guidelines or timelines. Failure to comply with such guidelines or timelines for the exchange of material and submissions may result in the matter not proceeding on the court date.

### Record of pre-trial agreements and admissions

(8)  At the completion of the pre-trial, any agreements or admissions may be signed or otherwise recorded, transcribed and attached to the information for the assistance of the trial judge.

### Focus hearing, preliminary inquiry

4.3(1)  A proceeding that is to have a preliminary inquiry shall have a hearing under section 536.4 of the Code if the preliminary inquiry judge so directs.

(2)  The hearing shall be attended by

(a)  counsel who will be conducting the preliminary inquiry, or another counsel designated by him or her with authority to make binding decisions; and

(b)  the accused, if he or she is self-represented.

## Materials

(3)  The party who requested the preliminary inquiry shall serve the following materials on the opposing parties, together with the statement of issues and witnesses required by section 536.3 of the Code, and file them with proof of service, at least three days before the hearing:

(a)  a list of witnesses whom the parties seek to have testify in person at the preliminary inquiry and, for each witness named in the list,

(i)  a brief synopsis of the expected evidence,

(ii)  an explanation of why in-person testimony is necessary, and

(iii)  an estimate of the time required to examine or cross-examine the witness;

(b)  a list of witnesses whom the parties propose to examine through a discovery process;

(c)  a brief statement as to whether committal for trial is in issue, and on what basis; and

(d)  a statement of admissions agreed upon between the parties.

### Commentary

The purpose of a focus hearing is to ensure that the process is streamlined and witnesses with non-contentious evidence are not inconvenienced or that non-contentious evidence is not unnecessarily called. If the parties cannot agree on the witnesses to be called or the manner of receiving their testimony, then a hearing on the record can be scheduled under s. 540 before the preliminary inquiry judge and may result in the judge making binding orders for the conduct of the inquiry.

## Absence of agreement

(4)  At the conclusion of the hearing, if the parties do not agree as to the witnesses to be called at the preliminary inquiry, either party may schedule a hearing in accordance with subsections 540(7), (8) and (9) of the Code.

## Discovery, preliminary inquiry

4.4(1)  At any time before committal for trial, the evidence of a witness may be taken by means of a discovery process if the parties and the preliminary inquiry judge agree.

## Official record

(2)  Evidence taken under subrule (1) forms part of the official record of the preliminary inquiry.

### Exception, vulnerable witness

(3) Subrule (1) does not apply to a witness who is

    (a) less than 18 years old; or

    (b) the complainant in a proceeding involving sexual or physical violence.

#### Commentary

The discovery process is most useful for expert or non-controversial witnesses. The discovery will take place on the record at the courthouse in a courtroom or motions room or in a location agreed to by the parties. The witness will be sworn and the evidence will be taken in the absence of the judge.

### RULE 5—PRACTICE DIRECTIONS, FORMS AND NON-COMPLIANCE

### Power to issue practice directions

5.1(1) The Chief Justice or his or her delegate may issue practice directions that are consistent with these rules.

(2) A practice direction may apply to the whole of Ontario, to one or more of the seven regions of Ontario designated by the Ontario Court of Justice or to one or more local offices within those regions.

(3) A practice direction does not come into effect before it is posted on the Ontario Courts website (www.ontariocourts.ca).

#### Commentary

Practice directions can address the issues and court culture of our regions and local courts. In creating practice directions the judiciary, in their discretion, will consult with local members of the justice community.

### Forms

5.2(1) The following forms, which are available on the Internet through www.ontariocourtforms.on.ca, shall be used where applicable and with such variations as the circumstances require:

Form 1 (Application)
Form 2 (Response)
Form 3 (Consent)

(2) The Chief Justice or his or her delegate may issue additional forms and require their use.

(3) A requirement to use an additional form does not come into effect before

    (a) the form and the requirement are posted on the Ontario Courts website (www.ontariocourts.ca); and

    (b) the form is available on the Internet through www.ontariocourtforms.on.ca.

### Power of Court to excuse non-compliance

5.3 The Court may excuse non-compliance with any rule at any time to the extent necessary to ensure that the fundamental objective set out in rule 1.1 is met.

**Commentary**

It is expected that the parties will be familiar with these rules of court and will comply with them. It is a professional obligation to do so. However, on rare occasions, there may be circumstances that prevent compliance. The Court in its discretion may excuse non-compliance with the rules to the extent required to ensure a fair hearing. Consequences may result from non-compliance, including dismissal of the application without a hearing on the merits.

## REPEAL AND COMING INTO FORCE

### Repeal

**Repeal**

6. The *Rules of the Ontario Court of Justice in Criminal Proceedings* are repealed.

### Coming Into Force

**July 1, 2012**

7. These rules come into force on July 1, 2012.

# Form 1, Application, *Criminal Rules of the Ontario Court of Justice*

N

**Form / *Formule* 1**
**APPLICATION**
***DEMANDE***

(Rule 2.1. *Criminal Rules of the Ontario Court of Justice*)
(*Règle 2.1. Regles de procedure en matiere criminelle de la Cour de justice de l'Ontario*)

ONTARIO COURT OF JUSTICE
*COUR DE JUSTICE DE L'ONTARIO*

Court File No. (if known)
*N° du dossier de la cour (s'il est connu)*

Region / *Région*

BETWEEN: / *ENTRE*

HER MAJESTY THE QUEEN / *SA MAJESTÉ LA REINE*

- and / *et* -

(defendant(s) / *défendeur(s)*)

1. APPLICATION HEARING DATE AND LOCATION
   *DATE ET LIEU DE L'AUDIENCE SUR LA DEMANDE*

   Application hearing date:
   *Date de l'audience sur la demande*

   Time:
   *Heure*

   Courtroom number:
   *Numéro de la salle d'audience*

   Court address:
   *Adresse de la Cour*

2. LIST CHARGES
   *LISTE DES ACCUSATIONS*

| Charge Information / *Renseignements sur les accusations* | | | |
|---|---|---|---|
| Description of Charge<br>*Description de l'accusation* | Sect. No.<br>*Article n°* | Next Court Date<br>*Prochaine date d'audience* | Type of Appearance (e.g. trial date, set date, pre-trial meeting, etc.)<br>*Type de comparution (p. ex., date de procès, établissement d'une date, conférence préparatoire au procès, etc.)* |
| | | | |
| | | | |
| | | | |
| | | | |

3. NAME OF APPLICANT
   *NOM DE L'AUTEUR DE LA DEMANDE*

4. CHECK ONE OF THE TWO BOXES BELOW:
   *COCHEZ LA CASE QUI CONVIENT CI-DESSOUS*

   ☐ I am appearing in person. My address, fax or email for service is as follows:
   *Je comparais en personne. Mon adresse, mon numéro de télécopieur ou mon adresse électronique aux fins de signification sont les suivants :*

   ☐ I have a legal representative who will be appearing. The address, fax or email for service of my legal representative is as follows:
   *J'ai un représentant juridique qui sera présent. L'adresse, le numéro de télécopieur ou l'adresse électronique de mon représentant juridique aux fins de signification sont les suivants :*

COR-OCJ-1 (rev. 04/12) CSD

APPLICATION
*DEMANDE*
(Rule 2.1, *Criminal Rules of the Ontario Court of Justice*)
*(Règle 2.1, Règles de procédure en matière criminelle de la Cour de justice de l'Ontario)*
PAGE 2

5. CONCISE STATEMENT OF THE SUBJECT OF APPLICATION
*BRÈVE DÉCLARATION DE L'OBJET DE LA DEMANDE*

(Briefly state why you are bringing the Application. For example, "This is an application for an order adjourning the trial"; "This is an application for an order requiring the Crown to disclose specified documents"; or "This is an application for an order staying the charge for delay.")
*(Expliquez brièvement pourquoi vous déposez la demande. Par exemple : « Il s'agit d'une demande d'ordonnance d'ajournement du procès. », « Il s'agit d'une demande d'ordonnance exigeant de la Couronne qu'elle divulgue les documents précisés. », ou « Il s'agit d'une demande d'ordonnance d'annulation de l'accusation pour cause de retard. »)*

6. GROUNDS TO BE ARGUED IN SUPPORT OF THE APPLICATION
*MOTIFS QUI SERONT INVOQUÉS À L'APPUI DE LA DEMANDE*

(Briefly list the grounds you rely on in support of this Application. For example, "I require an adjournment because I am scheduled to have a medical operation the day the trial is scheduled to start"; "The disclosure provided by the Crown does not include the police notes taken at the scene"; or "There has been unreasonable delay since the laying of the charge that has caused me prejudice.")
*(Énumérez brièvement les motifs que vous invoquez à l'appui de la demande. Par exemple : « J'ai besoin d'un ajournement parce que je dois subir une intervention médicale le jour prévu pour le début du procès. », « Les documents divulgués par la Couronne ne contiennent pas les notes de la police prises sur les lieux. » ou « Un retard excessif a suivi le dépôt des accusations qui m'a causé un préjudice. »)*

7. DETAILED STATEMENT OF THE SPECIFIC FACTUAL BASIS FOR THE APPLICATION
*DÉCLARATION DÉTAILLÉE DES FAITS PRÉCIS SUR LESQUELS SE FONDE LA DEMANDE*

8. INDICATE BELOW OTHER MATERIALS OR EVIDENCE YOU WILL RELY ON IN THE APPLICATION
*INDIQUEZ CI-DESSOUS D'AUTRES DOCUMENTS OU PREUVES QUE VOUS ALLEZ INVOQUER DANS LA DEMANDE*

☐ Transcripts  (Transcripts required to determine the application must be filed with this application.)
*Transcriptions  (Les transcriptions exigées pour prendre une décision sur la demande doivent être déposées avec la demande.)*

☐ Brief statement of legal argument
*Bref exposé des arguments juridiques*

☐ Affidavit(s)  (List below)
*Affidavits  (Énumérez ci-dessous)*

☐ Case law or legislation  (Relevant passages should be indicated on materials. Well-known precedents do not need to be filed. Only materials that will be referred to in submissions to the Court should be filed.)
*Jurisprudence ou lois.  (Les passages pertinents doivent être indiqués dans les documents. Les arrêts bien connus ne doivent pas être déposés. Il ne faut déposer que les documents qui seront mentionnés dans les observations au tribunal.)*

☐ Agreed statement of facts
*Exposé conjoint des faits*

☐ Oral testimony  (List witnesses to be called at hearing of application)
*Témoignage oral  (Liste des témoins qui seront appelés à témoigner à l'audience sur la demande)*

☐ Other  (Please specify)
*Autre  (Veuillez préciser)*

_____     _____
(Date)             Signature of Applicant or Legal Representative / *Signature de l'auteur de la demande ou de son représentant juridique*

To: _____
À :      (Name of Respondent or legal representative / *Nom de l'intimé ou de son représentant juridique*)

_____
(Address/fax/email for service / *Adresse, numéro de télécopie ou adresse électronique aux fins de signification*)

NOTE: Rule 2.1 requires that the application be served on all opposing parties and on any other affected parties.
*NOTA : La règle 2.1 exige que la demande soit signifiée à toutes les parties adverses et aux autres parties concernées.*

COR-OCJ-1 (rev. 04/12) CSD

# Form 2, Response, *Criminal Rules of the Ontario Court of Justice*

**Form / *Formule* 2**
**RESPONSE**
*RÉPONSE*

ONTARIO COURT OF JUSTICE
*COUR DE JUSTICE DE L'ONTARIO*

(Rule 2.2, *Criminal Rules of the Ontario Court of Justice*)
(*Règle 2.2, Règles de procédure en matière criminelle de la Cour de justice de l'Ontario*)

Region / *Région*

Court File No. (if known)
*N° du dossier de la cour (s'il est connu)*

BETWEEN: / *ENTRE*

HER MAJESTY THE QUEEN / *SA MAJESTÉ LA REINE*

- and / *et* -

(defendant(s) / *défendeur(s)*)

1.  NAME OF RESPONDENT
    *NOM DE LA PERSONNE INTIMÉE*

2.  CHECK ONE OF THE TWO BOXES BELOW
    *COCHEZ LA CASE QUI CONVIENT CI-DESSOUS*

    ☐ I am appearing in person. My address, fax or email for service is as follows:
    *Je comparais en personne. Mon adresse, mon numéro de télécopieur ou mon adresse électronique aux fins de signification sont les suivants :*

    ☐ I have a legal representative who will be appearing. The address, fax or email for service of my legal representative is as follows:
    *J'ai un représentant juridique qui sera présent. L'adresse, le numéro de télécopieur ou l'adresse électronique de mon représentant juridique aux fins de signification sont les suivants :*

3.  CONCISE STATEMENT OF REASONS FOR RESPONDING
    *BRÈVE DÉCLARATION DES MOTIFS DE LA RÉPONSE*

    (Briefly state why you are opposing the Application. For example, "The Applicant has not provided any medical evidence about pending surgery"; "The Crown disclosure is complete"; or "The length of time is not unreasonable, the Applicant has acquiesced to any delay, and there has been no prejudice flowing from the time to trial.")
    (*Expliquez brièvement pourquoi vous vous opposez à la demande. Par exemple : « L'auteur de la demande n'a pas produit de preuve médicale au sujet de son intervention chirurgicale imminente. », « La Couronne a divulgué tous les documents qu'elle pouvait. », « Le temps écoulé n'est pas excessif. L'auteur de la demande a accepté n'importe quel retard et le temps écoulé jusqu'au procès ne lui a causé aucun préjudice. »*)

4.  RESPONSE TO THE APPLICANT'S GROUNDS TO BE ARGUED IN SUPPORT OF APPLICATION (#6 on application)
    *RÉPONSE AUX MOTIFS DE L'AUTEUR DE LA DEMANDE QUI SERONT INVOQUÉS À L'APPUI DE LA DEMANDE (point 6 de la demande)*

5.  DETAILED STATEMENT OF SPECIFIC FACTUAL BASIS FOR OPPOSING APPLICATION
    *DÉCLARATION DÉTAILLÉE DES FAITS PRÉCIS SUR LESQUELS SE FONDE L'OPPOSITION À LA DEMANDE*

COR-OCJ-2 (rev. 04/12) CSD

RESPONSE
*RÉPONSE*
(Rule 2.2, *Criminal Rules of the Ontario Court of Justice*)
*(Règle 2.2, Règles de procédure en matière criminelle de la Cour de justice de l'Ontario)*
PAGE 2

**INDICATE BELOW OTHER MATERIALS OR EVIDENCE YOU WILL RELY ON IN RESPONSE TO THE**
6. **APPLICATION**
*INDIQUEZ CI-DESSOUS D'AUTRES DOCUMENTS OU PREUVES QUE VOUS ALLEZ INVOQUER EN RÉPONSE À LA DEMANDE*

☐ Brief statement of legal argument
*Bref exposé des arguments juridiques*

☐ Affidavit(s)   (List below)
*Affidavits*   *(Énumérez ci-dessous)*

☐ Case law or legislation   (Relevant passages should be indicated on materials. Well-known precedents do not need to be filed. Only materials that will be referred to in submissions to the Court should be filed.)
*Jurisprudence ou lois. (Les passages pertinents doivent être indiqués dans les documents. Les arrêts bien connus ne doivent pas être déposés. Il ne faut déposer que les documents qui seront mentionnés dans les observations au tribunal.)*

☐ Agreed statement of facts
*Exposé conjoint des faits*

☐ Oral testimony   (List witnesses to be called at hearing of application)
*Témoignage oral*   *(Liste des témoins qui seront appelés à témoigner à l'audience sur la demande)*

☐ Other   (Please specify)
*Autre*   *(Veuillez préciser)*

_____     _____
(Date)                                                        Signature of Respondent or Legal Representative / *Signature de l'intimé ou de son représentant juridique*

To:  _____
*À :*                (Name of Applicant or legal representative / *Nom de l'auteur de la demande ou de son représentant juridique*)

_____
(Address/fax/email for service / *Adresse, numéro de télécopie ou adresse électronique aux fins de signification*)

NOTE:  Rule 2.2 requires that a response to an application be served on the applicant and on any other affected parties.
*NOTA : La règle 2.2 exige qu'une réponse à une demande soit signifiée à l'auteur de la demande et aux autres parties concernées.*

COR-OCJ-2 (rev. 04/12) CSD

# Form 3, Consent, *Criminal Rules of the Ontario Court of Justice*

P

**Form /** *Formule* **3**
**CONSENT**
***CONSENTEMENT***
(Rule 2.7, *Criminal Rules of the Ontario Court of Justice*)
(*Règle 2.7, Règles de procédure en matière criminelle de la Cour de justice de l'Ontario*)

ONTARIO COURT OF JUSTICE
*COUR DE JUSTICE DE L'ONTARIO*

Court File No. (if known)
*N° du dossier de la cour (s'il est connu)*

Region / *Région*

**BETWEEN: /** *ENTRE*

**HER MAJESTY THE QUEEN /** *SA MAJESTÉ LA REINE*

- and / *et* -

(defendant(s) / *défendeur(s)*)

The Applicant
*L'auteur de la demande*

and the Respondent
*et l'intimé*

consent to the granting of the Application as follows:
*consentent à ce que la demande soit acceptée, comme suit :*

(Date)

(Date)

(Signature of Applicant's licensed legal representative / *Signature du représentant juridique titulaire d'un permis de l'auteur de la demande*)

(Signature of Respondent's licensed legal representative / *Signature du représentant juridique titulaire d'un permis de l'intimé*)

(Name (please print) / *Nom (en caractères d'imprimerie)*)

(Name (please print) / *Nom (en caractères d'imprimerie)*)

(Address / *Adresse*)

(Address / *Adresse*)

(Telephone no. / *N de téléphone*)

(Telephone no. / *N de téléphone*)

| **FOR JUDICIAL USE ONLY /** *RÉSERVÉ AUX MAGISTRATS* |
|---|

Date

☐ Order to go as requested:
*Ordonnance rendue telle que demandée*

☐ Application to be heard in Court:
*Demande sera entendue devant le tribunal*

NOTE: Rule 2.7(3) states:

(3) An application in which a party is not represented by counsel or by a licensed paralegal may be dealt with on consent if

  (a) a party files an application consent in Form 3;
  (b) the self-represented party appears before the Court; and
  (c) the Court is satisfied that the party understand the nature of the consent and the consequences of giving it.

*La disposition (3) de la Règle 2.7 stipule ce qui suit :*

*(3) Une requête pour laquelle une partie n'est pas représentée par un avocat ou par un parajuriste titulaire d'un permis peut être traitée sur consentement si les conditions suivantes sont réunies :*

  *a) une partie dépose son consentement rédigé selon le formulaire 3;*
  *b) la partie autoreprésentée comparait devant le tribunal;*
  *c) le tribunal est convaincu que la partie comprend la nature du consentement et les conséquences d'un tel consentement.*

COR-OCJ-1 (rev. 04/12) CSD

# Template for Probation Order, Form 46 of the *Criminal Code*

Q

FORM 46

*(Section 732.1)*

PROBATION ORDER

Canada, Province of _____ , *(territorial division)*.

Whereas on the _____ day of _____ at _____ , A.B., hereinafter called the offender, (pleaded guilty to *or* was tried under (*here insert Part XIX, XX or XXVII, as the case may be*) of the *Criminal Code* and was (*here insert convicted or found guilty, as the case may be*) on the charge that (*here state the offence to which the offender pleaded guilty or for which the offender was convicted or found guilty, as the case may be*);

And whereas on the _____ day of _____ the court adjudged*

*Use whichever of the following forms of disposition is applicable*:

(*a*) that the offender be discharged on the following conditions:

(*b*) that the passing of sentence on the offender be suspended and that the said offender be released on the following conditions:

(*c*) that the offender forfeit and pay the sum of _____ dollars to be applied according to law and in default of payment of the said sum without delay (*or within a time fixed, if any*), be imprisoned in the (*prison*) at _____ for the term of _____ unless the said sum and charges of the committal and of conveying the said offender to the said prison are sooner paid, and in addition thereto, that the said offender comply with the following conditions:

(*d*) that the offender be imprisoned in the _____ (*prison*) at for the term of _____ and, in addition thereto, that the said offender comply with the following conditions:

(*e*) that following the expiration of the offender's conditional sentence order related to this or another offence, that the said offender comply with the following conditions:

(*f*) that following the expiration of the offender's sentence of imprisonment related to another offence, that the said offender comply with the following conditions:

(*g*) when the offender is ordered to serve the sentence of imprisonment intermittently, that the said offender comply with the following conditions when not in confinement:

Now therefore the said offender shall, for the period of _____ from the date of this order (*or, where paragraph (d), (e) or (f) is applicable*, the date of expiration of the offender's sentence of imprisonment or conditional sentence order) comply with the following conditions, namely, that the said offender shall keep the peace and be of good behaviour, appear before the court when required to do so by the court and notify the court or probation officer in advance of any change of name or address and promptly notify the court or probation officer of any change of employment or occupation, and, in addition,

(*here state any additional conditions prescribed pursuant to subsection 732.1(3) of the Criminal Code*).

Dated this _____ day of _____ A.D. _____ , at _____ .

_____
Clerk of the Court, Justice *or* Provincial Court Judge

# Worksheet:
# Voluntariness of the Statement

R

| What was the statement? | | |
|---|---|---|
| 1. Was the statement made to a person in authority? | NO | YES—who was the person? |
| 2. Was the statement made voluntarily? Answer the questions below—if your answer is YES, provide an explanation. | NO | YES |
|    a. Were there any threats or promises made by the person in authority that had an effect on the accused? | | |
|    b. Was the accused under oppressive circumstances when the statement was made? | | |
|    c. Did the person making the statement lack an operating mind when he or she made the statement? | | |
| 3. Was any unfair trickery used by the police to get the person to make the statement? | | |

# Worksheet:
# Exclusion of Evidence

S

| | | |
|---|---|---|
| Was the evidence obtained by the authorities in a way that infringed (limited) or denied a right or freedom guaranteed in the Charter? | NO | YES—Section:<br><br>Explanation: |
| Would admitting the evidence harm the reputation of the justice system (i.e., society would think less of it or lose respect for it)?<br><br>To determine this, answer the three questions below: | NO | YES— explain: |
| 1. Is it a serious breach or just technical/minor? Fairness is a fundamental principle of the justice system. Consider: | | |
|   a. Was the violation committed in good faith or was it wilful and deliberate? | | |
|   b. Was it serious or technical? | | |
|   c. Was the violation due to urgency? | | |
|   d. Could the authorities have used other investigative tools? | | |
| 2. What is the impact on the individual's protected interests?<br><br>The more serious the impact on the accused's protected interests, the greater the risk that admission of it would undermine public confidence in the system. | | |
| 3. What is the societal interest in adjudication on the merits of the case?<br><br>Consider the reliability of the evidence and whether the truth-seeking function of the criminal justice system is better served by admitting the evidence or excluding it. | | |

# Glossary

## A

**absolute discharge** when the accused is found guilty of an offence but is discharged without a probation order or conditions, and no conviction results

**absolute jurisdiction offences** offences for which a provincial court judge has absolute jurisdiction to try an accused person charged with certain offences

**acquittal** formal judicial finding that the accused is not guilty of the offence(s) charged

*actus reus* a Latin term for the "guilty act"; wrongful physical acts that make up the offence

**aggravating factor** circumstance that may increase the severity of the sentence imposed

**agreed statement of facts** circumstances of the offence that are agreed upon by the Crown and the defence and are submitted before the court

**air of reality test** threshold test in which the trial judge considers the totality of the evidence in order to determine whether there is an evidentiary foundation for a particular defence

**appearance notice** formal document, signed by the accused, that sets out details of the accused's first court appearance and is given to the accused before he or she is charged with an offence

**application** request made before the court seeking an order for some sort of remedy or relief

**arbitrary detention** a random or unjustified restraint of liberty

**arraignment** formal reading of the charge or charges against the accused, in which the accused is asked to enter a plea

**attempt** intention to commit the offence, along with actions that extend beyond mere preparation

**automatism** a defence that applies when the accused's physical actions are involuntary as a result of either a disease of the mind or a non-mental disorder

*autrefois acquit* a special plea available to a defendant when he or she has previously been tried and acquitted of the same offence and therefore cannot be tried for it again

*autrefois convict* a special plea available to a defendant when he or she has previously been tried and convicted of the same offence and therefore cannot be tried for it again

## B

**balance of probabilities** standard of proof based on more likely than not

**bench warrant** warrant issued by the court

**beyond mere preparation** a legal test applied by a judge to determine whether the accused has taken steps toward committing the offence beyond simply planning it

**burden of proof** obligation of a party to prove what it is asserting

# C

**charge screening form**  form, typically included as part of a disclosure package, that contains information on how the Crown is proceeding and the Crown's position on sentencing on a guilty plea and after trial

**circumstantial evidence**  evidence that relies on an inference or reasoning to connect it to a conclusion of fact

**commission**  execution of an act that causes harm

**common law**  a legal system developed from judicial decisions

**community justice worker**  person who attends court on a regular basis, receives referrals from the Crown for diversion, and assists the accused in registering in and fulfilling the conditions of a diversion program

**compellability**  whether a witness may be forced to testify

**competence**  ability of a witness to testify and give evidence in court

**concurrent sentence**  sentence for two or more separate offences that are served at the same time

**conditional discharge**  when the accused is found guilty of an offence but is discharged with conditions placed on him or her, and no conviction results

**conditional sentence**  jail sentence of no longer than two years that is served in the community

**confession**  written or verbal statement made by the accused suggesting or implicating guilt

**consecutive sentence**  sentence for two or more separate offences that are served one after the other

**consent**  a defence that arises when the accused has an honest yet mistaken belief in the complainant's consent to an action

**conspiracy**  agreement between two or more parties to commit an offence

**counselling**  deliberately encouraging or actively inducing another person to commit an offence

**count**  specific details pertaining to an offence that are set out in the information

**Crown pre-trial conference**  meeting between the Crown and defence to discuss the evidence, the position of the parties, plea negotiations, or other issues related to a charge

# D

***de minimis non curat lex***  a defence that arises when the criminal conduct of the accused is so trivial that it is not worthy of the attention of the law

**denunciation**  a sentencing principle that is aimed at condemning or demonstrating disapproval of an offence committed or of the conduct of an offender

**derivative evidence**  evidence obtained as a direct result of violating the accused's legal rights

**disclosure**  the constitutional right of an accused person to obtain all information in the possession of the Crown that is relevant to establishing the guilt or innocence of the accused

**dismissal**  decision of the court that terminates proceedings against an accused once the trial has commenced

**diversion program**  alternative to a criminal proceeding; typically available to an accused person who does not have a criminal record and who is charged with a less serious offence

**dual procedure offences**  offences for which the Crown may elect to proceed by way of summary conviction or by indictment

**duress**  a defence both available under common law and statute that applies when an accused person is compelled to commit an offence by way of threats of death or bodily harm

# E

**endorsed warrant**  type of warrant in which the justice authorizes the accused to be released after arrest

**estreatment proceeding**  an application brought by the Crown to collect the money promised by a surety when the accused breaches a condition or conditions of bail

**exculpatory evidence**  evidence that tends to exonerate or clear the accused

**exigent circumstances**  danger that evidence will be lost, removed, or destroyed

**express consent**  consent that is clear and unmistakable; may be given verbally or by gestures

## F

**forensic identification specialist** specially trained police officer responsible for the collection of physical evidence from a crime scene

## G

*Gardiner* **hearing** hearing to establish facts in dispute during a sentencing

**general deterrence** a sentencing principle aimed at discouraging the public from committing a similar offence

## H

*habeas corpus* a Latin term for the accused's right to be brought before a judge

**hybrid offences** another term for dual procedure offences—offences for which the Crown may elect to proceed by summary conviction or by indictment

## I

**identification** evidence showing that a person charged with an offence is the one who committed the offence

**implied consent** consent that is inferred from a person's actions or silence based on the circumstances of the situation

**inchoate offences** offences that are not fully completed; the *mens rea* is present but not all of the elements of the *actus reus* are present

**inculpatory evidence** evidence that tends to establish the guilt or blameworthiness of the accused

**indictable offences** the most serious category of offences under the *Criminal Code*, which may only be tried on indictment

**inducements** threats or promises made by a person in authority that are meant to influence or persuade someone to do something

**informant** person who has reasonable grounds to believe that an offence has been committed and who appears before a justice to swear an information on oath

**information** charging document for criminal offences that is sworn and commences the prosecution

**information to obtain** document setting out reasonable grounds for the basis of a search warrant

**informational privacy** privacy rights relating to when, how, and to what extent personal information is communicated to others

**inherent jurisdiction** a concept based on the common law doctrine that a superior court has the authority to hear any matter that appears before it; may be overridden by statute or legislation

**intermittent sentence** sentence of incarceration of 90 days or less, to be served during days and times specified in the order

**intervenor status** a legal status granted to a non-party to an offence to participate in the proceedings

*intra vires* within the legal authority of a level of government to create a law

**issuing process** a procedure in which a justice issues a summons or warrant or confirms the form of release that the accused is on

## J

**joinder** joining charges or co-accused together

**joint retainer** contractual relationship in which the paralegal represents more than one client in the same matter

**joint submission** a sentencing submission in which the Crown and defence recommend the same sentence for the judge's consideration

**judicial interim release** formal term for bail; the release of an accused person before trial or sentencing

**judicial pre-trial conference** meeting between a judge who will not be presiding at the trial, the Crown, and the defence to discuss matters related to the trial such as disclosure, applications, witnesses, or other legal issues

**judicial stay of proceedings** ruling by the court that halts further legal process in a matter

# K

**Kienapple principle**  principle of law that states that when the accused is found guilty of more than one offence arising out of the same transaction, and the elements of the offences are substantially the same, the accused ought to be convicted of only the most serious offence, and the other offences should be stayed by the court

# L

**limitation period**  specific time period by which a charge must be laid

# M

**mens rea**  a Latin term for "the guilty mind"; the criminal intention or knowledge of committing an offence

**mistake of fact**  a defence that applies when the accused does not possess the *mens rea* to commit an offence as a result of being mistaken as to an essential fact, which would not result in a criminal offence, if the accused is to be believed

**mitigating factor**  circumstance that may decrease the severity of the sentence imposed

**motion to sever**  application to separate co-accused or charges from being heard together on an information

**multiple count information**  information that contains more than one count

# N

**necessity**  a defence that applies when the accused is forced to break the law in order to avoid a greater harm

# O

**obstructed view testimony**  use of a device in court so that the witness does not have to see the accused, but the accused can see the witness

**omission**  failure to do an act that one has a legal duty to do that results in harm

**onus**  responsibility or obligation to prove

**oppressive circumstances**  circumstances that deprive an accused person of basic necessities or the right to counsel and serve to overbear the accused's will

# P

**pardon**  a special plea available to a defendant when he or she has previously been pardoned for the same offence and therefore cannot be tried for it again

**parole**  provisional release of a prisoner prior to the completion of the entire sentence

**peace bond**  recognizance order with conditions that the court orders an accused person to abide by when the complainant has reason to fear the accused

**person in authority**  person who is formally engaged in the arrest, detention, examination, or prosecution of the accused

**personal privacy**  privacy rights relating to the bodily integrity of an individual

**plain view doctrine**  common law authority that permits the police to seize illegal items that are in plain sight while in the execution of a lawful search

**plea bargaining**  an agreement between the Crown and the defence in which the offender pleads guilty to a lesser charge, fewer charges, or in which the Crown proposes a reduced sentence

**precedent**  principle or rule established in a previous legal case that is binding or persuasive on other courts in deciding similar cases

**pre-enquete hearing**  private hearing in the absence of the parties

**preliminary inquiry**  evidentiary hearing during which the Crown must prove that there is sufficient evidence to proceed with an indictment against the accused

**pre-sentence report**  report prepared by a probation officer after interviewing the accused and other sources for use in sentencing

**principles of fundamental justice**  core values within the justice system that society believes ought to prevail over an individual's right to life, liberty, and security

**privilege** an evidentiary rule that excludes certain confidential communications from being admissible as evidence in court

**promise to appear** formal document, signed by the accused, in which he or she promises to appear in court on a certain date

# Q

**quash** a ruling by the court that nullifies a proceeding, a document, or an order

**quasi-criminal** non-criminal but may carry a penalty similar to that of a criminal offence

**quid pro quo** a Latin term that stands for the proposition of something granted to a person in exchange for that person giving something up or doing something in return

# R

**reasonable grounds** a set of facts or circumstances that would cause a person of ordinary and prudent judgment to believe beyond a mere suspicion

**rebuttal** refuting or contradicting the evidence put forth

**recklessness** consciously disregarding the fact that an action may result in a substantial and unjustifiable risk of harm to another person

**recognizance** form of release whereby an accused person agrees to be bound by a monetary amount and certain conditions in order to secure his or her release from custody

**record suspension** status that allows people who have been convicted of an offence but have served their sentence and demonstrated their ability to abide by the law to have their criminal record kept separate and apart from other criminal records

**rehabilitation** a sentencing principle aimed at reforming offenders through treatment or programming

**remedy** legal redress for harm or injury

**reparation** a sentencing principle aimed at having offenders make amends for harm or injury caused to a victim or to society

**responsibility** a sentencing principle aimed at holding offenders accountable for their actions

**restitution** financial compensation for injury or loss to a victim

**reverse onus** situation in which the burden of proving or disproving something shifts from the Crown to the accused

**rule against duplicity** rule against duplicate or ambiguous offences set out in one count

**rule of inevitable discovery** exception to the inadmissibility of derivative evidence when the evidence would have been discovered regardless of the Charter breach

# S

**segregation** a sentencing principle aimed at separating offenders from society

**self-crimination** a statement made or action taken by a person that supports a finding of guilt

**self-defence** a defence that applies when the accused must use reasonable force to defend himself or herself or another person

**show cause hearing** another term for a bail hearing, during which the Crown prosecutor must show cause why the accused should continue to be detained

**specific deterrence** a sentencing principle aimed at discouraging the particular offender from committing a similar offence

**spousal privilege** a legal concept that recognizes that communications between spouses are confidential and do not have to be revealed in court

**standard of proof** level or extent to which facts must be proven

**stare decisis** a legal principle that requires judges to follow previous rulings made by other judges in higher levels of court within the same province or territory and rulings of the Supreme Court of Canada on the same issue

**statutory law** written law passed by Parliament; takes precedence over common law

**subpoena** formal court-ordered document ordering a witness to attend a hearing

**summary conviction offences** less serious types of offences under the *Criminal Code*, which are punishable by lesser penalties and involve more simplified trial procedures than indictable offences

**summons** formal document served on the accused after a charge is laid that sets out the details of the accused's first court appearance and compels the accused to attend court

**super-summary offences** a category of hybrid or summary conviction offences that carry a greater penalty than the general penalty for summary conviction offences

**surety** person who agrees to take responsibility for and supervise the accused while he or she is out on bail

**suspended sentence** suspension of a jail sentence, in which the offender is placed on probation

**sympathetic witness** witness whose testimony supports a party, even though the party may not be calling the witness to testify

# T

**territorial privacy** privacy rights relating to places where an individual has a reasonable expectation of privacy

**third party records** records that are in the possession of parties other than the Crown and the defence

**tunnel vision** a situation in which a particular suspect is believed by investigators to be guilty of an offence and any evidence inconsistent with this theory is dismissed as irrelevant, incredible, or unreliable; may result in the elimination of other suspects who should be investigated

# U

*ultra vires* beyond the legal authority of a level of government to create a law

**undertaking** formal document, signed by the accused, in which the accused promises to do or refrain from doing certain things in order to be released

**unendorsed warrant** type of warrant that requires the accused to be brought before a justice to apply for bail after his or her arrest

**unsympathetic witness** witness whose testimony supports the opposing party, even though the witness is not necessarily being called by the opposing party

# V

**verdict** formal decision made by the judge or jury at the end of a trial

**victim impact statement** written statement describing the harm or loss suffered by someone harmed by, or who has suffered physical or emotional loss as a result of, an offence

*viva voce* a Latin term that means "with living voice"

*voir dire* trial or a hearing held within a trial, typically to determine the admissibility of contested evidence or the eligibility of prospective jurors

# W

**"will say" statement** a statement summarizing what a person will testify to in court

# Index

# U

# V

# W

# Y